The Foreign Exchange Matrix

A new framework for traders to understand currency movements

By Barbara Rockefeller and Vicki Schmelzer

HARRIMAN HOUSE LTD

3A Penns Road
Petersfield
Hampshire
GU32 2EW
GREAT BRITAIN

Tel: +44 (0)1730 233870
Fax: +44 (0)1730 233880
Email: enquiries@harriman-house.com
Website: www.harriman-house.com

First edition published in Great Britain in 2013

978-0-85719-130-4

Printed in the UK by Lightning Source.

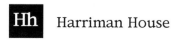

eBook edition

As a buyer of the print edition of *The Foreign Exchange Matrix* you can now download the eBook edition free of charge to read on an eBook reader, your smartphone or your computer. Simply go to:

http://ebooks.harriman-house.com/foreignexchangematrix
or point your smartphone at the QRC below.

You can then register and download your eBook copy of the book.

www.harriman-house.com

Contents

About the Authors

Barbara Rockefeller

Barbara Rockefeller is an international economist and forecaster specializing in foreign exchange. She was a pioneer in technical analysis and also in combining technical analysis with fundamental analysis. She publishes two reports daily using both techniques (**www.rts-forex.com**) for central banks, professional fund managers, corporate hedgers and individual traders. The trading advice newsletter has an average annual hypothetical return over 50% since inception in 1994 and has never posted a losing year. She is the author of three books on trading, including Technical Analysis for Dummies, and contributes a regular column to *Currency Trader* magazine. Her education includes a BA in economics from Reed College, with a year at the University of Keele in Staffordshire (UK), and MA from Columbia University in international affairs.

Vicki Schmelzer

Vicki Schmelzer has worked in the professional foreign exchange industry for over 25 years. Today she is a senior financial journalist at Market News International, with foreign exchange as her main beat. She is the creator and author of TheFXSpot a daily feature that looks at financial market happenings from the FX perspective, including fixed income, intermarket analysis, and emerging markets. Before becoming a journalist, Ms. Schmelzer worked as a senior currency dealer at major U.S. and international banks including Dresdner Bank, Citibank, Manufacturers-Hanover/Chemical Bank, and Westdeutsche Landesbank. She has appeared on ForexTV and in Alain Lasfargues' 2009 documentary *The Marvelous History of the Dollar*. Her education includes a BA in German (and Mathematics minor) from Clarion State University and the study abroad program with the Goethe Institut in Staufen, Germany.

Foreword

As you will undoubtedly gather from reading the introduction to this book, foreign exchange is a complex topic. It is complex in the number of factors that impact currency valuation, it is complex in the relative weighting of these factors and it is complex in the timing of these factors. Barbara Rockefeller and Vicki Schmelzer have done a masterful job of making sense of a market that some of the best and brightest have regarded as enigmatic if not utterly incomprehensible. Much of this scepticism is driven by what the authors refer to as the perverseness of markets – the habit of currency prices to respond contrary to what fundamental analysis would suggest. Further scepticism is caused by the perceived absence of financial market theory to explain currency valuation. Additional scepticism comes from the poor track record of many market professionals in managing foreign exchange risk – some infamously. The default view is that foreign exchange markets are random and that one should hedge away any underlying currency exposure and focus on the business at hand, whether that is investing in global equities or fixed income or managing a profitable multinational corporation.

Currency hedging is very common in global markets, but it is by no means ubiquitous. The rule of thumb is that global bond investors hedge on average 80% of their foreign exchange exposure, while global equity investors hedge on average only 20% of their exposure. Much of this is due to the positive correlation between equity market performance and appreciation of the local currency. The accepted explanation is that equity markets rally during periods of relative economic strength that are accompanied by rising inflation and interest rates. The combination of these factors attracts foreign investment into the country, which lifts the value of the local currency. Furthermore, currency hedging is more common in developed markets than in emerging markets, owing to the lack of an organised futures market in many developing countries that is needed for hedging. While some players have attempted to solve this problem through proxy hedging, their track record is not particularly encouraging. Moreover, proxy hedging tends to be more expensive than many assume, particularly in the longer term. Slippage in economic and policy variables, such as inflation or interest rate differentials, ensures that no currency is a perfect proxy for another. However, as foreign exchange exposure has grown with the globalisation of asset management over the past 30 years, there has been an increasing interest in understanding currency markets. While some portfolio managers attempt to beat their benchmarks by creating alpha from actively managing foreign exchange risk, an increasing number are even trading currency as an asset class.

The absence of a widely accepted economic model for foreign exchange valuation does not imply that currencies are random any more than equity or fixed income securities are random. As in other asset classes, currency prices are driven by supply and demand. So, we should revert to the balance of payments to determine the net inflow or outflow of trade and investment. Ideally, net trade and investment flows (or what economists refer to as the broad basic balance) should be used to explain real effective exchange rate rather than spot exchange rates. Why? The value of a currency is more than simply its relative value to the US dollar or euro. Rather, it is the trade-weighted average of a given currency with its trade and investment partners. Moreover, no two countries have exactly the same level of inflation every year over the indefinite future. Consequently, we need to work with real rather than nominal exchange rates, as inflation is corrosive to the value of a currency as demonstrated by the law of one price and the theory of purchasing power parity. While this approach is relatively uncontested, it falls short of fully explaining currency price movements. Currencies are not fully floating (determined by market supply and demand), but are often subject to intervention or even active management to limit a currency's movement over time.

There are as many foreign exchange regimes as there are countries, with only a handful truly fully floating. While major currencies such as the Japanese yen and the Swiss franc have been subject to intervention and price management recently, even the euro and US dollar have experienced market intervention over the past ten years. The reason is two-fold: first, central banks covet orderly market conditions; and second, governments prefer stable currencies to avoid threats to growth that accompany large currency movements. For these reasons, it is very difficult to use fundamental analysis to forecast foreign exchange prices. Just when a strong, fundamentally-driven currency trend is unfolding, the local authorities are most likely step in to stop it. Market intervention by the Swiss National Bank several years ago to arrest the Swiss franc's appreciation against the euro is a good example. Rather than it being driven by speculators, as suggested by SNB officials, it was largely due to the Swiss franc's safe-haven status amidst crisis-ridden Europe. Once you have controlled for all of these variables, you need to acknowledge the size of the interbank market and the large amount of cash it is able to move on a speculative basis. Trading for short-term profit in foreign exchange makes fundamental analysis useful only in the longer term. As the authors of this book point out, technical analysis is an indispensable tool of the foreign exchange trader.

The Foreign Exchange Matrix fills an important need in the market today regarding currency valuation and trading. With more than 50 years of foreign exchange market experience between them, Rockefeller and Schmelzer boldly go where few have dared. While they flatly admit to a lack of an elegantly simplistic theory to currency valuation, what they provide is a vigorous and comprehensive examination of the factors that weigh on foreign exchange markets. What the reader comes away with is not only a better understanding of what moves currency prices, but a better understanding of global markets and the interconnectedness of the world we live in. The historical anecdotes alone are worth the effort of reading this book, as the authors move effortlessly from the Asian Financial Crisis to the LTCM Crisis to the Lehman Crisis with deft and skill. While the reader may not decide to quit their day job to day trade foreign exchange spot, forward and option markets, they will have a greater understanding of what factors drive currency prices and a greater degree of comfort in managing foreign exchange exposure – whether that exposure is by default or design.

Michael J. Woolfolk, PhD

Managing Director and Senior Currency Strategist,
Bank of New York Mellon,
New York, NY
December 2012

Introduction

The FX market is a mystery to most people, including some of its participants. Pundits on other financial markets and legislators in most countries don't fully understand it, either. Everyone notes how big the FX market is – bigger than all other global markets combined at $4 trillion per day – but no one ever asks "What is the purpose of all this trading volume?" There are other unanswered questions about FX too.

We also want to know whether FX secretly drives all other markets, or whether it is the passive end-product of all the other markets. Neither assertion is wholly accurate, but knowing that doesn't help us understand where FX *does* fit into the grand scheme of things. Further, why do exchange rates always overshoot any reasonable estimate of *value*, such as comparative purchasing power? Does this mean the FX market is inherently unstable, as financier George Soros has said?

Most of all, FX is money, and money has many different roles. Money is not only how we pay the electric bill (*medium of exchange*), how we measure economic sustainability (*unit of account*), and how we measure wealth (*store of value*), it is also a symbol of a country.

For example, the French were so attached to the now-defunct franc that they continued to hoard as much as €1 billion worth of them, or some 3% of the francs that were in circulation, when the euro was introduced in January 1999. In February 2012, the French government made a windfall gain of about €500 million when the franc finally hit its expiration date. Germany continues to allow the Deutsche Mark to serve as legal tender; the Bundesbank estimates that citizens hold as much as DM 13.2 billion as of end-June 2012. Then think of all the nicknames for the US dollar – such as greenback and buck – and most interesting, food names – including bread, clams and cabbage.

How do the non-functional, reputational aspects of money affect FX trading and, while we're on that theme, is it justified that the dollar is seemingly in perpetual crisis?

It is possible to provide easy answers to these questions.

Easy answers

What is the purpose of FX trading volume?

The FX market is so big because accounting convention allows it to be largely hidden. FX is a contingent asset/liability on the balance sheet of both banks and corporations, and is reported only in the footnotes of financial statements. Even then, FX is lumped together with "other securities."

Further, the FX market is so big also because FX is a market dominated almost entirely by private speculators, including banks and hedge funds, who are trading almost entirely on private credit. The positions are not reported, nor are the credit lines backing the trading. You will search in vain for a number representing the gross credit lines of any bank to other banks for the purpose of FX trading.

FX trading outcomes are reported on the income statement, but do not have to be broken out from other securities trading. You will never discover how much profit Citibank, Deutsche Bank or Goldman Sachs made last quarter trading FX. And because FX traders are not burdened like equity and bond traders by having to meet a benchmark rate of return, relative performance among competitors is not in the public eye. FX traders have only cash profit targets and sometimes these are the bare minimum to justify the expense of the desk, quote terminal and telephone.

Finally, FX traded by institutions is not directly regulated by governments, although retail trading by individuals is usually regulated. FX escapes new efforts at regulation, as in exemption of FX derivatives in the US during 2010 and 2011, because self-regulation actually works, and works with impressive efficiency. This is in part because FX is a market on the leading edge of technology advances. We have not had a global problem due to FX since the Herstatt Bank failure in 1974, which was even then actually a credit risk issue and not strictly an FX issue. In essence, Herstatt accepted FX payments due to it and then declared bankruptcy, avoiding paying out its side of the FX trades. Note that credit risk always starts with the *character* of the counterparty.

Does the FX market drive other markets, or is it a passive end-product? Why do FX markets overshoot?

FX is both the driver of economic conditions and the end-product of economic conditions, mainly through a single factor set – inflation and expected inflation, and its financial market manifestation, interest rates. The government entity most associated with inflation is the central bank and its interest rate policies. FX traders watch inflation and its evil cousin, deflation, tirelessly and obsessively, even when they are low and flat.

It is true that exchange rates often overshoot reasonable estimates of their true value, but in the absence of any objective measurement of true value we count on market participants to judge when they have gone too far and to correct this themselves. If governments do not agree with the market's valuation, and desire a correction to be forced, they may order their central banks to intervene directly in the FX market.

The FX market is the only financial market in which governments intervene and such intervention is intermittent and fairly rare. Its rarity may suggest that governments dislike quarrelling with the market's valuations because they actually do believe the best policy is to *let the market decide*, or alternatively they may be lily-livered in the face of such a behemoth. It would in fact be easier and cheaper to change the policies that led to a *wrong* currency valuation than to intervene.

If the FX market is inherently unstable, it would be because governments engage in policies that lead to overshooting, including inadequate advance signalling of policy changes. So, if governments make bad decisions and manage policy poorly, it may be justified to say FX is inherently unstable.

Exchange rates also overshoot because we misinterpret economic data and do not have a universally accepted theory of how exchange rates should be determined. The absence of a single theory of FX determination allows overshooting to occur on the influence of other markets. A shop-keeper in Lucerne will glibly comment that the dollar is down against the Swiss franc because oil is up. An amateur retail FX trader in Hong Kong will say it's obvious that the S&P 500 and the FTSE 100 will follow the Shanghai Composite index down in a nerve-wracking big move, and a drop in global stock markets logically harms the dollar. *Really?* This is true only in the sense that greed and fear can easily jump asset boundaries. As for real-world fundamental connections, nearly everything posited about intermarket relationships is badly formulated, mistaken and often easily refuted.

But note that professional traders and key players like hedge funds are required to behave as though they accept the cause-and-effect relationship of FX and other markets because this is how they earn a living. A trader may know perfectly well that a big change in the price of oil or gold has no fundamental relationship to currencies in any particular situation, but will trade as though it does because that's the profitable strategy. This is one of the more vital of the insights into the FX market that we want to convey in this book – data *proving* intermarket correlations may be undeniable, but correlation is not causation and to assume intermarket relationships are valid and long-lasting can be dangerous.

Finally, sometimes the FX market overshoots because a technical pattern is being completed. FX is always heavily influenced by chart-reading, more so than any other market. Traders use technical analysis because it is an effective tool to measure sentiment and reliably leads to profitable trading. Anyone with a bias against technical analysis will not fare well in FX.

How do the reputational aspects of money affect FX trading and is it justified that the dollar is in perpetual crisis?

Sentiment has many faces but can be boiled down to one concept – risk appetite or risk aversion. Preconceptions and bias toward nationalities is incorporated in the rolling risk appetite/risk aversion calculation. The euro, for example, has magic, and the dollar does not. The euro is able to withstand a major sovereign debt and banking crisis with less loss of value and less volatility than the history of currencies would suggest.

In contrast, the dollar can't get a break and is sold heavily on the slightest pretext, with bad economic news exaggerated and good news dismissed or undervalued. This is the fate of all reserve currencies, including the dollar, because to serve the reserve currency needs of the rest of the world, the reserve country always has to issue more currency than it needs for purely domestic uses. And yet the reserve currency is a safe haven in times of financial market panic.

Decoding how the FX market really works

Many economists and financial professionals view the foreign exchange market as the pinnacle of sophistication. FX rates embody all the important Big Picture Macro developments of the day as well as the hidden undercurrents of the international capital markets. The FX market is linked to core economic health, central bank monetary policies, various countries' fiscal conditions, and trends in stocks and commodities. FX is the glamorous top of the heap.

And yet the professional bank traders who actually move the market minute by minute and day by day are like any other traders. They rarely have PhDs in international economics and finance. They are not paid to have analytically correct opinions. Their sole job is to make a speculative profit for the employer, literally out of thin air. It is thin air they are trading with because banks, hedge funds and other big players do not allocate actual cash or collateral to trade FX

– it's all done on credit lines. Professional FX traders can be viewed as the biggest speculators on the planet, with the primary currency traders at each of the big banks, sovereign risk funds and hedge funds having a credit line *stake* of hundreds of millions of dollars.

So which is it, pinnacle of high finance or grubby profit-seeking? It's both. How, then, do we get FX prices that reflect all those high-level economic factors and links to governments and other markets? Well, we don't. The reflection is like that in a fun-house mirror. Currencies *do not* equilibrate disparate conditions and imbalances, as economists theorise they should. Imbalances persist not for brief periods, but for decades. We see big exceptions to seemingly classic and timeless rules, like capital following the highest real rate of return and exiting a currency when returns fall. This is just one of the many strange and seemingly contradictory characteristics of the FX market that we seek to explain in this book.

Our goal is to describe how the FX market works in practice and to demystify as many of these puzzles as we can. Together we have about 50 years of experience in the FX market as big-bank spot desk dealer, big bank corporate FX trader, market economist, technical analyst, risk manager, and wire service reporter/financial advisor. Between us, we know or have heard of just about everything, and are equipped to verify or to debunk much of it.

Our purpose, however, is not to present a primer on FX. We assume that the reader already has a high level of knowledge about financial markets generally and a particular curiosity about the FX market. We can't puncture every misleading or inaccurate idea about FX that has been published as fact in the past decade, but we can offer a perspective that is both true and useful.

To help us do this, we use the overarching concept of risk appetite and its opposite side, risk aversion. Risk appetite is the only explanation that bridges the tangle of contradictory facts and theories about FX. For example, how can a crisis in Europe trigger an already overvalued Japanese yen to become stronger, even in the face of Japanese economic data that dictates the yen should be weaker? The answer lies in risk aversion inspiring Japanese investors to repatriate funds into the *safe-haven* home currency, the yen. The explanatory value of risk appetite/risk aversion is powerful, and much needed. Before we go further it is important to understand what risk aversion is and how it came to be used in analysis of the FX markets.

Risk aversion

Risk aversion is a concept arising from economists in the insurance industry (later applied with great efficacy in designing lotteries). Academic work on this area includes measuring and modelling such things as the effect on absolute and relative risk aversion of a change in wealth. For example, a rich man fears losing 0.01% of his wealth more than a poor man fears losing 10% of his, which is one of the great mysteries of the human brain. Following the Lehman debacle in the autumn of 2008, the use of the concept of risk aversion to explain FX market behaviour was quickly adopted. Application of the concept to financial markets and especially FX quickly went viral and became universal within weeks.

In financial markets generally and the FX market in particular, we observe that players mostly act like the rich man – risk aversion starts out high and goes higher as a one-time specific threat to wealth appears. The Lehman Brothers bankruptcy was a spectacular example of a variable outside the usual scope of the FX market that became internal to the FX market through the transmission mechanism of short-term interest rates. The perception of excessive riskiness in the interbank lending market morphed in to a perception of excessive riskiness in the euro/dollar currency market. Risk aversion is what they have in common – it's a force through which price actions are produced.

As liquidity dried up and interbank lending tapered off to a trickle everywhere in the world, the US 4-week bank discount rate shifted from 1.92% at the beginning of June to 1.35% on 12 September – and 0.28% on 15 September, the date of the Lehman bankruptcy announcement. By year-end 2008, it was 0.11%. Yields fell all along the curve, too. The yield on the 10-year note was 4.324% on 13 June and dipped to 3.25% on 16 September. It bottomed near year-end at 2.038% on 18 December 2008. Around the same time, the euro fell from 1.5948 on 16 July 2008 to 1.2738 on 22 October 2008.

The drop in return reflects a massive safe-haven inflow to the dollar that violates the usual rule that *currency follows yield*. In other words, if all other things are equal, we expect a currency to fall if its yield is falling, especially the after-inflation, *real* yield. In 2008, investors were happy to get return *of* capital and never mind return *on* capital. The Treasury's report on capital flows bears out this thesis. The net capital flow to the US, including Treasuries, Agencies and equities, rose from $14.76 billion in August 2008 to $59.10 billion in September. This is risk aversion in action.

It's probably fair to say that risk appetite/risk aversion were known for decades under a different name: *greed* and *fear*. But whereas greed and fear arise from personal emotions that overcome rational cognition, risk aversion is entirely rational. The new *flat* world of international finance consists of players who recognise *shocks* and *events* outside their own securities' factor set as capable of jumping barriers into their own factor set. In a sense, all factors, however exogenous-seeming, are potentially endogenous, and that's not even counting *unknown factors*.

It's not only the FX market that sees this effect. In US equities, after a 40-year delay, securities analysts started to acknowledge that multinational corporation earnings are influenced by FX rates; they were forced to start accounting for the FX effect of overseas earnings along with less difficult things like cash flow, EBITA and book value.

Information overload

Risk appetite and risk aversion are handy proxies for a broader and more thorough analysis, but if you want to follow FX and understand why prices are moving the way they are, you need to hold in your head a mix of economic data, institutional factors, and technical indicators on six or ten currencies, not to mention that ineffable thing called *sentiment*, which includes what the majority in the market are thinking and thus how they are positioned.

Each country has, at a minimum, ten variables you need to follow, including rate of growth of GDP, inflation, industrial production or some proxy for it like the purchasing managers index, unemployment, consumer sentiment, debt-to-GDP ratios, and so on, plus the viability of the banking system, political developments and the policy bias of the central banks and resulting interest rates. In addition, you want to know the technical condition of the currency – is it trending up or down, and with what robustness?

This is clearly impossible.

To make life more complicated, the foreign exchange market is driven by factors that constantly shift. One week, the market is focused on interest rate differentials, the next on the trade balance or fiscal deficit, and after that, an upcoming election. One minute, the market is risk-averse and clamouring for safe-haven US Treasuries, and the next minute it is willing to dive head-first into frontier markets.

How do you know whether a factor will dominate trading for months to come or is merely a one-day wonder? How do you make wise trading decisions when a driver is brand new and the market is trading in response to this driver for the first time? When has one trend run its course and another trend begun? More importantly, how do you know when to believe commentators and when to intuit they are talking through their hats?

A difficulty commentators and traders alike face is that the economics industry has failed to offer up a coherent theory of exchange rate determination (see Chapter 5). The FX industry has failed to give us basic information, so easily available in other asset classes, on positions and flows (see Chapter 6). Even the most accessible of explanations, relative interest rates (see Chapter 4), fails with great regularity. Conventional thinking would have it that the country with the highest real rate of return (real denoting *after-inflation*) will get the biggest capital inflows and thus a rising currency. But in 2009 and 2010, Australia was the first to start raising interest rates and had the highest real rate of return among all the developed countries, and yet the Australian dollar fell about 14% from the April peak to the May low in 2010 and again in the fall of 2011 as global risk aversion got all markets by the throat. Obviously the relative differential is not the only factor at work.

The effect of events on other asset classes, including equities and commodities like oil and gold, has a spotty record (see Chapter 7). When one big market, like equities, is in a tizzy, it tends to infect other markets. This is a variation of the *falling tide lowers all boats* market lore. But it takes falling stock markets in more than one market to affect currencies – usually.

And even if the fundamentals, relative interest rates and other markets all line up to point to a single conclusion, the FX market still may not obey – if the chart dictates otherwise. The chart is one of the few ways we have to get some idea of how a consensus of traders is positioned. Traders resist negative news when they are long and exaggerate the importance of negative news when they are short, and this can be seen on the chart. Unlike equity and other markets, FX embraces technical analysis with open arms – it pretty much has to, given the shortage of other information (see Chapter 8).

So, why bother to try to understand mountains of conflicting and contradictory data when a simple application of risk appetite/risk aversion will cut through the mess? The answer is that sometimes the most unlikely things can promote risk appetite and FX traders need to be like Boy Scouts – prepared. When Lehman failed, no one expected that the failure of one bank in the US would set off a global liquidity crisis, the failure of European banks, the drop in the price of oil from $146 to $36 in less than six months, or volatile gyrations in the EUR/USD as money flowed to safe haven US Treasuries.

Even when you can see risk appetite or risk aversion developing in the news day-by-day, you still want to be able to judge whether it has lasting power. As the sovereign debt crisis in Europe has evolved over several years and encompassed 19 summits (as of July 2012), the market has been mostly willing to give the European Monetary Union (EMU) the benefit of the doubt. But periodic euro rallies after summits have not been inspired by any measurable progress toward repairing problems, but rather by the extent the outcome was expected.

For example, the euro rally after the end-June 2012 summit was not set off by the seeming capitulation of Germany to a looser interpretation of Treaty conditionality, but rather because expectations of any progress at all were practically zero. A small change in conditions was seen as a breakthrough and worthy of a currency rally, even though, at the time, the euro zone was facing worsening recession and a central bank interest rate cut to boot. On the dire institutional conditions and bad economic data, the euro *should* have fallen. In this instance, though, risk appetite came roaring back to lift the euro on the triumph of hope over experience. In order to trade the euro correctly through this period, you had to be able to judge whether the risk appetite embodied in the euro rally was strong enough to overcome the economic data and interest rate outlook, for how long the sentiment might last, and what other institutional factor might jump up out of the shrubbery and bite the market.

The bottom line is that risk appetite/risk aversion is a handy tool but it's no substitute for having a bird's eye overview of economic and other conditions that may become the source of change in the current risk sentiment or the source of a reversal in sentiment. Judging risk appetite is an *ex-post* exercise – you can identify the sentiment only after it has started to appear in the form of changes in prices. In fact, many commentators are lazy and attribute anything they can't otherwise explain to a change in risk sentiment. And, in fact, sometimes we cannot go back and retrace the route taken by risk appetite or risk aversion through the winding path over which it touched and changed various asset prices and data. The transmission of risk appetite and risk aversion is as yet an uncharted mechanism. We know that wild fear in one market, say a bond market, may sometimes bleed over to fear in another market, say a stock market or FX, but we can't count on it happening every time in exactly the same way.

To overcome the tangle of data and questionable or unknown transmission routes, we propose a matrix of factors as the core organising principle. We describe this matrix in Chapter 1. What we cannot describe is the route by which a change in one factor will invariably affect another factor, or even if a change in one factor will affect other factors at all. It's wiser to assume that risk sentiment attached to any factor has the capability to affect the risk sentiment associated with other factors, but not always in a predictable way. The lack of predictability is no excuse for not having a firm grip on what the factors are in the first place. Again, the motto is "Be prepared."

A secondary motto might be "Drop ideology." If you assume, for example, that gold must go up and the dollar must go down as the Federal Reserve balloons its balance sheet with massive amounts of new money supply that will induce high inflation, you might be shocked to see gold fall and the dollar rise as other factors sometimes take centre stage. These factors might include on a drop in demand for gold from Asia, the rise and fall of the popularity of gold as a diversification commodity, contraction of bank lending in the US so that no inflation appears, and safe haven inflows to the dollar. One thing that watching the FX market will teach you is that ideology is a poor guide to trading success.

The FX market is not what you think

Chances are the realities of the FX market are not what you might think. In this book, we point out that:

- FX is driven more by pure speculation and global investment flows than by economic facts and ideas.

- FX players thumb their noses at the efficient market hypothesis and the concept of rational expectations.

- FX has a *disconnect puzzle* in which factors that should move the market do not, such as the three decades of persistent trade surpluses in Japan and deficits in the US. The exchange rate does not work as an equilibrating factor, as economists insist it should.

- While we cannot forecast exchange rates systematically, we can trade FX systematically.

- FX does not have a benchmark rate of return that traders or investors must try to match and surpass.

- FX traders are vastly more disciplined than traders in other sectors, in part because they use technical analysis.

- We do not have volume statistics in FX, except in the most delayed and roundabout forms.

In summary, the FX market is endlessly fascinating, not least because figuring out some of its puzzles and perversities leads to profound insights into the human heart and mind, albeit sometimes all you get is the same old insight that the profit motive always rules in markets and it doesn't pay to attribute mystical properties to mere prices.

CHAPTER 1 -
THE MATRIX CONCEPT

"I do not believe such a quality as chance exists. Every incident that happens must be a link in a chain."

Benjamin Franklin

What is the matrix?

The FX Matrix refers to a grid format of the multiple factors and players in the FX market and the way they interact. The term matrix is borrowed from *random matrix theory* and we use the matrix concept as a metaphor to help you avoid reaching or accepting oversimplified explanations of why the market behaves the way it does.

In random matrix theory, the maths is truly advanced. Graduate students, hedge funds and governments devise models of complex dynamic systems. Most of us can't get past page one of their articles and books because of the daunting calculations, but the metaphor is helpful to get a general grasp of the idea. In finance, random matrix theory was borrowed from physics and used to do things like remove idiosyncratic noise from correlation studies in designing optimum portfolios, leading to better estimates of component risk. The factor modelling includes weighting endogenous variables, exogenous variables and unobserved factors, and measuring their vectors.

Most relevant to the FX market today is estimating effects like sovereign risk contagion. Central bankers, including the Federal Reserve, are avid practitioners.[1] As the European Monetary Union (EMU) grapples with bank capital adequacy and sovereign credit issues, it's a pretty good assumption that European economists are using matrix theory, too.

The 2008 failure of Lehman Brothers (considered a *local behaviour*) jumped the boundaries of its own (large) matrix and became a *universal* factor independent of the pre-existing probability distributions of the other matrices. In the vernacular, a falling tide lowers all boats. But we want to know whether the factors involved in the Lehman failure (including the behaviour of the US government) were random noise to the FX market, or an exogenous factor (out of left field), or maybe an endogenous (inherent) factor in the FX matrix. Some correlations are, after all, just coincidence. Millions of random correlations exist in the financial world. We want to know how much weight to give *Big Financial Institution Failure* and *Government Refusal to Intervene* in the FX matrix.

Lehman Brothers declared bankruptcy on 15 September 2008. Before then, the rumour mill was already active with word of the bankruptcy. We heard of European banks closing lines to Lehman several months before the final collapse. Lehman wasn't the only factor in the FX market, but consider the trajectory of the dollar index. It had bottomed in March 2008 (at 70.698) and put in a second low in July (71.314) but then rose to 80.375 by 11 September. Over the next week, encompassing the Lehman debacle, the dollar index fell to what turned out to be an intermediate low of 75.891 on 22 September. The index then rose to a high of

88.463 by late November. The dollar's rise was a surprise to those FX players accustomed to selling the currency of a country in trouble. The dollar's use as a safe-haven trumped the negativity of Lehman's bankruptcy and therefore gave the safe-haven status more weight in the matrix.

The dollar index was already on the upswing when Lehman went bankrupt and the sell-off on the actual bankruptcy news was very short-lived; only one week. Smart FX analysts were detecting that overall financial market risk aversion was in play over the summer of 2008 and the dollar kept rising. The Lehman bankruptcy in hindsight was an exogenous *shock*, mostly because it was inconsistent with our assumptions about how the US government behaves and how the financial sector had behaved in the past. Up until the very last minute, some observers expected a bailout like the one of Long-Term Capital in 1998, and a return to risk positioning. But once the news was digested, the FX market returned to its previous mode of shunning risk. At that time (and up to the S&P downgrade of the US sovereign rating in August 2011), to be risk averse was to buy the safe-haven dollar.

Why the matrix is useful

The Lehman case is an example of a factor from a relatively distant corner of the FX matrix wending its way to FX prices themselves via interbank liquidity and interest rates, coupled with a major change in perception of the banking sector and US government – the *Establishment*. We would normally not expect an exogenous variable like the bankruptcy of a single financial institution to have such broad-reaching effects. It remains a puzzle why the rumours of the bankruptcy and then the event itself caused such an exaggerated reaction among international investors, sending them rushing to the safe-haven dollar.

The Lehman bankruptcy marks a dividing line in FX history between a time when price determinants encompassed an already wide range of factors to a new period in which price determinants range even more widely and reach into even more unexpected corners. This is why the concept of risk appetite and risk aversion is so useful – today, just about any exogenous variable has the potential to fly over the standard cause-and-effect factors and land on FX.

In the next sections of this chapter, we see examples of the new power of exogenous variables in FX. Pre-Lehman, for example, a popular uprising in an emerging market seldom had any effect on FX prices. But in 2011, regime change in North Africa had a pro-dollar effect, but in limited and varying ways. The effect of the Egyptian change differed from the effect of the change in Libya, in part because of Libya's role as an oil producer and the presence of foreign military forces. The addition of geopolitical events to the universe of FX determinants through the medium of risk appetite/risk aversion has made the FX world a vastly more complicated place in just a few years.

We now have to enter into consideration issues to which we used to give little thought, such as what will happen to oil prices if and when the current Venezuelan leader Chavez leaves office? We can suppose that the oil market will respond but we do not know whether a resulting rise or fall in oil prices will be correlated with the dollar – or the euro. The matrix helps us to make sense of all these interconnecting strands and thus of the FX market.

The primitive matrix

When an economist sits down to map out a hierarchy of fundamental factors that determine exchange rates, he may come up with something like Table 1.1. For each exchange rate on the left, the factors that affect it can in theory be checked off to reach an understanding of what affects that rate. Note that the factor list is incomplete – we could add dozens of other fundamentals such as labour market flexibility, tax rates, etc.

Table 1.1 – fundamental factors

Currency	Interest rate	Inflation rate	Terms of trade	Purchasing power parity	GDP growth	Degree of market freedom
USD						
EUR						
GBP						
JPY						

But if an economics-minded trader tries to apply incoming data to real-time trading, very quickly he discovers that economic fundamentals are sadly insufficient to explain FX price action – you also need the institutional context, as in the Lehman case and European sovereign risk contagion in 2009-2011. So now we need the mindset of *political economy* (as it was named in the 19th century). Table 1.2 shows how this grid might look.

Table 1.2 – institutional factors

	Public deficit as a percentage of GDP	Demographics	Central bank stances	Financial market size, liquidity and freedom	Reserves	Alliances, including military	State of the sovereign and politics
USD							
EUR							
GBP							
JPY							

For example, the European Central Bank (ECB) famously has a single mandate – to maintain price stability – whereas the US Federal Reserve has an additional mandate, to promote employment. In addition, as the issuer of the reserve currency, the US has a unique responsibility to lend to other central banks in time of crisis. Meanwhile, the euro is a currency without a state, which circles around to public deficits and to several factors in the economic factors spreadsheet, like the terms of trade.

Just when the analyst is trying to figure out how to combine the two sets of factors, he realises something else is missing, and it's big – the goals and attitudes of the FX market players themselves. In this grid (Table 1.3) it's the players that are on the y-axis rather than the currencies.

Table 1.3 – market player factors

	Correlation with other assets	Risk on-risk off	Technicals	
			Trend-following	Momentum
Bank professional				
Hedge fund				
Sovereign fund				
Multinational corporation (MNC)				
Retail trader				
High frequency trader				

In short, the fundamentals matrix introduced first doesn't include all the factors you need to analyse the FX market, and by the time you add institutional factors and market player factors, you need a three-dimensional matrix more like a Rubik's cube than a spreadsheet.

No sooner can you fix on a matrix like the one above than something will come along and show its inadequacy, if only because financial markets evolve. China opened a gold and precious metals commodity futures exchange in 2011, and is exploring reserve diversification not only in other currencies, especially the euro, but also in the form of bigger equity investments at the expense of US Treasury and Agency paper. European peripherals may default on sovereign debt, an event that has never happened in quite the same way throughout all history because we never before had a currency union quite like the EMU. So even if you build a system for analysing the FX market, you have to be prepared for it to be out of date, or for a factor you didn't think to take account of to occur, quite soon.

As for two-dimensional charts that appear to illustrate that Factor X is highly correlated with Currency Outcome Y and must be causative, this is often misleading. Two-dimensional charts are deceptive – correlation is not always causation, and worse, they result in emphasis on outcomes instead of processes. The salient question in FX analysis is in fact: *how do traders rank various multiple variables and events to determine whether they want to buy or sell a currency?*

Charts in two dimensions lack explanatory power and analytical depth – they don't enable us to answer the question just posed. Worse, they are static. It would be nice to be able to display interactive, dynamic effects, but that would take video, and even then it's not clear we could see cause-and-effect clearly.

We can try another matrix. Along one axis are the players in the FX market and along the other axis are the factors that influence FX prices. The grid should be imagined like a standard spreadsheet so that a big change in one cell is transmitted to other cells.

For example, we know that not only current interest rate differentials influence FX traders and investors, but also interest rate expectations. When a big change in expectations arises, as when Federal Reserve Chairman Bernanke announced in August 2010 that a second round of quantitative easing was pending, it dominates the market. When news of this magnitude is released we can grey out all the other variables on the matrix until bigger news about a key factor comes along. Because the graphic process is not a dynamic one, we need to prepare additional matrices and throw away the old ones as conditions change.

As a practical matter, you could combine and simplify to produce a master matrix that looks something like the one shown in Table 1.4.

Table 1.4 – combined master matrix

	Exogenous factors, shocks	Global attitude toward risk	GDP growth	Trade deficit	Capital flows	Interest rate	Interest rate forecast	Fiscal position	Politics	Other asset classes	Technicals, trend-following	Technicals, breakout/ momentum
Bank trader												
Position trader											X	
Carry trader												
Fund manager, equities												
Fund manager, bonds												
Individual retail trader												
High frequency trader												X

The two Xs mark the primary factors for just two types of FX market participants, the position trader and the high-frequency trader. The position trader, which includes the deep pockets of sovereign wealth funds and hedge funds (as well as hedgers from the equity and bond markets), will probably analyse the market using trend-following technicals, while high-frequency traders will use short-term breakout and momentum technicals. They may be on opposite sides of the same trade. Fund managers, whether of money market instruments, stocks or bonds, may have their antennae tuned to GDP growth and capital flows, while the carry trader cares about only thing; the stability of interest rate differentials.

The matrix process

We are still missing an important component, namely the weights to attach to each player and his favoured factor, and the vectors by which the factor invades another player's consciousness. In the set of matrices shown below, we start out with an allocation of the importance of various factors to professional bank traders. We chose bank traders as the leading edge of FX price determination – these are the players who cause directional breakouts based on their interpretation of factors. Don't forget that the professional bank traders are informed by the trading decisions of hedge funds and others who have a global worldview and make value judgments; the bank trader is not going to *fight the tape* if he sees sentiment shifting in a particular direction.

Let's say that over the summer of 2010, professional traders attributed a weight of 50% to interest rates and expected interest rates (Period 1 in the tables below). We can quibble over the weights, but let's take 50% for the minute.

Period 1 – June 2010 to end-August 2010

	Interest rates	Expected interest rates	Geopolitical risk	Equities	Commodities	Technicals
Bank traders	25%	25%	10%	10%	20%	10%
Sovereign funds	X	X	X	X	X	X
Hedge funds	X	X	X	X	X	X
Long-term investors	X	X	X	X	X	X
MNC's	X	X	X	X	X	X
Retail market	X	X	X	X	X	X

Then Ben Bernanke pre-announced QE2 at the Kansas City Fed summit in Jackson Hole, Wyoming in August 2010. The focus immediately shifted to interest rate expectations, which now get a much higher weight in Period 2. The other players, seeing the dollar fall on the pros building a wider differential against the dollar, increased their weight to that factor, too. The weight attributed by the pro bank traders bled into the other players' evaluations of factors.

Period 2 – Quantitative Easing 2: end-August 2010 to end-December 2010

	Interest rates	Expected interest rates	Geopolitical risk	Equities	Commodities	Technicals
Bank traders	25%	75%	0%	0%	0%	X
Sovereign funds	X	X	X	X	X	X
Hedge funds	X	X	X	X	X	X
Long-term investors	X	X	X	X	X	X
MNC's	X	X	X	X	X	X
Retail market	X	X	X	X	X	X

In Period 3, Eurostat released data showing that inflation was over the ECB cap of 2%, raising the spectre of the ECB tightening rates faster than the US. The interest rate expectation factor thus got stronger, the dollar fell more, and because the FX market is reactive, all the other players imputed a higher weight to this factor, too.

Period 3 – euro zone inflation rises: January 2011

	Interest rates	Expected interest rates	Geopolitical risk	Equities	Commodities	Technicals
Bank traders	0%	100%	0%	0%	0%	X
Sovereign funds	X	X	X	X	X	X
Hedge funds	X	X	X	X	X	X
Long-term investors	X	X	X	X	X	X
MNC's	X	X	X	X	X	X
Retail market	X	X	X	X	X	X

At end-January 2011, Tunisia experienced rioting and the government fell (Period 4). Civil unrest broke out in Egypt, and in a single day, geopolitical factors became the dominant factor. Oil rose, returning the commodity correlation story to the fore.

Period 4 – revolution in Egypt, 28 January 2011

	Interest rates	Expected interest rates	Geopolitical risk	Equities	Commodities	Technicals
Bank traders	5%	5%	90%	0%	0%	X
Sovereign funds	X	X	X	X	X	X
Hedge funds	X	X	X	X	X	X
Long-term investors	X	X	X	X	X	X
MNC's	X	X	X	X	X	X
Retail market	X	X	X	X	X	X

If these matrices were on a set of cards and you could fan them in order, you would get a moving picture that would show first the interest rate expectation gaining dominance, then bleeding to the other players, and then the geopolitical factor taking over. In other words, you'd get a moving picture showing how the weight of factors increases and then bleeds into other factors.

Flickering off to the side would be the technical factors. Technical factors never really go away but can always be trumped by institutional factors. This is a useful way to think about how and why exchange rates move – better than two dimensional charts labelled with world events – but obviously it is too cumbersome and impractical for anyone but a programmer to attempt.

That brings us to the thorny problem of factors that are temporarily not at the top of the list but which are still present; a form of *known unknowns*. On the day in January 2011 when the Egyptian riots took over the imagination of traders in all markets, nobody was talking about fiscal sustainability in Greece, Ireland, Britain, Japan or the US. In fact, S&P had downgraded Japan's sovereign rating just the day before, but the yen didn't move an inch on the downgrade. Still, a new geopolitical issue coming along does not kill a factor, it just supersedes it for a while.

Perversity of the FX market

While the various matrices are a handy metaphor for market behaviour, not everything can be explained in a rational way. On any day, a sane interpretation of events may suggest the dollar should move up when in fact it goes on to move down. In the middle of the worsening euro zone peripheral debt crisis, the euro rose for almost a full year (June 2010 to May 2011).

What's going on here? Why does the FX market behave in this perverse fashion?

Understanding this perversity

In a way, perverse FX responses to events are a form of *irrational rationality*, like the prisoner's dilemma. Both parties (bulls and bears) would benefit if they both stay silent, but often the first prisoner will confess because he doesn't know whether the second prisoner appreciates that his self-interest lies in staying silent. Translated to FX, it pays to jump to conclusions on the assumption that others will jump to those conclusions, even if they are nonsensical conclusions. One such perversity, after the 2008 global financial crisis, is the dollar reliably, consistently and persistently falling on good economic news – it occurs because good US data implies the environment is safe for risk-taking in non-US dollar currencies and assets.

To get oriented in trying to answer the perversity question, you have to accept two ideas mentioned in the Introduction: the first is that the price of a currency is set at any one moment in time by traders whose only goal is to make a profit. FX traders usually do not know, nor do they care about, *fair value*. They want to buy low and sell high, or buy high and sell higher. The second idea is that a key tool in this quest for profit is technical analysis.

Technical analysis in the FX market

Like the addition of hitherto exogenous variables to the basic FX matrix, the spread of technical analysis is relatively new. While technical analysis has been used since right after the dollar was first floated in 1974 – as a remedy to mass confusion over the determinants of FX prices – it was the advent of the personal computer in the 1990s that made it widespread. Technical analysis is more efficient than fundamentals – you use three or four indicators on a single chart against a complicated, interactive matrix of fundamental and institutional factors.

Moreover, technical factors can drive and override fundamentals, at least sometimes, even if in the end the fundamentals always have the last word. Unlike in other securities fields, in FX there is no clear-cut dividing line between the fundamental and the technical. Fundamental and technical effects are as interactive with one another as fundamental and institutional factors. For example, once the euro bottomed in June 2010 and started rising, it had upward momentum and upward-pointing patterns that set a new stage for evaluating the later worsening of sovereign debt and the banking crisis.

This is called Bayesian analysis, wherein what you think you knew is changed by subsequent knowledge. You literally go back and remember your original thinking differently from what it really was at the time. In a nutshell, everything is relative. The first appearance of a crisis is more shocking (and causes a bigger price move) than a later worsening of the same crisis, when the effects of the first shock have worn off and the first shock has become part of the background environment. In the case of the euro, the second shock was buffered significantly by its healthy image, which was both cause and effect of the first rebound.

Pinpointing how multiple factors – fundamental and technical – interact is tricky because in FX there are no absolutes. We might postulate that at the beginning of a price move, fundamentals drive the technicals, but once the fundamental event is known, the technicals can lead. For instance, a key level will be resisted solely because the probability of a negative news release is high, even when traders don't have anything specific in mind. The trader has an existing position to defend and therefore a bias against reversing from pessimism to optimism – unless and until it becomes profitable to drop the position.

Technical analysis is so important in FX trading that we can say that a FX market event gets some of its importance from what is happening on the chart at the time. Untangling what is technical and what is fundamental in any specific move thus becomes complex. Unlike the situation in equities, where price-earnings ratios are a fixed (if evolving) number, fundamental events do not have a fixed hierarchical ranking in FX but rather gain or lose power over the minds of traders depending on how the chart looks. A bad news release will be dismissed if a currency has just made a decisive upside breakout, but the same news may be fatal to an existing upmove if it comes when the price is already flirting with reversal.

It's a mistake to dismiss technical analysis as some strange sideline of a minority. Professional traders bet hundreds of billions of dollars per day using technical analysis and they would not do that if technical analysis failed to help achieve profits and avoid losses. Virtually everyone in FX applies some concepts from the technical analysis world, even if they are not self-described techies; a trader who does not subscribe to technical analysis concepts will still be aware that others in the market are using them.

Every once in a while, you may meet a brilliant, intuitive trader who uses no technical indicators at all and yet succeeds in generating winning trades. He is almost certainly using the same ideas as the technical trader, just not measuring and labelling the ideas with the same terms. After all, most of the indicators in technical analysis derive from long-standing trading practices. Ask an intuitive trader why he changes from long to short, and he may say "I couldn't see any more buyers out there – the bid was gone." The technical trader will point to three or four indicators and say "It was overbought." Same thing.

The pinball effect

Sometimes a price change comes out of left field and we literally cannot find an explanation for it in the fundamentals, technicals or what little information we have on professional positioning. It's as though one deep-pocket trader had an epiphany that inspired him to take a huge new position. Some of these initiatives fail and are never heard of again, but in the time-honoured way of crowd behaviour, others take a profitable ride. As recounted in the many books about the Soros 1992 sterling trade, many other FX players declined to believe the statements of UK officials and instead put their money on the same trade as Soros, short the pound, because they could see a clear trajectory on the chart. Soros did the hard work of analysing the situation, but it was his positioning that everyone could see, even if they didn't know exactly who was behind it.[2]

Where do these inspirations come from? Oddly enough, they often come from outside the immediate conditions in the financial markets themselves, from perceiving a historical analogy, from maths, or even from superstition. Thus is created a *pinball effect*, where a new idea (or an old idea resurrected) shoots around several markets along multiple interconnecting and criss-crossing pathways. An inspired trade in oil futures can pinball to emerging market currencies, to advanced country fixed income securities, to mutual fund valuations, to the new-technology energy names on the NASDAQ, to the Shanghai and Nikkei indices, to the dollar/yen… and so on. Transactions are conducted at such speed and the world is so interconnected today that we can't explain everything, and often, ex-post explanations are unconvincing. Explanations do exist, but we may never know them. This is a wonderful and frightening thing.[3]

The actors

Let's take the actors, or *agents* as academics might call them. How you interpret FX market developments depends on what sort of trader you are, so it is important that we consider how various actors think.

Let's say, for example, a key technical level is being hit – but it's Friday at 3 pm. The FX market's reaction to the key level is entirely different from when a key level is hit at 8:30 am on a Monday morning. More nuanced than this, a key level being hit at 3 pm in London on any day is different from the level being hit at 3 pm in New York. In the London case, traders still have several hours to see what the New York market will make of the development. If New York responds predictably to the key level, London traders have a new profit opportunity, although it means working late.

The New York traders do have an overlapping time zone – New Zealand opens around 3 pm New York time, Australia opens around 5 pm and Tokyo opens around 7 pm. But these are much smaller markets than London and New York, and New York traders have different work habits. They arrive at work early to partake of the London and European action, rather than staying late to join the Asian markets. The importance of the key level is far lower in New York at 3 pm on any day than at 8:30 am on any day.

Now consider which group of actors cares the most about a key level at any time of day – technical traders. After all, with algorithm-trading and pre-set electronic entries and exits, the trader doesn't have to be physically at the trading terminal to respond to a technical event like a key level. If the key level is a match of a past benchmark high or low, or a round number, or widely publicised (like a Fibonacci level), then non-technical traders know about it, too. If the technical group responds as expected, the non-technical groups feel compelled to react, whether defensively or opportunistically.

In other words, the sets of players are interactive. Because we have so much news and chatter in the electronic age, we are all getting a great deal of information about the other players, and we are getting it 24 hours a day. A good case is when the FX newswires have reported where a big buy-side client has an option strike, often a round number. The existence of the option and its strike price is a mechanical aspect of the market and not strictly speaking *technical*, but the strike level is almost always set by technical considerations. It may be just past a moving average, a historical benchmark level, or some other calculation.

The financial institution that wrote the option will have hedged at least part of its position (although not all, or it wouldn't make a profit on the transaction), but still probably prefers not to have to pay up, while other market players know that a failed test of the level opens the door for a big move in the opposite direction of the strike. This is a case in which the widespread knowledge of the option strike is the top factor and it would take a big event in the macroeconomic world to overwhelm it.

Positions

The option strike price case illustrates the most important aspect of the player groups – their positions. When the vast majority of the market holds a particular belief, their positions reflect those beliefs. If a set of factors lines up against the pound sterling, for example, a short sterling position is rewarded with every news release reinforcing the negative tone. Good news is dismissed and disregarded. Every trader is gunning for sterling. It doesn't matter that by any objective measure on a fundamentals matrix, five factors are negative and two factors are positive.

But there is always a tipping point at which the market gets oversold sterling – something experienced traders can smell and that technical analysts can measure – whereupon a key level gets hit and a cascade of short-covering ensues. The tipping point may appear with or without a news announcement pertaining to a factor. Sometimes the factor is directly relevant, whereupon the press says "the release of the XYZ data caused the pound to firm." In other instances, and we say it's the majority of the time, the release of the XYZ data is just an excuse for traders to get out of Dodge. If you can't sell it (anymore), buy it.

Hence the seeming perversity of the FX market. The objective measure would still have four negative factors versus the new count of three positive ones; it would still be net negative. Logically, we say the pound *should* remain in a falling trend and the factor weights do not line up to support a rise, but the market is not responding only to the factors, but to the quickly disappearing probability of making a profit from the existing short position.

This is the sense in which the market is not *always right*, as the old law has it. The market is always right in the sense that every trader has to accept the prices offered and a single trader cannot change the market's mind about what is the correct price. The market can be dead wrong about factor analysis but it doesn't matter. You have to trade the prices in front of you, not what you think prices should be.

Making sense of the information

Now enter the poor retail trader, who often has no idea that FX trading is not easy, as the TV and website ads proclaim. Retail FX trading is rapidly expanding, hot on the heels of professional asset managers diversifying their base. How do these new traders make sense of the market? FX commentary is keeping pace, but much of it is of dubious quality.

One book author asserts the Canadian dollar is 40% correlated with the price of oil – without naming the time period over which the statistic was calculated, rendering it literally useless. In practice, you can manipulate the CAD to be correlated with the price of oil to any number that suits your argument by changing the correlation timeframe. In the funniest case, a publisher was so eager to get a book in print and capitalise on the demand for market commentary that it failed to notice a whole chapter and multiple other references devoted to "rouge" traders (when "rogue" was the intent).

The lesson here is to be careful what conclusions you draw from what you read. And also, to come back to our matrix, that single-factor explanations of FX market behaviour are always wrong. To explain a move, you need:

1. fundamental factors;

2. technical measurement of the sentiment derived from those factors;

3. technical dynamics, and

4. existing positions of the key players.

Once you have these four things and decide which weight each should have, you can begin filling out your matrix and deciding how best to position yourself for a move. In the chapters ahead, we will go deeper into the specific factors that drive currencies.

It's probably fair to say that very few, if any, highly sophisticated FX market players have programmed a matrix to include all the factors or succeeded in figuring out how a change in one fundamental feeds the technicals and then how the resulting positions create a feedback effect on other technicals and sometimes the fundamentals themselves. A computer program that is capable of taking new data and have it light up the relevant variables in some kind of logical order and have it all result in a price deduction would be a splendid machine, indeed. If some advanced hedge fund or sovereign fund has created a working matrix, they are keeping it a deep, dark secret.

Until such a thing can be devised, we mere mortals must struggle with the sets of variables the old-fashioned way, using our brains. It should come as no surprise that some of the best traders are fairly ignorant of economics and historical context, but are cracker-jack at game theory. In the chapters that follow, we do not actually mention the matrix very often. Instead our goal is to describe the FX market in ways that will be useful to the reader in creating his own matrix in his imagination, if not in programming code.

CHAPTER 2 -
REVIEW OF RISKS

"If this were a logical world, men would ride sidesaddle."

Ron Frost, Agricultural Markets Manager, Chicago Mercantile Exchange

Markets are increasingly global in scope, so that a Mumbai investor can trade a US equity issue or the euro/dollar exchange rate with equal ease of execution (although we may question whether he should). A symptom of this globalisation is that global financial markets move together in a way that they did not before; events in one market have repercussions for others.

There are many risk indicators that players watch to try to help them understand the risk that movements in one market will affect another they are interested in, but we do not yet have a single risk index to explain market behaviour.

In this chapter, after discussing the globalisation of FX markets and contagion, we move on to the tools the market uses to gauge risk. We discuss VIX, the highly-watched fear-factor gauge, risk reversals, stress indexes, and credit default swaps.

Risk and contagion

Contagion arises from the Asian Crisis

Before the Asian Crisis of 1997-98, a big risk event was fairly well contained to the country in question; now a Brazilian limit on foreign investor inflows has a spillover effect not only on the Mexican peso, but also the Korean won. The Asian Crisis was the first time we saw the attitude toward risk shifting from a single country basis to a global basis. What began as a run on the Thai baht in May 1997 (leading to devaluation in July 1997) spread to investor selling of the Malaysian ringgit, Philippine peso and Indonesian rupiah, among others. In the autumn of 1997 and early 1998, Asian currency jitters sent shock waves around the world, with other emerging market currencies feeling the heat as investors exited existing emerging market long positions and sought safe-haven currencies.

By May 1998, the Russian stock and bond market had collapsed, along with the Russian ruble. Russian officials were forced to triple interest rates to 150% to prevent the ruble from falling further. In June of that year, the Japanese yen succumbed to downward pressure, with the Bank of Japan and the US Federal Reserve intervening to prevent further yen weakness. The dollar-yen topped out at ¥147.65 before ending the year at ¥113.45.

By August 1998, the Dow Jones Industrial Average had fallen over 500 points and, by September, Federal Reserve Chairman Greenspan promised to lower US interest rates as the Nikkei 225 hit a 14-year low and other global stock indices also fell dramatically. In addition, troubled US hedge fund Long-Term Capital Management (LTCM) received a $3.5 billion bailout. LTCM had been counting on the convergence spread in fixed income to make tiny arbitrage gains magnified by high leverage, a strategy designed by not one, but two, Nobel Prize winners. Like others, they had never heard of contagion on this scale.

In the autumn of 2008, the Fed initiated a series of interest rate cuts to stabilise US financial markets. The International Monetary Fund (IMF) announced bailout packages for Russia and Brazil. The market began to stabilise in the first quarter of 1999 and the Dow Jones Industrial Average climbed back to over 10,000. Investors breathed the first sigh of relief in nearly two years. While traumatic, the events of that period provided investors with a valuable education. They learned the hard way that, as *New York Times* columnist Thomas Friedman would later write, "The World is Flat."

Globalisation of risk

While we were not looking, economic globalisation had occurred far faster than anyone was accounting for. No longer can risk be confined to the properties of a specific security and its environmental conditions, but an investor has to look at risk on a worldwide basis. In the first decade of the 2000s, you couldn't open a newspaper without seeing reference to the *butterfly effect*, whereby a butterfly flapping its wings in China results in a tornado in Kansas. Note that the formal name for the butterfly effect is *sensitive dependence on initial conditions*, giving rise to just about any observation about an economy becoming expandable into grand deductions about markets near and far.

Since the Asian Crisis, when a big risk event occurs, market players judge whether the risks will be contained to one country or region or are global in nature, and react accordingly. Investors' collective attitude towards risk becomes a factor in its own right and influences how markets react to shocks. As a report of the Bank for International Settlements (BIS) put it:

> "Bad news in a market situation where investor risk appetite is already low is likely to result in a much greater repricing of risky assets than in periods where it is high. The dynamic stance of the risk appetite of market participants as a sentiment could thus serve as an important contributing factor in the transmission of shocks through the financial system. Furthermore, as it might itself be influenced by the situation in financial markets, it could work as a multiplier. Accordingly, taking into account the risk appetite/risk aversion of investors and its evolution has become an important element of assessing the condition and stability of financial markets."[4]

In recent years, larger risk aversion on a global scale has been triggered most often by events taking place in the United States. The market panicked after the NASDAQ Composite crash in 2000, in the wake of the 9/11 attack of the World Trade Center, in the lead-up to the Iraq War in 2003, following Hurricanes Katrina and Rita in 2005, and during the subprime mortgage crisis that began to unfold in late 2008.

In contrast, the euro zone, which came officially into existence in January 1999, was the root cause of fewer worldwide risk events until recently. Small effects in the euro/dollar exchange rate were occasioned by the French and Dutch No vote on the referendum in favour of the European Union's proposed constitution in 2005 and Ireland's rejection of the Lisbon Treaty in 2008 (later accepted in the 2009 vote), but these events were contained to Europe. Having previously avoided being the source of a shock catalyst, Europe has more than made up for it with the peripheral country debt crisis that began in the fall of 2009, with Greece admitting it had cooked the budget books on the Olympics. This set off a chain of developments that has ended up endangering the structure and composition of the euro zone itself.

Asia had a chance to offer a shock again, in the form of the Shanghai Surprise from October 2007 to October 2008. The SSE Shanghai Composite Index was already falling from a peak in October 2007 when (on 28 February 2008) it fell 9% in a single day. The S&P fell the next day by the most since 9/11/01. European and Japanese markets fell. Certain other emerging market stock markets, like Brazil, Russia and Turkey, also suffered big declines – but not all emerging markets.

The Shanghai event was curious for many reasons, not least that at the time the exchange had limited international participation and the drop was triggered by reports of impending new restriction on transactions, including a proposed tax. By what logic does this isolated market – and why do other regional markets – have such an outsized effect, such as is illustrated in Figure 2.1, globally?

Figure 2.1 – the Shanghai Surprise (SSE Shanghai Composite Index (Dark) vs. S&P 500, Nikkei 225 and FTSE 100

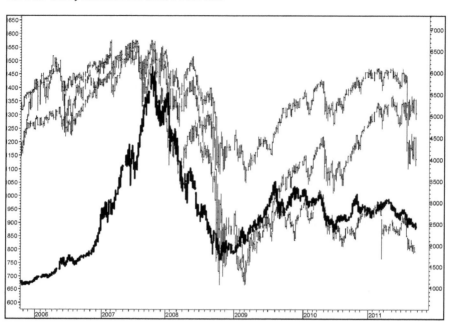

Explaining large-scale contagion

Analysts don't have a good explanation for large-scale contagion. To call it a Pavlovian or herd-instinct response is both insulting to the investor class and insufficient. Why should one market drop in sync but not others? One reasonable-sounding scenario is that economies that are already vulnerable – due to trade and budget deficits, stressed institutions, inadequate legal and regulatory institutions, etc. – will be affected the most by a shock. These are the countries that sophisticated and knowledgeable investors will exit first. But that doesn't account for the major markets in advanced countries following the Shanghai stock index. It also doesn't account for a shock in one asset class in one country affecting different asset classes in other countries that are linked only in the most indirect ways. Something else is going on.

The *something else* is perception of riskiness in the world at large, and perception of riskiness is heavily influenced by what academics call *information asymmetry*. At a basic level, if one party to a transaction has more information than the other party, the informed party has more power and will likely be the profitable one. Think of inside information, moral hazard and why governments impose disclosure rules on minimum safety conditions in real estate.

Information asymmetry is illustrated perfectly in every home sale – the seller knows the furnace is on its last legs, the roof will need replacement in two years, and there is some asbestos lurking in the cellar ceiling. The selling agent may or may not know these things, and the buyer certainly doesn't know them and will not be told them unless the law requires disclosure of each specific drawback by name. The buyer is at risk of overpaying for the house, and cannot count on the agent to volunteer adverse information because the agent works for the seller.

In the home sale case, the seller is more knowledgeable about the asset than the buyer. In the case of financial market information asymmetry, emerging market investors generally tend to have less information than advanced country investors about emerging markets overall, including their home market. The foreign investors tend to have more news sources, including sources that may not be permitted in the emerging market itself. In fact, sometimes the flow of adverse information runs from one emerging market through the advanced investors to a second emerging market before the domestic investors in the original emerging market catch on. That's just one example of how a lopsided flow of information can move.

In market contagion, the less-knowledgeable party knows that he is less knowledgeable and fears being cheated, so that he sells even when there is no evidence that the quality of the asset has changed. When an investor knows he is less-knowledgeable, he assumes the more-knowledgeable parties have information he does not have, so he joins the stampede. Thus, when the presumed knowledgeable parties started a sell-off in overvalued Thai equities, it spread to other risky assets elsewhere in Asia and then Argentina and Russia, even though Malaysians, for example, complained it was unfair to be tarred with the Thai brush.

In many instances, the domestic investors were authentically more knowledgeable about their home assets and knew perfectly well that there was, objectively, no change in the conditions that should determine their prices – except that advanced country investors were fleeing emerging markets indiscriminately (in what investment managers term *cross-market rebalancing*). By assuming that emerging markets share the same market and economic risks to the same degree, the managers can transmit contagion in the form of falling prices even in the absence of directly relevant news, and sometimes between markets that do not, in fact, share the same risks.

It can work the other way around, too, like the home seller failing to disclose asbestos in the cellar ceiling. Unscrupulous asset sellers can offer fraudulent products, like some Chinese companies listed on the New York Stock Exchange and other exchanges, that are the paper equivalent of knock-off Rolex watches and Hermes scarves. The buyers who know they are less-knowledgeable about the true financial condition of these companies are the first to exit on news of a regulatory investigation.

The second important point is that information flow and thus market effects are not linear – they ricochet around in the pinball motion mentioned in Chapter 1. Sometimes contagion can occur in the absence of information and is based on unfounded assumptions.[5] Therefore, what traders and investors need is a general indicator of global riskiness. If global riskiness is low, the probability of a shock in a small context becoming a major crisis is also low. If the market feels riskiness is high, the slightest rumble can set off shock waves, and perhaps in some asset classes linked to the source by many degrees of separation.

Unfortunately, we do not yet have a single index of global riskiness that works in all instances. But we do have a selection of indicators and indices that send out warning sounds ahead of shocks that cause global stock markets to plummet and safe-haven buying of developed market bonds.

Let's look at these now.

Risk gauges

There are a selection of indictors that can be used to assess risk in financial markets. Many of these are based on markets or areas other than FX, but conclusions can be extrapolated from these to the FX market. These risk gauges give FX traders reliable guidance towards direction, but not necessarily about the magnitude of moves. Traders use these risk gauges mostly to red flag potential trend changes.

These indicators are:

1. The VIX

2. Risk reversals

3. Federal Reserve stress indexes

4. Bank stress indexes

5. Inflation breakevens and inflation swaps

6. Corporate spreads/credit default swaps

7. Prices of commodities

1. The VIX

One of the most closely tracked risk instruments is the Chicago Board Option Exchange's (CBOE's) volatility index or VIX (also called the *fear factor*). The CBOE describes the VIX as "an up-to-the-minute market estimate of expected volatility that is calculated by using real-time S&P 500 Index (SPX) option bid/ask quotes." It is seen as a proven risk gauge.

To calculate the VIX, the CBOE uses "near-term and next-term out-of-the money SPX options with at least eight days left to expiration, and then weights them to yield a constant, 30-day measure of the expected volatility of the S&P 500 Index." While the VIX is quoted as a percentage, most analysts drop the percentage sign and just use the number itself. When the VIX price goes up, it means risk aversion is kicking in and the S&P 500 typically falls. Conversely, when the VIX falls, there is more risk appetite in the market and the S&P usually will rise. A graph of the S&P 500 juxtaposed over the graph of the VIX would provide roughly a mirror image of the risk indicator. See Figure 2.2.

Figure 2.2 – VIX and S&P 500 (inverted scale, monthly)

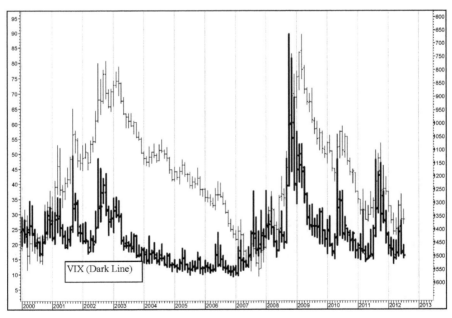

As well as VIX, the CBOE calculates other volatility indexes including the NASDAQ-100 Volatility index (VXN) and the DJIA Volatility Index (VXD). In

2008, the CBOE introduced other indexes incorporating VIX methodology. These new contracts include the Crude Oil Volatility Index (OVX), the Gold Volatility Index (GVZ) and the EuroCurrency Volatility Index (EVZ), all of which use exchange-traded options based on the United States Oil Fund LP(USO), SPDR Gold Shares (GLD) and CurrencyShares Euro Trust (FXE), respectively. While traders may occasionally use these other tools, the focus remains on the VIX and the latest signal that the fear factor is emitting.

A VIX level below 20 is deemed positive for risk and a VIX level over 40 is deemed negative for risk, with the range in the middle deemed indecisive. A timeline of the VIX shows that after starting the millennium around 24.15, the index soared to a high of 43.74 in the wake of the 9/11 attacks and then slipped back into the 20s and 30s in 2002/2003. The VIX stood at 29.15 at the start of the Iraq War in March 2003, before closing the year at 18.31. At the time of Hurricane Katrina in August 2005, the VIX was trading below 15.

The index remained offered in subsequent years, with the low volatility indicative of the extreme risk appetite present in the market. The VIX bottomed at a 13-year low of 9.39 in December 2006, very close to the life-time low of 9.31 seen in 1993. By October 2008, at the peak of the US financial crisis, the index had reached a life-time high of 89.53. During key stress points of the euro zone peripheral crisis, the VIX topped out a bit below 50 on two occasions, first at 48.20 in May 2010 and again at 48.00 in early August 2011. The velocity of the VIX rise or fall can be a factor affecting risk also. On 8 August 2011, when the VIX topped out at 48.00, the index rose 50% in a single day.

The VIX and the S&P 500 do not always move in lockstep with each other; there is often a sizeable time lag. In October 2008, the VIX topped out close to 89.00 and subsequently edged lower into the end of 2008 and early 2009, suggesting diminishing risk aversion. In contrast, the S&P 500 continued to decline into late 2008 and early 2009, bottoming at 666.92 only in March 2009 (VIX closed at 49.33 that day). A trader trying to buy US stocks cheaply in late 2008/early 2009, thinking they had bottomed, would have experienced buyer's remorse by getting in too early. The lesson to be learned is that while the VIX can be considered a good predictor of future direction of the S&P 500, a turn in market sentiment suggested by a drop or rise in VIX volatility may not translate to an immediate shift in stock positioning.

Currency traders use swings in the VIX as a gauge of risk appetite for US and global stocks and, depending upon the FX link at the time, buy and sell currencies accordingly. Starting in September 2010, the CBOE began to offer weekly options (both puts and calls) on VIX futures, which allowed investors to bet on VIX direction for the first time. In the past, if an FX trader saw the VIX falling sharply, he would conclude that US stocks might also fall and drag the dollar with it. More recently, since the US and euro zone financial crises, a falling VIX would suggest risk friendly positions were being pared and red flag the potential for safe-haven demand. Under this scenario, the dollar might firm on safe-haven demand.

It's not only FX traders that use VIX as a risk gauge. Figure 2.3 shows VIX against the oil futures contract. Oil *led* the VIX up from 2004 to 2008 and as oil crashed at end-2008 so did the VIX. In fact, VIX stayed low as oil resumed its rise, except for spikes in both 2010 and 2011. The correlation is not very strong and it lags, but fear of equity market volatility arises from economic conditions and in turn has economic implications that affect perceived demand for oil. It can be bit head-spinning, but it's not without a certain logic. Since FX traders watch oil prices as well as VIX, when they are both signalling rising risk we can expect magnification of a pro-dollar bias.

Figure 2.3 – VIX and Crude Oil Futures (monthly)

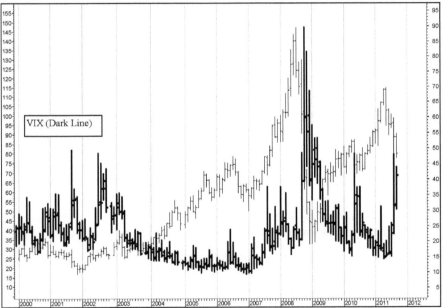

2. Risk reversals

Another measure of bias or directional preference used by currency traders involves risk reversals. Market players, especially those trading FX options, watch the skew in option risk reversals to see which way sentiment is leaning in a given pair. A *risk reversal* is the difference between the implied volatility of an OTM (out of the money) call (right to buy a currency) and that of a put (right to sell a currency) option of similar maturities. Typically, 25-Delta calls and 25-Delta puts are tracked by the market players.

If a risk reversal is positive (calls are more expensive than puts) it means that for a given maturity (one-month, two-months, three-months, etc.) buying option protection or *insurance* in the event of a currency move higher is more expensive than buying protection for a move lower. Conversely, if a risk reversal is negative, then it means that buying insurance to protect against a currency move lower is more expensive than buying insurance to protect against a currency move higher. When risk reversals hit extended levels, it may indicate that a directional expectation has become excessive.

"This bias helps in assessing the excessive sentiment toward a directional preference and the common wisdom is to use it as a contrarian indicator," explains Bashar Azzouz, Founder and Managing Director of 2 Rivers Consulting. Azzouz, who manages money and educates on option strategies, says the common practice is to generate two sets of observations from positive and negative risk reversals. The upper limit will be the mean (pick a historical time frame such as six months or a year) of the positive observations, plus one standard deviation of the positive observation. If the upper limit is exceeded, then the bias indicates excessive bullishness and therefore can be viewed as overbought. The lower limit will be the mean of the negative observations, minus one standard deviation of the negative observations. If the lower limit is exceeded, then the bias is indicating excessive bearishness and can be deemed oversold.

Risk reversals and their ranges can vary greatly between FX pairs. These instruments are quoted like forward foreign currency swap rates, typically from one week to one year, with the most attention paid to the one-month risk reversal. There are occasions where one period suggests future bullishness and another future bearishness. "When there is a divergence in the skew, say one-month (risk reversals) shows calls are bid over puts, while three-months shows puts are bid over calls, this may indicate a corrective short-term bullish outlook in a longer-term bearish trend," Azzouz suggests.

3. Federal Reserve stress indexes

Currency traders seeking a more detailed picture look beyond the one dimensionality of the CBOE's VIX and seek out other risk indicators that factor in multiple variables, such as Federal Reserve stress indexes. The Federal Reserve Banks of Kansas City and Cleveland release monthly Financial Stress Indexes (FSIs) and the Federal Reserve Bank of St. Louis releases a weekly Financial Stress Index (FSI). These Fed risk gauges are becoming more popular as FX tools. With all stress indicators, the higher the stress, the more pro-dollar bias we see in the FX market.

Kansas City Federal Reserve Financial Stress Index (KCFSI)

The Kansas City Federal Reserve Bank describes its FSI as "a monthly measure of stress in the US financial system based on 11 financial market variables." These variables are: the three-month LIBOR/T-Bill spread (TED spread), the two-year swap spread, off-the run/on the run 10-year Treasury spread, Aaa/10-year Treasury spread, Baa/Aaa spread, high-yield bond/Baa spread, consumer ABS/5-year Treasury spread, the negative value of correlation between stock and Treasury returns, the implied volatility of overall stock prices (VIX), idiosyncratic volatility (IVOL) of bank stock prices, and a cross-section dispersion (CSD) of bank stock returns. "A positive value indicates that financial stress is above the long-run average, while a negative value signifies that financial stress is below the long-run average."[6]

The Kansas City Fed explains the root causes of financial stress as arising from:

- increased uncertainty about fundamental value of assets
- increased uncertainty about behaviour of other investors
- increased asymmetry of information
- decreased willingness to hold risky assets (flight to quality)
- decreased willingness to hold illiquid assets (flight to liquidity)

In discussing the uncertainty about the fundamental value of assets, the Kansas City Fed observed that financial innovations can "make it difficult for lenders and investors to even assign probabilities to different outcomes. This kind of uncertainty, in which risk is viewed as unknown and unmeasurable, is often referred to as Knightian uncertainty." As example of financial innovation, the Fed pointed to "complex structured products such as collateralised debt obligations (CDOs) in the recent subprime crisis, or program trading in the Long-Term Capital Management crisis of 1998."

On the issue of transparency the Kansas City Fed stated, "asymmetry of information is said to exist when borrowers know more about their true financial condition than lenders, or when sellers know more about the true quality of the assets they hold than buyers." These information gaps can "lead to problems of adverse selection or moral hazard, boosting the average cost of borrowing for firms and households, and reducing the average price of assets on secondary markets."

In the past 15 years, the KCFSI flashed warning signals on several occasions. See Figure 2.4. In the period from October 1998 to October 2002, the KCFSI saw six distinct peaks in a short period of time. The index peaked in the wake of the Russian debt moratorium in August 1998 and the bailout of Long-Term Capital Management in September 1998, and then peaked in October 1999 ahead of Y2K.

Figure 2.4 – Kansas City Fed Stress Index (monthly)

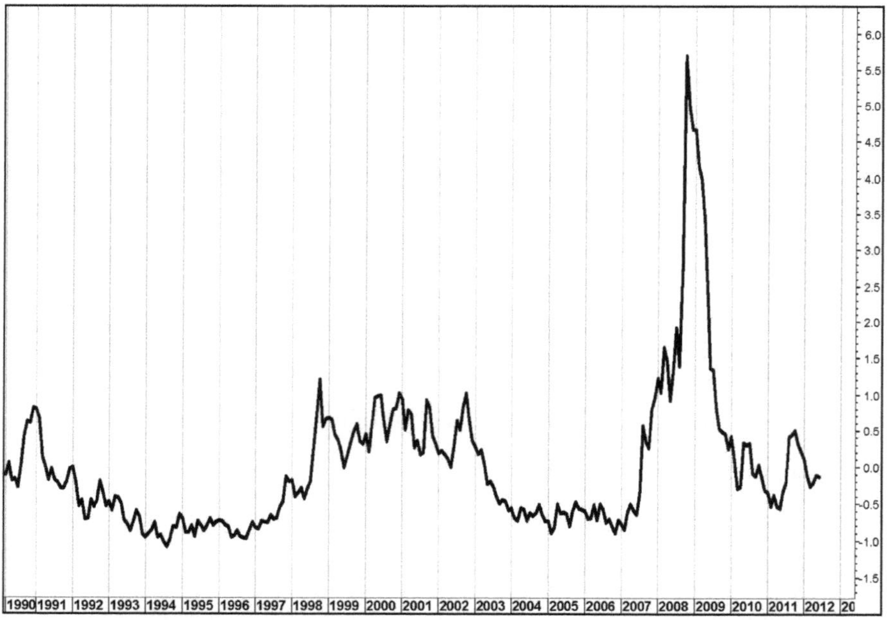

Source: **research.stlouisfed.org/fred2**

In 2000, the KCFSI peaked twice, first in line with the bursting of the technology bubble and subsequent sharp NASDAQ Composite decline and then again later in the year. "The second peak was December 2000, when there were no obvious reasons for increased financial stress other than the approach of recession. The next peak came after the 9/11 attacks and the most recent peak came in October 2002, amidst widespread accounting scandals (Enron/World Com).

During the subprime crisis, the KCFSI has spiked on a few occasions, first in response to mortgage-related concerns in August and November 2007, and then again in March 2008, when Bear Stearns collapsed. Later in July 2008, the index again spiked when IndyMac failed and Fannie Mae and Freddie Mac had their issues. The following year saw the largest spikes seen ever in the index, first in September 2008, following the Lehman Brothers bankruptcy, AIG bailout, and forced merger of some institutions (such as Bank of America and Merrill Lynch). The index spiked again in October 2008 amidst debate about the $700 billion Troubled Asset Relief Program (TARP).

To give a sense of magnitude of the moves, the Kansas City Financial Stress Index peaked at 5.57 in October 2008 (after Lehman Brothers bankruptcy and around the TARP debate) and remained elevated (at 4.68) at year-end. In the first quarter of 2009, despite wider deleveraging of positions in equities and commodities, the index edged lower (3.99 in March). By August 2009, the KCFSI had dipped below 1.0 and has remained below there ever since, even slipping into negative territory on several occasions in 2010, 2011 and 2012.

St. Louis Federal Reserve Financial Stress Index (STLFSI)

The St. Louis Federal Reserve's Financial Stress Index (STLFSI) is similar to the KCFSI, but with 18 variables. It is updated weekly on a Thursday at 10 am Central Standard Time.[7] The STLFSI takes into account interest rates (the effective fed funds rate and two, ten, and 30-year Treasury yields, Baa-rate corporate yields, Merrill Lynch High-yield Corporate Master II index, Merrill Lynch Asset-Backed Master BBB rated rates), yield spreads 10-year Treasury minus 3-month Treasury yield curve, Corporate Baa-rated bond minus 10-year Treasury, Merrill Lynch High Yield Corporate Master II index minus 10-year Treasuries, 3-month London Interbank Offering Rate-Overnight Index Swap (LIBOR-OIS) spread, 3-month Treasury-Eurodollar (TED) spread, 3-month commercial paper minus 3-month Treasury bill, and other indicators including the JP Morgan Emerging Markets Bond Index Plus, the CBOE's volatility index VIX, Merrill Lynch Bond Market Volatility Index (1-month), 10-year nominal Treasury minus 10-year Treasury Inflation Protected Security (TIPS) yield or breakeven inflation, and S&P 500 Financial Index (equities).

The STLFSI peaked at 5.572 in the week ending 17 October 2008, a month after the Lehman bankruptcy, and closed the year at 4.596, which was still an elevated level when compared to the 0.676 reading seen the week of 4 January 2008. The index proceeded to edge lower into the first quarter of 2009, despite the near panicked deleveraging going on that sent the S&P 500 to a twelve-and-a-half year low of 667. By September 2009, the STLFSI was back under 1.0 and the index ended the year at 0.254, even with the admission by Greece that its books had been cooked. In 2010 and into early 2011, the index traded in negative territory at times and at worst edged up but never managed to break over 1.0. Even as euro zone peripheral tensions and US fiscal concerns increased in the summer of 2011, the STLFSI saw only the smallest of moves higher, topping out just over 1.0 on two occasions only in the weeks of 30 September and 7 October 2011. The STLFSI subsequently has remained below 1.0.

Cleveland Federal Reserve Financial Stress Index (CFSI)

In March 2012, the Cleveland Federal Reserve announced the creation of its own monthly financial stress index, which looks at 11 variables that are slightly different to those measured by the other Fed indexes. The CFSI is constructed using daily data from components that reflect credit, equity, foreign exchange and interbank markets. The Cleveland Fed offers four grades of stress:

- Grade 1: below normal stress with the index in a range of less than or equal to -0.50

- Grade 2: normal stress with the index in a range of -0.50 to 0.59

- Grade 3: moderate stress with the index in a range of between 0.59; and 1.68

- Grade 4: significant stress, with the index above 1.68

In the fall of 1998, at the peak of the Long-Term Capital Management crisis, the CFSI "neared a value of 2.0," a level that was not seen again until the start of the subprime mortgage crisis. The Cleveland Fed noted that the CFSI "climbed into the 'significant stress period' grade in late 2007 and remained there throughout the middle of 2009."

While the CFSI has not moved back into this 'significant stress period', it rose throughout 2011 and remained in 'moderate stress' territory in early 2012 before falling into 'normal stress' mode later in the year.

4. Bank stress indexes

Various banks have developed their own versions of the Federal Reserve stress indexes, which like the Fed stress indexes are popular tools for FX traders.

Goldman Sachs Financial Stress Index (GSFSI)

Global banking powerhouse Goldman Sachs has had its Financial Stress Index (GSFSI) in place since the collapse of Lehman Brothers in September 2008.

"Goldman's FSI consists of four equally weighted variables: the spread between the London interbank offered rate (LIBOR) and the overnight index swap (that is, the spread between the bank funding rate and the market's perception of future official rates); the spread between the United States government's repo rate (the discounted rate at which a central bank repurchases government securities from commercial banks to manage the level of money supply) and the mortgage repo rate; the amount of commercial paper issuance; and the ratio of money market funds to the value of equity market capitalisation in the US, a measure of risk aversion," explains Jim O'Neill, former head of global economic research at Goldman Sachs, now Chairman at Goldman Sachs Asset Management.

BofA/Merrill Lynch Global Financial Stress Index

In November 2010, BofA/Merrill Lynch Global launched its own Global Financial Stress Index. Their GFSI is touted as "a comprehensive, cross market gauge of risk, hedging demand and investment flows." BofA/Merrill's goal is to "to help investors identify market risks earlier and more accurately than commonly used risk indicators, such as the VIX index." In the launch statement for the index in November 2010, BofA/Merrill said:

> "The GFSI composite index aggregates over 20 measures of stress across five asset classes and various geographies, measuring three separate kinds of financial market stress: risk, as indicated by cross-asset measures of volatility, solvency and liquidity; hedging demand, implied by the skew of equity and currency options; and investor appetite for risk, as measured by trading volumes as well as flows in and out of equities, high-yield bonds and money markets."

The statement noted that "back-testing of the GFSI since 2000 illustrates that sharp rises in the index over short periods of time would have had a high degree of accuracy in forecasting sell-offs in assets, particularly global equities, commodities and US high-yield bonds."

"Since the global financial crisis, risk appears to have become as important to investors as return," said Michael Hartnett, chief Global Equity strategist at BofA Merrill Lynch Global Research. "The GFSI measures risks not normally visible in public markets by incorporating assets trading in the over-the-counter market. We believe its breadth and depth make it a better measure of financial market stress than the VIX, which is based on US options data alone."

Citicorp's Macro Risk Index

Citicorp devised a Macro Risk Index, which uses a slew of measures to estimate risk aversion, including emerging market credit spreads, US credit spreads, US swap spreads, and implied volatility in FX, equity and swap spreads. The factors are equally weighted.

The index ranges from zero (no stress) to 1 (white hot risk aversion). Citicorp admits the level of correlation among many of these components is quite high, implying that sophisticated traders who detect mispricing could use it to jump on an opportunity. The index is relatively new (its inception was in 2009) and has yet to prove itself.

5. Inflation breakevens and inflation swaps

Fixed income traders, Federal Reserve Board members and a growing number of currency, commodity and equity traders watch inflation breakevens and swaps. The inflation *breakeven* level is the difference between the nominal yield on a given fixed income instrument and the real yield on an inflation-linked instrument of the same maturity.

US market players refer to the *breakeven spread* as the difference between a Treasury instrument and a TIPS instrument with a comparable maturity. For instance, the 10-year US Treasury note might offer a 4.0% yield, whereas a Treasury Inflation Protected Securities instruments (adjusted for consumer price inflation) might only offer a yield of 3.0%. If (CPI-U) inflation is greater than 1.0%, then the TIPS would be the better deal.

The other factor to consider is that the TIPS market is far less liquid that the larger Treasury market, which can also skew prices at times. In addition to looking at US/TIPS breakevens, traders also track breakevens in the euro zone, UK, Japan and other countries that offer an inflation-protected alternative to their benchmark bond instruments.

Breakevens and inflation swap movements give insight not only into inflation, but also risk for other asset classes. If breakeven spreads are widening globally and market players are willing to pay more for inflation swap protection, as was the case at the start of 2011, this suggests that inflation expectations are growing and it might be wise to look at an inflation hedge. Investors might buy gold or other commodities, or look to buy commodity currencies like the Canadian and Australian dollars, for protection.

We go in to more detailed discussion of breakevens and interest rate swaps in Chapter 4 on interest rate differentials and expectations.

6. Corporate spreads/credit default swaps

In determining the market's appetite for risk, traders also keep a close eye on the spread between US corporate high-yield debt and the equivalent US investment-grade bond (US Treasuries). If the spread between the two instruments widens dramatically because the corporates need to offer a higher yield to woo investors, this is a red flag for risk, whether for the market as a whole, or that particular company. Whether a triple-A corporate or a junk name, savvy FX players try to watch how these spreads are trading.

A company or country's credit default swap (CDS) is also monitored by traders. A Federal Reserve research paper updated in February 2011[8] explains the fundamentals of a credit default swap agreement:

> "Under a CDS contract, the protection seller promises to buy the reference bond at its par value when a predefined default event occurs. In return, the protection buyer makes periodic payments to the seller until the maturity date of the contract or until a credit event occurs. This periodic payment, which is usually expressed as a percentage (in basis points) of the bonds' notional value, is called the CDS spread. By definition, credit spread provides a pure measure of the default risk of the reference entity. We use CDS spreads as a direct measure of credit spreads. Compared to corporate bond yield spreads, CDS spreads are not subject to the specification of benchmark risk-free yield curve and less contaminated by non-default risk components."

Country risk can be gauged by watching CDS spreads also. Indeed, throughout the euro zone debt crisis, traders kept a close eye on peripheral spread widening, in both the CDS market and in spreads over German Bunds. Greek five-year CDS spreads (Greek CDS over the equivalent of German Bund CDS) widened to a record 1,385 basis points in April 2011, only to push well over 1,600 basis points in June.

What exactly does this *insurance policy* mean? It would cost $1.6 million dollars annually to insure $10 million in Greek debt for five years. Greek five-year spreads over Bunds, which already stood at a stretched 950 basis points in early January 2011, widened to a record 1,509 basis points in early August.

It should be noted that, despite Greek CDS spreads hitting record highs and two-year Greek yields reaching nearly 43% in August, the euro exchange rate maintained roughly a $1.40 to $1.45 range, far closer to the 2011 highs near $1.4850-$1.4940 seen in May than the 2011 lows around $1.2875 seen in January. The widening of Greek CDS, while a clear euro negative, was not enough to offset the combination of uncertainty about the US dollar and reserve diversification by world central banks (a topic covered in more detail in Chapters 10 and 11).

7. Price of commodities

FX traders watch commodity prices as an inflation barometer as well as for insight into which commodity currencies to buy or sell. Select commodities, especially the precious metals, are viewed as a gauge of risk. For instance, spot gold prices and futures prices are closely eyed, along with gold exchange traded funds (ETFs). Rising gold prices may mean that the market is concerned about inflation or that investors are too afraid to buy anything else. Similarly, the rapid run-up in crude oil prices in 2011, especially Brent crude, indicated that market players were concerned less about reduced supply in the wake of Middle East/North African turmoil, and more about the risk of prices doubling. Fear of the unknown drove prices, rather than pure supply and demand concerns.

Ask a precious metals trader why spot gold reached a life-time high of $1911.46/oz in August 2011 and he will give you a laundry list of reasons, namely low US interest rates, inflation concerns and rising global demand. At the same time, he will say that fear of the unknown and fear of investing in other instruments also played an important role.

Some traders track the Thomson Reuters-Jefferies CRB Index and watch for anomalies in its price action as a risk gauge. The CRB has been around for over 50 years and began in 1957 when the Commodity Research Bureau constructed an index comprised of 28 commodities, two spot markets and 26 futures markets for investors to trade. The index has evolved over the years, with the number of commodities later pared back. In June 2005, the index was renamed the Reuters/Jefferies CRB index and included 17 commodities, all on a futures basis. The present Thomson Reuters-Jefferies CRB Index includes 19 commodities.

Of the weightings given to the various commodities, Group One (WTI crude the highest weight of 23%, heating oil and RBOB gasoline each 5%) has a 33% weight, Group Two (natural gas, corn, soybeans, live cattle, gold, aluminum, copper all 6%) has a 42% weight, Group Three (sugar, cotton, coffee, cocoa all 5%) has a

20% weight, and Group Four (nickel, wheat, lean hogs, orange juice, silver all 1%) has a 5% weight.

As of 4 January 2012, the CRB has a ten-year annualised return of 4.73%.[9] This is favourable compared with other tradable commodity indexes – the Dow Jones UBS commodity index return was at 4.58% and the S&P GSCI commodity index was at 3.46%. The Sharp ratio (measure of risk premium per unit of risk) is 0.4x for the CRB, 0.3x for the Dow/UBS commodity index and 0.1x for the S&P GSCI. What this signals to FX traders is that commodities are, as the portfolio optimisation orthodoxy has it, a high-risk but profitable alternative investment to conventional equities and bonds. When investors are feeling frisky and want to embrace risk, they will buy commodities and this is a signal that demand for the dollar as a safe-haven is waning.

Conclusion

Currency traders, like soldiers in battle, utilise the best available radar to ascertain how the war is going and how to develop the best offensive and defensive tactics. The use of risk indicators helps them formulate their worldview. We must stress that these indicators are not infallible and don't always dictate dollar direction exactly, or how long an FX trend will last. In terms of a shift in the risk trend or the extension of a risk trend, while there are clear ramifications for FX, it is not always clear what they are.

For example, during the first half of 2012, the CBOE's VIX spent a good portion of its time in risk friendly, sub-20 territory. Even as the crisis in the euro zone escalated and Greece held a second run-off election and Spanish banks were bailed out, the VIX could not even break above 30, let alone retest the 47.56 high seen in 2011. An FX trader using the VIX alone as a risk gauge might not have known to expect the sizable safe-haven dollar demand that was seen during the first half of the year.

In addition to risk indicators, FX traders keep a close eye on existing positions and country flows, which we will explore more in Chapter 6.

CHAPTER 3 –
GLOBAL ATTITUDE TOWARD RISK

"Glass, china and reputation are easily cracked, and never mended well."

Benjamin Franklin

Investors have become better informed in recent years as technology has levelled the playing field in terms of data and research delivery. Now small-bank and retail traders get the same information in the same timely manner as those at larger banks.

But human emotion about risk has not changed throughout the years. Investors' attitude toward risk versus reward is the same today as 500 years ago, or longer. The reasons for caution in the past are the same reasons for caution now; price risk, country risk, credit risk, political risk and liquidity risk are timeless. One main difference is that trading in the new millennium presents a new risk in the shape of technology risk.

In this chapter we look at the different types of risk to be considered before entering into FX positions.

Overview of risks

In FX, as in securities markets generally, the risks are:

1. *Settlement risk*: one party fails to pay or the payment mechanism or agency makes errors, delaying or denying payment.

2. *Price risk*: the price unexpectedly changes by a large amount, causing a loss or a windfall gain.

3. *Country risk*: the country has inadequate institutions, including customs and a legal system, to protect the rights of securities holders; and *sovereign risk*, where the state refuses to pay its debt, allows excessive currency depreciation, or engages in outright expropriation.

4. *Credit risk*: the borrower cannot or will not repay debt.

5. *Liquidity risk*: so few participants are in the market that no price is available to exit a position.

6. *Political risk*: the country has a change of attitude toward markets because of an uprising, military coup, election or other event.

7. *Contagion (intermarket) risk*: one market has a rally or a meltdown that carries over to other markets, even though the supply/demand metrics are not really linked.

8. *Technology risk*: risk from inadequate systems and controls.

Let's look at these types of risk in more detail.

1. Settlement risk

Settlement risk in FX is not a big issue. FX is settled on the next day, or most commonly in two days, so that a trade on Monday is settled on Wednesday.

The spot FX contract is the most basic and well-established contract in history – it is literally an "I owe you" (IOU) contract wherein Party A agrees to pay Party B a specific sum of money into a specific bank account in a specific currency, and in return, Party B agrees to pay Party A a specific sum of money into a specific bank account in a specific currency on the same date. Forward contracts for delivery on dates longer than two days have the same terms.

Since 2002, most banks (and all the major banks) use the Continuous Linked Settlement (CLS) system, located in Switzerland, which processes about 58% of turnover (by value) and essentially eliminates credit risk through counterparty exposure netting and simultaneous payment verification.[10] In September 2011, the CLS reported that it settled a new record amount of 1.96 million sides, with a gross value settled of $8.99 trillion, on a single date.[11]

The clearing houses are the only financial institutions to emerge from the global financial crisis that started in 2008 with their reputations intact, if not enhanced. Clearing appears to be a tedious back-office function, so the herculean efforts of the clearing houses continue to go unsung. But if you want to understand the plumbing of the international financial system and accordingly the safety of FX trades, you should consult Peter Norman's *The Risk Controllers*.[12]

One area where settlement risk remains an issue is the retail market. Retail FX brokers are sometimes accused of settling trades at incorrect prices and engaging in other acts contrary to traders' interests. When retail FX first became popular, brokers were able to invent any interest rate carry charge they liked for positions held longer than the usual two days of a spot transaction. Other abuses included failure to confirm trades. Even today, finding a human being to correct an error can be an ordeal.

In 2000, the US Commodity Futures Trading Commission, a government agency that regulates and oversees trading in futures, asserted its authority over the retail FX market in spot. Capital requirements for brokers were raised, and enforcement actions taken for bad behaviour, including false advertising. Many retail brokers left the business.

The most dramatic events in the retail sector were the failure of Refco in 2005, in 2011 the failure of MF Global and, in 2012, the failure of Peregrine Financial. Refco was the biggest commodity trading firm on the Chicago Mercantile Exchange (CME) and a publicly traded company. The Refco CEO was discovered to have concealed $430 million in losses in ten customer accounts, including the account of famed hedge fund manager Victor Niederhoffer. When Refco was forced into bankruptcy, traders who had been using the Refco spot facility, technically a subsidiary headquartered in Bermuda, lost everything. In contrast, traders who had been using Refco to broker FX futures trades got 100% of their account value. This is because the CME members guarantee the trades of each member and keep a reserve fund to maintain the integrity of the exchange.

The Refco case illustrates that in practice, unless there is a computer failure, settlement risk often boils down to credit risk. The MF Global failure is more complicated since in addition to credit risk, the firm also exposed clients to operational or bookkeeping risk. Some $900 million of customer funds remained unaccounted for as of year-end 2011. The Peregrine case is also an operational risk in the sense that the manager of the firm stole the customers' money and falsified bank statements.

2. Price risk

Price risk is the risk that a position is not exited before a large change in price pushes it into a big loss. The price change is usually sudden and unexpected, although sometimes a stubborn trader who refuses to exit a losing position will be caught out. The normal way for banks to measure price risk is to assume a normal distribution of prices around a median in the usual bell-shaped curve, albeit with very fat tails to reflect surges in price volatility. But since the vast majority of bank FX trades are held for minutes or seconds, the fat-tail issue is of lesser import than among corporations or fund managers that hold positions for weeks and months.

In a nutshell, the holding period is the key to price risk in FX. More advanced risk management techniques at some banks are frighteningly sophisticated but you will search in vain for hard information on in-house price risk management at banks because the policies and statistical measurements are confidential.

Because the big FX market participants are able to keep their transactions confidential, losses tend to be a secret unless they are so big they must be disclosed. Therefore, we know very little about price-risk induced losses in FX. Of the 50 biggest losses over $100 million in securities trading over the past 50 years, 11 were in FX, as shown in the Table 3.1. Fraud is involved in some, but not all. Some of the giant losses, like the Nick Leeson incident at Barings Brothers in 1995, involved non-FX securities (Nikkei futures) with an FX component, even through FX was not the *security* being traded directly.

Table 3.1 – trading losses over $100 million due to FX and FX options

Rank of 50	Nominal amount lost (bn)	Real amount lost (USD bn)	Country	Company	Year
6	BRL 4.62	2.43 bn	Brazil	Aracruz	2008
10	JPY 166	2.14	Japan	Showa Shell	1993
11	JPY 154	2.09	Japan	Kashima Oil	1994
12	HKD 14.7	1.82	China	CITIC Pacific	2008
15	EUR 1.4	1.56	Austria	BAWAG	2000
19	BRL 2	1.05	Brazil	Sadia	2008
23	USD 0.69	0.80	United States	AIB/Allfirst	2002
24	DEM 0.47	0.76	Germany	Herstatt Bank	1974
32	EUR 0.30	0.41	Austria	Hypo Group	2004
34	AUD 0.36	0.34	Australia	Nat'l Australia Bank	2004
44	USD 0.1	0.12	Croatia	Rijecka Bank	2002

Source: en.wikipedia.org/wiki/List_of_trading_losses

3. Country risk and sovereign risk

Of all the risks associated with the FX market, participants are most highly attuned to country and sovereign risk as key components of price risk. Foreign exchange traders may not know the exact dates and circumstances of sovereign defaults throughout history, but they seem to be hard-wired with an instinct for exactly this kind of trouble.

A history of sovereign default

In July 1576, King Philip II of Spain instigated the first sovereign default of the modern era, stiffing his creditors as well as his own soldiers. In fact, Philip defaulted four times. Before him, his father Charles V had run up 37 million ducats in debt, two million more than Spain had taken from the Americas during his 40-year reign. Charles wanted to become the Holy Roman Emperor; Philip extended dominance over Portugal, the Philippines, the Netherlands, Belgium and England, and skirmished with Turkey.

The two Spanish kings squandered the greatest sovereign fortune of all time in just two generations. Philip II accumulated foreign debts equivalent to 60% of GDP and became the first serial defaulter in history – on four occasions. Spain became the record-holder for repeated defaults, at 13 times.[13]

France defaulted more times – eight – than Spain between 1300 and 1799. Even the English king Edward III (1312-1377) defaulted on the nation's external debt, the first of only two external debt defaults in English history. Portugal defaulted in 1560, Prussia in 1683, and Austria in 1796. In the 19th century, Greece defaulted four times, Spain defaulted another eight times, and even Sweden defaulted (1812). Seventeen Latin American countries defaulted 47 times in the 1800s.

In the 20th century, China defaulted twice (1921 and 1939) and Japan defaulted once (1942), with the rest of the sovereign defaults in Africa and Asia. Nigeria defaulted five times and Indonesia three times. The United States and Canada have never defaulted on external debt, nor have Australia or New Zealand.[14]

Greece not only lived through its first century as a sovereign state in perpetual default, but also takes the prize for the biggest currency crash of all time in 1944, another devaluation of 50% in 1953 and a drachma crisis in 1994. Spain has the longest history of the biggest defaults, and France, which runs a close second to Spain, has also a long history of virulent verbal attacks on its creditors, taking the stance that mere speculators should not be allowed to damage the reputation of the sacred state by actually examining the books.

How FX traders react to country risk

FX traders today respond with a hair-trigger to the slightest whisper of fiscal insufficiency in those states with a history of default. Greece and Spain in particular are contaminated by a dimly-glimpsed history of disregard for the property rights of others – from the perspective of the international investor, ownership of a sovereign bond is *property*. In the broadest sense, the foreign exchange trader acts as a steward of the interests of international bond investors.

In December 2009, the lesson was reprised when Fitch downgraded Greece's sovereign rating to BBB+ from A- with a "negative outlook." In response, Greek equity markets tumbled and the credit default swap for Greek government debt widened to 211 basis points (from 100 basis points in August). The Fitch downgrade was one of many straws on the camel's back that eventually led to a wider euro zone financial crisis, involving Portugal, Italy, Ireland and Spain.

As it emerged in late 2009 that Greece would have had to pay ever-higher yields to place sovereign paper, it was not only bond traders who took notice – FX traders went on high alert, too. From 26 November 2009, the euro/dollar fell from

1.5145 to 1.4218 by 22 December 2009. As the talk of sovereign risk contamination spread to Ireland, Spain and Portugal, the euro fell further to 1.1877 by 6 June 2011. The euro's decline was halted only when the EMU devised an institutional response, the European Financial Stability Facility, and euro advances since then can be traced directly to additional institutional initiatives, including the European Stability Mechanism and the European Central Bank's (ECB's) long-term financing operation in December 2011 and February 2012.

Why FX traders worry about country risk

FX traders are so finely attuned to sovereign risk because sovereigns facing insolvency almost always devalue their currencies. In the days before paper money, this took the form of debasing metal coins by adding cheaper metals or reducing the size but not the denomination. Dionysius of Syracuse in Greece during the 4th century BC was one of the first, calling in one drachma coins on pain of death and re-stamping them as two drachma coins. Expropriation through debasement was widespread in Europe from 1285 to 1799, according to Reinhart and Rogoff.[15]

Devaluation in turn has two effects that serve to restore economic stability, if at a lengthy remove. First, the cost of imported goods automatically rises after devaluation, pushing inflation higher. If the defaulter's central bank is on the ball, it raises interest rates and higher rates attract at least some risk capital.

Second, the devalued exchange rate promotes exports, supporting job creation and thus raising sovereign tax revenue. But the prospect of higher rates and improving fiscal conditions is not a clear path. Higher rates can also smother the very exporters on which the sovereign is depending. In any case, foreign exchange traders keep first things first, and first the currency has to be trashed. The classic recovery model may or may not work, and until the recovery story gets a grip, traders may safely postpone caring about the model.

Sovereign defaults are the flashy headliners in the pantheon of risks that traders must follow, but they are not the only country risk. Sovereign difficulties from excessive debt or budget mismanagement often lead to banking sector risk.

Banking sector risk

In the Greek sovereign debt crisis that started in 2009, many observers noted that the Greek banking sector itself had not misbehaved and, in fact, Greek bank balance sheets were relatively healthy, unlike those of Icelandic and Irish banks, which were the core source of the sovereign state's debt problem. As a practical matter, FX traders feel that they do not need to distinguish a sovereign crisis that arises from banking sector problems from sovereign debt problems that cause a banking sector crisis – either way, the country and its currency have a black cloud hanging over them.

Even the most stable and solvent bank can get into trouble. During the Greek crisis, Greek banks found themselves with much reduced credit lines from other international banks in a form of imputed credit risk, however unfair this was. Banks that really were in trouble, like those in Ireland, saw their FX lines of credit cut to the bone.

FX bank credit limits were cut back sharply starting in March 2009, when US rating agency Standard & Poor's downgraded Ireland's sovereign rating to AA+ from the AAA rating the country had held since 2001. Fitch and Moody's followed suit, leaving Ireland totally stripped of its AAA rating. Investors, who had flocked to Ireland earlier because of its investment grade, were forced to move monies to other AAA-rated countries. FX trading limits were pared back as a result of the downgrade.

This real or imputed credit risk arises despite simultaneous settlement having removed much of the credit risk inherent in conducting transactions with people whom one has never met. One reason credit risk remains in the equation is that the settlement mechanism can be overridden by the sudden imposition of new regulations or taxes – in other words, political or country risk.

4. Credit risk

Defining credit risk

Traders may have their own prejudices and biases toward specific countries and their institutions, but the ability to trade a specific security or instrument with a specific counterparty is a *credit risk* defined elsewhere in the trader's institution. In the big commercial and investment banks, credit officers approve currency trading limits and traders have no say in the matter. While they can request a limit or an increase in a line from time to time, final approval is in the hands of the credit officers and is not guaranteed. A trading desk's top customer, be it a corporate or a sovereign name, could see its FX limit cut in half or pulled entirely under certain circumstances. Limits on the electronic trading platforms as well as on in-house trading systems would all be adjusted, with a sharply worded memo circulated and warning of job consequences if the rules are broken.

Credit risk is almost always a function of the character of the counterparty, character being the banker's codeword for honesty. Bankers know that the efficient market theory is bunk. The core thesis of the efficient market hypothesis is that information is instantly distributed to all parties and that the information is accurate. But some market players deliberately start false rumours to favour their positions. In equities, traders are influenced by the distance between expected earnings and reported earnings when both numbers are likely to be engineered. Just as corporations inflate earnings, hide debt, claim nonexistent orders, and conceal failed product launches, countries lie about their growth, unemployment and inflation rates, misrepresent tax collection and hide sovereign debt.

Harbingers of credit risk

When China emerged in the late 1990s as an industrial powerhouse, economists wondered how growth could be so robust at 10%-plus when reported electricity usage was falling. It's a logical question for a good economist to ask but we never got an answer. In the end, the growth was real and the drop in electricity usage was a fluke, a statistical error, or a lie.

Similarly, markets were not really surprised when Greece confessed to hiding billions of euro of debt associated with the 2004 Olympics that then developed into a far larger sum of undisclosed debt. Greece had already been named in 1997 as the site for the 2004 summer Olympics, before adopting the euro in 2002. Greece continued to report that its budget deficit was 3% of GDP as late as 2009 before confessing that the deficit was actually 13% of GDP and a fair amount of the extra debt was due to the Olympics, which cost over double the original estimate at nearly €9 billion. This was the first chink in the armour of the fiction that Greece was a properly functioning member of the EMU.

Sometimes a credit event is abrupt, even though the watchful could have seen the event coming. This is what happened in September 2008 when Lehman Brothers declared bankruptcy and suffered what is called *reputational risk*. The Foreign Exchange Committee of New York defines reputational risk as relating to "the current and prospective impact on earnings and capital attributable to negative public opinion of an institution's products or activities." The FXC also warned of the dangers of *systemic risk*, which is where "the failure of one market participant to meet its required obligations" prevents "other participants or financial institutions from meeting their obligations when due" (i.e., the domino effect). Both of these risks came into play in the fall of 2008.

In the weeks heading into the event, FX and other trading limits with Lehman were already being removed or greatly reduced. At least one European bank had pulled all lines of credit to Lehman as early as May. Credit officers were uncertain what to do with the myriad currency deals already on the books, because (as was discovered during the Drexel Burnham bankruptcy in 1989), a company already in bankruptcy may choose to honour deals if they favour the stakeholders, while counterparties to a bankrupt company have the right not to allow transactions to go to settlement. As noted above, foreign exchange transactions are the simplest form of contract, but that doesn't make them an absolute obligation. FX transactions are contingent assets/liabilities on all bank balance sheets and thus there is uncertainty until payment is actually made and confirmed.

The lesson learned then, as in earlier situations such as Long-Term Capital Management in 1998, was that no matter how financially secure a counterparty might have been in the past, credit-worthiness can change in days or even hours. This is why the worst-case scenario for world welfare would be if the United States lost its high credit rating. In August 2011, the US was downgraded from Triple A to Double A, with no adverse consequences, so far. But a bigger downgrade below investment grade could be a disaster. It would take weeks, if not months, for credit officers around the world to start re-approving credit lines to US banks after a massive rating agency downgrade of the US as a sovereign. Most global banks have a permanent supply of dollars that they hold in their own name, but the combined amount may not suffice to cover all the booked dollar transactions, with over 70% of world trade denominated in dollars.

The Canadian importer of goods from, say, Vietnam has first to convert his Canadian dollars to US dollars, the numeraire or unit of account of most international trade transactions. If the Canadian bank credit officer forbids the FX trader to obtain dollars from the usual source – a US bank – the trade deal either cannot be done at all, must be done at a premium expense to get the dollars from another non-US bank, or has to be redenominated in some other currency, including the most logical one, the Canadian dollar. If the Vietnamese exporter has debt denominated in US dollars that he is counting on export proceeds to repay, he is now out of luck, and facing the same dollar shortage as everyone else.

Credit risk in practice

The credit limit for each country's banks is governed by an overall country limit that is decided by a financial firm's credit officers, who take into consideration the geopolitical situation as well as the country's fundamentals. Country limits tend to be changed more slowly than the credit limits for specific banks, in part because information about reduced limits tends to make its way to the affected country's ministry of finance. The repercussions can be felt in all kinds of odd and embarrassing ways, including official protests by ambassadors, the cold shoulder at diplomatic events, and more serious effects such as delays in bilateral trade agreements and even arms and environmental treaties.

For example, up until the Asian crisis of 1997, Russia was well regarded and portfolio managers flocked to buy any and all Russian instruments, whether higher yielding fixed income instruments or stocks deemed destined to outperform US equity markets. But in late 2007 and early 2008, world commodity prices saw a steep decline as market players deleveraged and bailed out of even profitable positions, leaving Russia – with 80% of its exports in natural gas, timber, metals and petroleum – vulnerable.

Russian yields shot higher, rising to over 200% at one point, while Russian equities collapsed, falling 75% from their peak before year-end. The Russian ruble tumbled on fears that the government would devalue the currencies or default on its debt, or both. Suddenly no one wanted to enter into financial transactions of any kind with a Russian financial firm, including foreign exchange deals. Even after a $22.6 billion World Bank/International Monetary Fund (IMF) bailout, it took Russia years to restore its credit and credibility.

In late 2010, concern about new regulations and taxes was renewed during the discussion of *currency wars* instigated by Brazilian Finance Minister Guido Mantega. In response to what was perceived to be active efforts on the part of the Federal Reserve and Treasury Department to engineer a lower dollar, global central banks took action to prevent excessive investor inflows. Several countries, including South Korea and Brazil, imposed new capital controls, such as taxes on foreign inflows and bank levies.

Up to this point in currency history, the mere mention of capital controls has led to fast-paced selling of the country's currency. In 2010, however, the Korean won and Brazilian real saw only limited selling in response to the new measures being taken and, even then, the selling pressure was not sustained and investors soon came back. This approach – using capital controls to manage hot money inflows – was even given the blessing by the IMF.

"Countries have a number of policy options in their toolkits – lower interest rates, reserves accumulation, tighter fiscal policy, macro-prudential measures, and sometimes capital controls. The response should depend on circumstances – there is no *one-size-fits-all* solution," then IMF managing director Dominque Strauss-Kahn said in October 2010. "For example, with a credit-fuelled housing bubble, prudential tools might be the way to go. If instead the problem is debt inflows fuelling a boom in foreign currency lending to unhedged borrowers, then the solution might be different and might include capital controls. Again, we should always be pragmatic... We need a holistic approach, which means a changing role for central banks in the years ahead."

5. Liquidity risk

Liquidity risk is the absence of bids and offers when a trader wants to buy or sell a security. With trading volume at $4 trillion a day, liquidity is not commonly an issue in the most-traded currencies unless there is a crisis, but it is more often an issue in less-traded currencies and exotic cross-rates.

There are plenty of traders with long memories who will recall pre-euro currency crises in some of the less major currencies. During the drachma crisis of 1994, for example, liquidity didn't exactly dry up, but the bid-offer spread was as much as 400 points wide. You could sell drachmas, but only at a deep discount. The same thing happened during the Asian crisis of 1997-1998, which spread to Argentina and Russia; market-makers prided themselves on always answering the phone and making a two-way price, but it was usually a price that sellers could not stomach. More than one hedge fund holding unhedged drachma, pesos or rubles to gain the extra yield failed to see that the extra yield was to compensate for sovereign risk, and the fast-moving FX market converted sovereign risk into liquidity/price risk in a matter of hours. They could get out the door, but they had to leave their bag and shoes behind, and sometimes their pants too.

Even major currencies can have their moment of being illiquid. A case in point was 17-18 March 2011 when in the US session, dollar-yen closed Thursday below ¥80 for the first time in history. In the transition period to Friday's Tokyo session, the pair plummeted well over three big figures from about ¥79.80 to a record low of ¥76.25 in less than an hour, sparking coordinated intervention. Later that year on 31 October, the Bank of Japan (BOJ) intervened at the Ministry of Finance's request after dollar-yen fell to a record ¥75.331 low in the lead into the Asian session. Dollar-yen soared in response, topping out around ¥79.50, before closing the day around ¥78.20. BOJ intervention, even though not unexpected at the time given rhetoric and fast-paced yen gains in recent sessions, was enough to quickly wipe out existing orders on the electronic dealing machines and create a temporary dearth of liquidity.

The important observation here is that liquidity risk in the foreign exchange market, at least in the major traded currencies, tends to take the form of pure price risk. This raises the chicken-and-egg question of which comes first, perception of sovereign weakness and lack of resolve that bleeds into bond yields and other prices in an economy, or a run on the currency that causes, at least in part, the very crisis the currency traders fear. We saw this phenomenon in the contagion from the Thai baht crisis to the Japanese yen in 1998 and in the contagion of bond yield spreads from Greece in late 2009 to Ireland, Spain and Portugal during 2010, a bond market event that was equally swiftly reflected in the euro/dollar exchange rate.

With less-traded currencies, you must weigh the prospects of a higher return against the risk of a loss of manoeuvrability. First, you pay the price of a wider spread for a South African rand or Mexican peso quote versus the dollar than you would for a euro or yen price versus the dollar. When Commodity Futures Trading Commission weekly data shows long Mexican peso futures positions are large (*extended*) and market sentiment turns bearish, dollar-peso may rise 10 to 20 *big figures* in a blink of an eye. What is perceived as extended in the peso (+/- 60,000 contracts) might only be a moderately large euro position. If market sentiment toward the euro shifts, a similar sized position might only result in a one or two *big figure* move.

Note that outside of FX futures, FX transactions are all private deals between the customer and the financial institution. We therefore never have hard data on volumes traded as is readily available in the equity and bond markets. FX traders at the big houses may report to the newswires that trading is heavy or thin, but we never get specific numbers or at least not in a timely manner. It is only the triennial Bank for International Settlements (BiS) survey and the bi-yearly Foreign Exchange Committee report in the US and the Foreign Exchange Joint Standing Committee in London that tells us aggregate volumes. We discuss this further in Chapter 6 on positions and flows.

6. Political risk

It is rare that elections or politics are a main driver of a foreign exchange move. It is usually the market's expectation about what the political party, either in power now or in the future, will do to influence the economy that causes long or short positions in a given currency to be taken, not the election itself.

Taking an example, in Canada in March 2011, when a vote of no-confidence was called against Stephen Harper's Conservative government, the Canadian dollar barely budged in response to the reports of a new election. Partly this was because the no-confidence vote was expected, but also partly because investors saw both the Conservative government and opposition parties (Liberals, new Democrats and Bloc Quebecois) as capable of leading the country.

This was not the case in the United States in the run-up to the controversial 2000 election between Al Gore and George W. Bush. Bush was deemed as more friendly for business and so US equities and the dollar suffered when polls had Gore leading. US instruments, as well as the dollar, later came under severe downward pressure when a tie was called and it took a month for the Supreme Court to decide the winner. The dollar index closed at 115.52 on the date of the election, 7 November 2000, and slipped to 114.15 by 13 December, the day after the Supreme Court issued its decision. From there, the dollar index fell to a low of 108.09 by January 2001. The drop in the dollar index was not necessarily a market vote on Bush, but rather a response to high uncertainty and a long-standing belief, not entirely unfounded, that the Republicans would favour a weaker dollar.

A National Bureau of Economic Research (NBER) study offers detailed insight into financial market swings around US elections, especially tight ones, starting in 1880. The NBER study found that stocks outperformed after a Republican win and US interest rates tended to edge higher. "In 2000, 2004, and over the entire 1880-2004 period, a Republican victory raised equity values by about 2%. On the other hand, since the Reagan Administration, Republican victories also have raised interest rates on government bonds by 0.12%."[16]

Intervention as political risk

Intervention, a key risk in foreign exchange, is a political risk. In Brazil, during President Luiz Inácio Lula da Silva's two terms (1 January 2003 to 1 January 2011), the country prospered and as one of the so-called BRIC countries (Brazil, Russia, India and China, the biggest four of the emerging markets) came to enjoy sizable foreign inflows, which were at first welcomed. Central Bank President Henrique Meirelles was well respected and investors felt comfortable buying Brazilian stocks and bonds. Even in the aftermath of the subprime-mortgage/credit crisis, select emerging market currencies maintained their allure, including the Brazilian real. In 2010, however, the government and central bank decided that further fast-paced Brazilian real gains would be negative for the economy. The central bank stepped up its interventions to twice and sometimes more times per day, and the government raised the financial transaction (IOF) tax on portfolio investments and local assets for a second time, with other capital controls announced as under consideration.

FX intervention can be done to benefit a single country or financial markets as a whole. In the aftermath of the March 2011 earthquake and tsunami in Japan, the yen rose when it might have been expected to fall. At the time, Japan was a current account surplus country, and Japanese investors, while keeping the lions' share of their savings at home in domestic Japanese government bonds, have sizable overseas investments. The market thinking at the time was that between insurance companies needing to buy yen to pay for reconstruction and Japanese investors bringing money home for that purpose, the yen would likely rise, not fall.

With many unknowns (reconstruction costs, total damage done, Japan's nuclear reactors in a precarious state) the yen began to race higher, with world financial markets reacting in a negative manner, tracking the yen nearly tick for tick. Global stocks fell sharply and there was heightened demand for safe-haven instruments such as US Treasuries and German Bunds as well as gold and select other commodities. Group of Seven (G7) central bank heads and finance ministers had a conference call just as dollar-yen was closing below the psychological ¥80 level on 17 March 2011. In the lead in to the Tokyo session, dollar-yen bottomed at a new life-time dollar low of ¥76.25, before a G7 communiqué was released, announcing joint intervention to weaken the yen:

> "In response to recent movements in the exchange rate of the yen associated with the tragic events in Japan, and at the request of the Japanese authorities, the authorities of the United States, the United Kingdom, Canada and the ECB will join with Japan, on 18 March 2011 in concerted intervention," the G7 said. "As we have long stated, excess volatility and disorderly movements in exchange rates have adverse implications for economics and financial stability."

After chastising the Chinese for "FX manipulation" regarding the Chinese yuan, it rankled G7 central bankers to intervene on behalf of the Bank of Japan, but they were required to under the unwritten law of world central bankers. Concerted intervention always packs a much harder punch than unilateral intervention. Co-ordinated intervention pushed dollar-yen higher in March 2011, but the BOJ was forced to step in again later in the year when the yen again posted new life-time highs.

7. Contagion risk

Contagion risk is the risk that a big price move in one market will infect another market, even when the two markets are not really well connected. An example is the Shanghai Surprise in the period October 2007 to October 2008, taking the SSE equity index from over 5,900 to under 1,700. Figure 2.1 in Chapter 2 shows how world stock markets tracked the Shanghai at this time. For a large part of this period, from October 2007 to July 2008, the dollar index was falling more or less in sync. We can understand why other equity indices around the world might track the Shanghai – it was a global rejection of equities out of fear of falling earnings and so on. But why should the dollar index track the Shanghai, as illustrated in Figure 3.1?

Figure 3.1 - SSE Shanghai Composite Index (dark) vs. Dollar Index

We may say that the dollar index was just tracking all or most stock indices, but this argument flies in the face of the supposed inverse correlation of equities and the dollar. This inverse correlation is based on the idea that risk appetite for equities reduces demand for dollars as a safe-haven and risk aversion to equities raises demand for dollars. Logically, a drop in global stock markets should lift the dollar as a safe-haven, but this time the Shanghai had nearly completed its massive decline before we see a divergence between the Shanghai and the dollar index, and restoration of the assumed inverse correlation. One idea is that for contagion to occur, it has to be pneumonia and not just a common cold. By August/September of 2008 when the inverse correlation kicked in, the Lehman Bros. crisis was coming to a head.

We see similar sharp moves in currencies when oil or gold move abruptly. We may say that so-called intermarket relationships are mostly bogus, at least with respect to true cause-and-effect based on measurable supply and demand factors, but if you are a trader with a position limit of several hundred million dollars, you are not going to ignore a stock market rout or a surprise rally in commodities. The purported relationships are created by those who expect to see them, a form of self-fulfilling prophecy.

Contagion risk shows itself in more understandable ways, too. The Australian dollar/US dollar and Australian dollar/Japanese yen are what we call the *canary in the FX coalmine*. The AUD has come to represent a commodity currency that is directly linked to demand for commodities from emerging markets in Asia. When China releases data showing a rising trade surplus, the AUD rises. This makes price risk in the AUD vulnerable to contagion from commodity prices, with the commodity prices themselves vulnerable to economic conditions in emerging markets. Figure 3.2 illustrates this situation.

Figure 3.2 – Australian dollar (inverted) vs. Commodity Index (weekly)

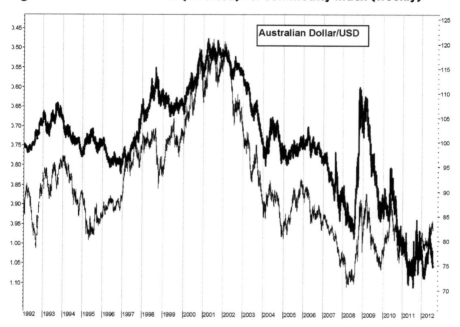

8. Technology risk

Technology risk is often associated with the rapid expansion in the use of technology in trading in the last 20 years but technology risk existed even when trading systems were primitive because the traders of yesteryear often trusted their hand-written blotter more than the back office system. The telephone seemed an easier way of getting prices than the electronic broker system. The advent of lightening-fast computing has brought new technology risks that some banks are still coming to grips with. What happens if there is an electrical blackout that prevents dealing, or a bank refuses to honour a trade?

The New York Fed-sponsored Foreign Exchange Committee (FXC) of New York, in its 'Guidelines for Foreign Exchange Trading Activities', addresses the fast-paced technological changes seen in recent years:

> "The explosive growth of electronic communication and electronic commerce has driven the foreign exchange industry headline into reassessment. Best practices that appeared appropriate a few years ago are now being rethought and reshaped to better understand the electronic age," the FXC says. While "automation has streamlined many transactions and procedures, the foreign exchange market may be becoming more, rather than less, complex."[17]

The FXC's list of risks associated with foreign exchange transactions includes not only the risks already mentioned in this chapter, but also *reputational risk*, which is a "negative public opinion of an institution's products or activities, plus operational/technical risk."

The FXC defines operational/technology risk as emanating "from inadequate systems and controls, human error or management failure. Such risk can involve problems of processing, product pricing, and valuation." This means that operational risk takes two main forms. The first is the occasional scandal involving a rogue trader. A rogue trader is one who fails to pass transactions through to the back office and the trade tickets sit *in the drawer*, accumulating losses. Every trade is confirmed separately by back office personnel, who are kept literally behind a locked door away from the trading floor, so it's hard to see how these trades can still occur – and yet they do. We are aware of two incidents in 20 years, although there may be more.

The other operational/technology risk is the failure of a computer or electrical system. For example, in March 2011, Thomson Reuters Corp (TRI)'s FX trading system suffered a major outage and was out of commission for roughly four hours. ICAP rival Electronic Brokerage System (EBS), along with other smaller FX dealing platforms, allowed market players to keep trading. A few days later, the *Wall Street Journal* reported that Barclays Capital took yen prices off its Barx trading system, when during the volatile transition period from the New York session to the Tokyo session dollar-yen prices began to widen dramatically. Reuters' matching system crashed again in October 2011, leaving traders without FX prices for an hour and a half.

These incidents come after the London Stock Exchange saw a similar four-hour outage in February 2011, which was the third outage in two weeks. In the last ten years, there have been various stock exchange shutdowns ranging from an hour to seven hours, with causes ranging from rats eating through cables (New Zealand exchange in 2005), to software bugs and platform problems.

Summary

As in all securities markets, the FX market faces an array of risks. The biggest risk is price risk – that a trader takes a large position without a pre-set stop-loss order and walks away from the trading desk. This can be done with or without management's knowledge, depending on the seniority of the trader. Given the high volatility in FX prices, losses can snowball very quickly. It is a tribute to the professionalism of the FX industry, plus the remarkable secrecy of the industry, that we seldom hear of big institutional losses due to FX trading.

CHAPTER 4 –
INTEREST RATES AND INTEREST RATE DIFFERENTIALS

"Lenin was certainly right. There is no subtler, no surer means of overturning the existing basis of society than to debauch the currency."

John Maynard Keynes, *The Economic Consequences of the Peace*, 1919

Of all the factors FX traders look at, relative interest rates and relative inflation expectations are at the top of the list. Interest rates are the single strongest conduit linking economic fundamentals to exchange rates – except when consideration of relative interest rates is overwhelmed by risk aversion.

In this chapter we will look at circumstances when interest rate differentials matter to a currency pair and circumstances when they do not. We will discuss interest rate expectations and why expectations, more often than actual interest rates themselves, can become the larger driver of FX direction.

Why interest rates matter

Of all the prices in the world – such as prices for raw materials like iron ore and oil, for labour, for factories and facilities – the price of money is the one most central to an economy.

The economist who first asserted the centrality of interest rates was Irving Fisher, called by Milton Friedman the greatest economist in US history. Fisher is the one who invented the quantity theory of money, although Friedman often gets credit for it. Today we take it as a given that the supply of money has a direct, quantifiable effect on price inflation of goods and services in an economy and it was Fisher who proposed the *equation of exchange*, whereby money supply (M) times the velocity of money (V) equals the price level (P) times *trade* or GDP (T). Here is the basic formula:

$$MV = PT$$

Most importantly, the formula represents a core belief of most traders, even those who don't know much formal economics – money is on one side of the equation and inflation is on the other. Fisher had more advanced things to say that are part of market lore today, including the observation, named *the Fisher equation*, that the real interest rate is the nominal interest rate minus the expected inflation rate.

Interest rates matter to FX traders because for long periods of time – but not always – there is a strong correlation between the inflation adjusted (*real*) interest rate differential of two currencies and the exchange rate. Figure 4.1 shows the correlation between the real return on the 10-year German Bund and the euro, and we can see that the inverse relationship is quite good.

Figure 4.1 – Real Bund Return vs. euro (monthly)

Figure 4.2, however, showing the *relative* real return between 10-year German and US notes and the EUR/USD, indicates less of an obvious correlation. In fact, the relative real return shows less of a trend and is choppier than the euro/dollar itself. We would expect the euro to rise when the relative real return of Germany is higher than the US real return, but this is not consistently the outcome. (In these charts, the euro data in the first period, from 1995 to 1999, is artificially created out of legacy currencies.) Because the relative real return as a key determinant of exchange rates is so central to FX trading, we need to find explanations for discrepancies between the two series.

Figure 4.2 – Relative Real 10-Year Yield of US and Germany vs. EUR/USD (monthly)

Explanations are not hard to find. From 1995 to 1999, the European yield advantage is falling and so is the euro, but when the euro actually came into existence in January 1999, the Bund's advantage rose and yet the euro fell. This could be because in the beginning of the euro experiment, investors were sceptical that the euro would survive. After all, previous versions of the European currency union had failed. From 2001 to 2006, the euro rose in rough correlation with a rising yield advantage, but in 2007-2008, the euro continued to rise despite a falling yield advantage. This, of course, is when the financial crisis started in the US and attention turned to more pressing matters than ordinary inflation differentials. In 2009, the euro rose in line with the rising yield differential, but continued firm into 2010 and 2011 despite a declining advantage. In both instances, institutional factors overrode the relative differential theory. In the first case, the euro zone was still an experiment. In the second instance, the solidity and viability of US financial institutions came into doubt.

To some extent, we should assume that absolute numbers have something to do with the euro rising despite a declining yield advantage. In both countries, Germany and the US, the 10-year real return is negative, i.e., ten-year yields are lower than the rate of inflation. But the market has more confidence in the inflation-fighting resolve of the ECB than in the Fed, since the ECB has a single-goal mandate and the Fed has the additional mandate of promoting employment. Thus, inflation expectations for the US are structurally, permanently higher no matter what policy actions each central bank is actually taking.

This is a new development in the history of exchange rate analysis – never before have we had negative real rates in the benchmark country pair at once. In 2012, Germany issued two-year notes at a negative nominal and real yield, and the US auctioned 10-year TIPS at negative yields. TIPS are inflation-adjusted notes, so a negative yield at issuance means inflation has to go higher for the investor to get the return of principal, let alone any interest earnings. This new development doesn't mean that inflation expectations are any the less powerful as a prime consideration of investors, but it makes yield comparisons vastly more complicated and, above all, raises institutional considerations above relative yields, at least temporarily.

Inflation dynamics

The single most dangerous thing in an economy is inflation and its mutations, deflation and stagflation. Interest rates are the tool with which governments tame, or try to tame, these monsters.

Inflation creates losses for creditors and investors. It discourages savings and capital investment. Inflation causes uncertainty, leading to hoarding of goods that are expected to cost more in the near future and thus shortages of these goods, and inflation may destabilise society. Popular discontent at the German inflation of 1918-1923 is believed to have been a factor in the rise of the National Socialist Party. To the foreign exchange market participant, inflation is the one factor that always and everywhere causes currency depreciation. Other factors may or may not cause depreciation, but inflation will do it for sure.

The Bank of Japan has maintained its Zero Interest Rate Policy (ZIRP) since the early 1990s to try to combat deflation. The BOJ tried on a few occasions subsequently to loosen policy to goose credit, activity and inflation, but deflation has been persistent. While nominal rates of return are near zero, the presence of deflation means the real rate of return is positive, from 2.20% to 3.85% during 2007-2011, according to the World Bank.[18] In addition, Japan's sizeable bond market has allowed the currency to maintain a level of allure.

The inflation most people look at is consumer price inflation and expected consumer price inflation. The dynamics of inflation starts with a rise in money supply feeding real demand for goods and services and also driving interest rates lower, inducing capital to flow to higher-yielding currencies abroad and depreciating the currency. This is the core linkage, but we can sometimes also see a rising trade deficit as higher prices make imports more attractive.

The rubber meets the road when inflation expectations come into the picture. Capturing all the different ideas of inflation expectations is extremely difficult. We have surveys, estimates based on the input supply chain, and the price of inflation-adjusted government notes. None of these approaches do a particularly good job of predicting actual inflation in later periods.

The central bank with the best grip on expected inflation is the Bank of England. The Bank of England Act (1998) calls for the bank to set an inflation target range, to forecast inflation every three months in detail, and to write a formal report to the Chancellor of the Exchequer when inflation exceeds the target range. The governor's letter has to explain how the forecast went awry, how long the violation will last, and what the bank plans to do about it. The process is transparent and the credibility of the bank's statisticians is high. The bank's continuous dialogue about inflation with financial markets has almost certainly contributed to a drop in the volatility of the UK pound/US dollar and UK pound/euro since 1998. During the 1980s, sterling was the most volatile currency among the majors. During the first decade of the 2000s, volatility fell so that today the GBP/EUR is the least volatile of the major currency pairs, using average daily range as the measure.

FX traders cheerfully admit that they may not know all the arcane economics, but they still believe themselves qualified to judge central bank actions. This is because FX traders see firsthand the reactions of various markets to changes in inflation and expected inflation, and central bank statements and policy decisions.

Interest rate curve shifts as FX drivers

With an abrupt change in one currency's yield curve, even if other differentials between the two currencies stay the same, a change in FX sentiment will be triggered.

In the second half of 2010, with the Federal Reserve increasingly expected to implement additional quantitative easing measures, two-year US Treasury yields began to creep lower, until eventually they posted what was then new life-time low yields below 0.40% in late summer. This occurred because investors wanted to hold US Treasuries, but not longer-dated instruments whose price might suddenly fall as yields rose. Investors preferred to park their monies in the short-end of the US curve rather than choose instruments such as a 10-year note or

30-year Treasury bond. The thinking at the time was that when the US economy rebounded, long-dated yields would rise faster and higher than short-dated yields. As US Treasury yields declined, dollar-yen began suddenly to be more impacted by yield changes in two-year Treasuries instead of swings in the 10-year note.

The dollar/yen fell 4% between the time Federal Reserve Chairman Ben Bernanke first mentioned the possibility of new quantitative easing measures, later dubbed QE2, in Jackson Hole on 27 August 2010 and the actual announcement of QE in November. The two-year US yield bottomed around 0.33% on 4 November 2010. US long-term yields had fallen so low that the yields were less attractive to Japanese investors, especially from a real (ex-inflation) yield perspective. Like other investors, as US investments matured, the Japanese preferred to either park the monies in a shorter-term instrument or repatriate the funds back to Japan, thus helping to drive dollar-yen lower.

And so we can see that when conditions are deemed *normal*, changes in the 10-year yield spread have a powerful effect on currency price direction, but as conditions become abnormal, and we must consider negative real returns as *abnormal*, the 2-year note differential becomes the ruling data set for FX rates. The correlation of the euro/dollar and the 2-year note differential between the US and Germany from 2010 is very high, as shown in Figure 4.3.

Figure 4.3 – EUR/USD vs 2-Year German Bund/T-Bond Differntial (since 2010, daily)

Remember that high correlation doesn't mean both data series move in perfect lockstep. There are exceptions. The EUR/USD was particularly jittery in June 2012 when Germany issued new 2-year notes at a coupon of zero, effectively forcing investors to pay for the privilege of parking their cash with the German government and accepting a loss due to inflation, then running at about 2.4%. At one point (2 June 2012) the return was minus 0.012 percent, the first time the rate has been negative in the history of German notes. At the time, the yield on US 2-year notes was 0.40%, so you would think that the flight to safety in German paper would favour the dollar. But it was not the case. The euro had fallen over May and June, to be sure, but right after the zero-coupon issuance, the euro rose in June due to hopes surrounding yet another EMU summit (on the 19th).

When the euro fell in July, nobody named negative yields as the reason. Instead, the reason was a renewed loss of confidence in European leadership and the nature of some of the changes proposed, including lack of clarity of whether the Spanish bank bailout would entail sovereign Spanish liability. The euro was already falling in early July when the ECB cut rates by 25 bp; some commentators blamed the rate cut for the falling euro, or perhaps the cut in the deposit rate to zero, but traders believed the rate cuts were secondary. In any case, the ECB cut had not much to do with the pricing of German debt.

The significance of this is that the German 2-year yield was pushed down by flight to safety from other European countries and, at the same time, the US equivalent yields were also lower on inflows diverted from Europe. The relative spread was jumpy but moving in tandem by similar amounts. There were plenty of occasions, such as May to August 2012, when the two series did not move together. Often what was moving the euro/dollar exchange rate was the evolving judgment on the viability of the euro zone, not interest rates.

Greenspan's yield curve conundrum and what it means for foreign exchange

Interest rate differentials may be among the very best of the indicators we have to forecast exchange rates on both a near-term and long-term basis, but sometimes central banks get unintended consequences when they manage interest rates for the benefit of the domestic economy without consideration of exchange rate effects. This is particularly true for the US as the issuer of the reserve currency.

During the early 2000s, the US Federal Reserve was raising interest rates at the short end but the news seemed not to reach the longer-end of the yield curve. This is Greenspan's conundrum and it throws a very large monkey wrench into the relationship of relative yields and currency levels.

Here's the story.

In the early 2000s, the US was trying to recover from the effects of the NASDAQ crash and the 9/11 attacks. In response, the Federal Reserve lowered interest rates to a then record low of 1.0% in June 2003 in order to stimulate the economy. Low US Treasury yields prompted investors to look abroad and the dollar came under downward pressure as world currencies rose. Other central banks were forced to intervene, buying dollars to prevent their currencies from strengthening too quickly. These central banks, in most cases, then took their dollar holdings and invested them in US Treasuries, which in turn weighed on US yields. This unexpected and persistent demand for Treasuries prevented yields, especially long-term yields, from rising a year later in June 2004 when the Fed raised the federal funds rate to 1.25%. The Fed proceeded to hike 17 more times, before stopping when fed funds hit 5.25% in June 2006. Over the course of this tightening period, US long-term yields moved lower, rather than higher, making it difficult for the Fed to be effective.

In February 2005, then Federal Reserve Chairman Alan Greenspan addressed this puzzling phenomenon in a speech to the Senate Committee on Banking, Housing and Urban Affairs:[19]

"In this environment, long-term interest rates have trended lower in recent months even as the Federal Reserve has raised the level of the target federal funds rate by 150 basis points. This development contrasts with most experience, which suggests that, other things being equal, increasing short-term interest rates are normally accompanied by a rise in longer-term yields. The simple mathematics of the yield curve governs the relationship between short and long-term interest rates. Ten-year yields, for example, can be thought of as an average of ten consecutive one-year forward rates. A rise in the first-year forward rate, which correlates closely with the federal funds rate, would increase the yield on ten-year US Treasury notes even if the more-distant forward rates remain unchanged. Historically, though, even these distant forward rates have tended to rise in association with monetary policy tightening.

"In the current episode, however, the more-distant forward rates declined at the same time that short-term rates were rising. Indeed, the tenth-year tranche, which yielded 6.5% last June, is now at about 5.25%. During the same period, comparable real forward rates derived from quotes on Treasury inflation-indexed debt fell significantly as well, suggesting that only a portion of the decline in nominal forward rates in distant tranches is attributable to a drop in long-term inflation expectations.

"Some analysts have worried that the dip in forward real interest rates since last June may indicate that market participants have marked down their view of economic growth going forward, perhaps because of the rise in oil prices. But this interpretation does not mesh seamlessly with the rise in stock prices and the narrowing of credit spreads observed over the same interval. Others have emphasised the subdued overall business demand for credit in the United States and the apparent eagerness of lenders, including foreign investors, to provide financing. In particular, heavy purchases of longer-term Treasury securities by foreign central banks have often been cited as a factor boosting bond prices and pulling down longer-term yields. Thirty-year fixed-rate mortgage rates have dropped to a level only a little higher than the record lows touched in 2003 and, as a consequence, the estimated average duration of outstanding mortgage-backed securities has shortened appreciably over recent months. Attempts by mortgage investors to offset this decline in duration by purchasing longer-term securities may be yet another contributor to the recent downward pressure on longer-term yields.

"But we should be careful in endeavouring to account for the decline in long-term interest rates by adverting to technical factors in the United States alone because yields and risk spreads have narrowed globally. The German ten-year Bund rate, for example, has declined from 4.25% last June to current levels of 3.5%. And spreads of yields on bonds issued by emerging-market nations over US Treasury yields have declined to very low levels.

"There is little doubt that, with the breakup of the Soviet Union and the integration of China and India into the global trading market, more of the world's productive capacity is being tapped to satisfy global demands for goods and services. Concurrently, greater integration of financial markets has meant that a larger share of the world's pool of savings is being deployed in cross-border financing of investment. The favourable inflation performance across a broad range of countries resulting from enlarged global goods, services and financial capacity has doubtless contributed to expectations of lower inflation in the years ahead and lower inflation risk premiums. But none of this is new and hence it is difficult to attribute the long-term interest rate declines of the last nine months to glacially increasing globalisation. For the moment, the broadly unanticipated behaviour of world bond markets remains *a conundrum*. Bond price movements may be a short-term aberration, but it will be some time before we are able to better judge the forces underlying recent experience."

Greenspan's *conundrum* has continued in subsequent years and the suppressive yield effect, stemming from world central bank and sovereign wealth fund demand for Treasuries, has only increased as global reserves have grown. This is another instance of an institutional factor, the US being the issuer of the reserve currency, trumping the relative real yield as a key FX determinant.

The relative real yield has logic, common sense and history on its side, but we have seen several times in the last two decades that institutional factors can override it. As a result, professional FX analysts and traders are more likely to watch institutional developments with as much care as the relative rates themselves. For example, Japan, the US and the UK are all engaged in quantitative easing, but as of July 2012, the European Central Bank has not accepted QE as one of its policy tools.

Rising global FX reserves and the effect on FX

China alone saw its foreign exchange reserves rise from about $155 billion at the end of 1999 to well over $3 trillion in 2011, with the bulk of these assets held in dollars and in US instruments. If China picks up its ball and goes home, US Treasury yields would skyrocket. China has stated, however, that selling any sizable portion of its US fixed income assets would only drive the price of the instrument lower and decrease the value of its holdings. The People's Bank of China (PBOC) has been increasing its diversification into the euro and other currencies, but the bulk of its holdings remain in US dollars.

Going forward, what the PBOC decides to do as their existing US fixed income instruments mature will be key for FX direction. Indeed, with total global official reserves doubling, if not tripling, over the past ten years, any larger diversification out of the US into other countries could hit the dollar hard. Analysts have stressed, though, that given the depth and breadth of the US financial system, the United States will likely remain the home of the lions' share of world central bank foreign exchange assets, but even a small percentage shift could lead to larger dollar sales. We will discuss this more in the chapter on Reserve Diversification and the Future of the Dollar.

China has not been the only world central bank actively intervening to prevent currency strength in recent years. The Bank of Korea, the Bank of Japan, the Monetary Authority of Singapore, just to name a few, have also at times stepped in buying dollars and selling their domestic currencies. In Latin America, Brazilian and Chilean central bank authorities increased their dollar purchases in 2010 and 2011 also. As these central banks purchase dollars to prevent foreign inflows from pushing their country's exchange rate higher, which would hurt exports, the dollar proceeds, if unsterilised (no change to the monetary base), typically end up back in the United States and mostly back in US Treasuries.

So the circular argument went. The more Treasuries the central banks bought, the lower US yields went, which made the dollar and US investments less attractive so investors were forced to look abroad instead, buying higher yielding assets elsewhere, continuing the cycle. If we assume that US yields will eventually rise in the 2014 to 2020 period, central banks will perceive less need to intervene and therefore there will be less demand for Treasury purchases, which may result in even higher US yields than being engineered by the Federal Reserve.

In the fall of 2011 these central banks got a respite, but not necessarily the kind they wanted. Because of the escalating euro zone peripheral debt crisis, investors scrambled to exit emerging market holdings, driving emerging market currencies sharply lower and the dollar higher in late September. Emerging Market central banks then had to contend with an unexpectedly weak currency instead of a strong one. Several central banks used this opportunity to sell their US Treasury holdings, making a profit on what was on some days 45-year low yields (in the 10-year Treasury) below 2.0%. The central bank could then use the dollar proceeds to sell dollars to panicked investors and buy back their currency at much lower levels than they sold them for.

This may have been a win-win in terms of profit for the central bank, but it came at the cost of steep domestic equity declines and in some cases higher domestic yields. This same scenario played out again in the first half of 2012. Many world central banks, including Banco Central do Brazil and the Bank of Korea, actively intervened in the first three months of the year, buying dollars to prevent investor demand from pushing their currency higher. A few months later, these central banks were forced to sell dollars to prevent investor outflows from unduly weakening their currency, which might force a larger exodus.

Foreign investment inflows and outflows have always been a dollar driver, but with the advent of more marked globalisation in the early 2000s, these flows began to have a larger effect than before. Central banks and sovereign wealth funds, which once came to the FX market to execute millions, are now doing deals in the billions.

Inflation expectations and what the market watches

Every central bank manages interest rates to promote growth without inflation, or at least with inflation held under a benchmark target, generally around 2%. That sounds simple, but it becomes hideously complicated when you acknowledge that keeping an eye on consumer prices and producer prices can only get you so far. Central banks have to look not only at existing data, which by definition is backward-looking, but also inflation expectations. This is a topic that features great disagreement among economists, and the amount of disagreement varies over time depending on what other economic data is showing. Worse, some people form their inflation expectations based on outdated information, the so-called *sticky-information model,* accounting for a wide dispersion of estimates. Not only do professional economists disagree, consumers and the public at large disagree.[20]

A good example of the sticky information model today is raging fear of inflation in the US arising from the Fed's ballooning balance sheet, money creation and quantitative easing. What is sticky is the connection between money supply and inflation, and quite rightly. But it's not the complete story. If the velocity of money is decelerating at the same or nearly the same pace as money supply is rising, then the right-hand side of the Fisher equation does not show a change in value and therefore the other side of the equation, GDP and inflation, are also unchanged.

You can see velocity and other monetary data at the St. Louis Fed's web database, charmingly named FRED
research.stlouisfed.org/fred2/series/M2V?cid=32242

This data shows the velocity or turnover rate of money falling off a cliff from 2.15% in 1996 to 1.65% at end-2010. In this instance, we would have to attribute high inflation expectations to more than outdated information – it's incomplete information, or rather an incomplete understanding of the mechanism by which money supply influences inflation.

Discussion of inflation expectations is one area where stockbroker economics is definitely not sufficient. In fact, to evaluate inflation expectations, analysts and traders give more focus to the semi-academic literature, in the US chiefly from the Federal Reserve, than to any other aspect of economics. Traders who wouldn't be caught dead studying trends in export prices (say) can be caught checking out FRED, which fortunately has nice graphics.

In addition, both the central banks and market players keep close tabs on inflation swaps and inflation breakevens. As core inflation accelerates, spreads on inflation swaps and inflation breakevens begin to widen and, conversely, as core inflation decelerates, spreads on these instruments narrow.

Inflation swaps

An inflation swap acts to transfer inflation risk from one party to another. This is done through the use of inflation derivatives, which may be traded either over-the-counter or on an exchange. In December 2010, Joseph G. Haubrich and John Lindner of the Cleveland Fed wrote a research piece on inflation swaps. They said:

> "One way to find out what markets expect for future inflation is to look at the inflation swaps market. In an inflation swap, one side makes a variable payment that is based on the realised inflation rate, and the other makes a fixed payment. To make the swap fairly priced, the fixed payment must

approximate the expected value of inflation. Since actual inflation is uncertain, however, there is a risk premium involved as well."[21]

Haubrich and Lindner advise looking at complex configurations, such as the expectation for the 3-year inflation rate two years into the future.

Inflation breakevens

Inflation breakevens came into being shortly after the US Treasury began to offer Treasury Inflation Protected Securities (TIPS) in 1997. The breakeven inflation rate is the difference between the nominal yield on a conventional bond and the real yield on an inflation indexed bond of the same maturity.

The first US Treasury TIPS offer was for $7 billion of 10-year notes and market demand quickly grew. By 2005, there were about $200 billion TIPS outstanding of the total $4 trillion in overall Treasury instruments, with maturities of five-year, 10-year, 20-year, and 30-year offered intermittently. At the end of 2010, there were roughly $550 billion in TIPS outstanding as part of a total of about $4.3 trillion in overall Treasury instruments. The US Treasury changed the name of these instruments to Treasury Inflation Indexed Securities (TIIS) shortly after TIPS came into being, but the market continued to keep the more popular acronym.

The Treasury Department explains [22] how the TIPS product works:

> "Interest payments on TIPS are made semi-annually and are linked to the Consumer Price Index for Urban Consumers (CPI-U). The underlying value of the principal grows at the same rate that prices (as measured by CPI-U) rise. When the principal grows, interest payments grow also since interest payments are a fixed percentage of principal. At maturity, if inflation has occurred and increased the value of the underlying security, Treasury pays the owner the higher inflation-adjusted principal. If, however, deflation has occurred and decreased the value of the underlying security, the investor receives the original face value of the security."

Federal Reserve banks and traders watching breakevens

As investor interest in TIPS took off, market players began to watch the spread between the Treasury yield and the TIPS yield, with five-year and 10-year spreads watched most carefully. Indeed, various regional offices of the Federal Reserve have mentioned their interest in using breakevens as a gauge of inflation expectations on several occasions. In October 2005, the San Francisco Fed said in an economic letter entitled 'Inflation Expectations: How the Market Speaks'[23] that "comparing yields between conventional Treasury securities and TIPS can provide a useful measure of the market's expectation of future CPI inflation."

The San Francisco Fed tracked the breakeven inflation rate for Treasury yields versus TIPS for both five and ten-year instruments, noting that:

> "the breakeven inflation rate overstated inflation expectations because of the inflation risk premium in Treasury yields, but it understates inflation compensation because of the liquidity premium in TIPS yields. With a more mature TIPS market and over relatively short time periods, both the inflation risk premium and the liquidity premium are likely to be fairly constant. Thus, the changes in breakeven inflation rates can be interpreted as the market measure of changes in inflation expectations".

In 2006, the Kansas City Fed noted[24] that "many market participants and policymakers are interested in the yield spreads between nominal Treasuries and TIPS because the spreads contain information about market expected future inflation rates." Figure 4.4 is a chart of the yield spreads between 10-year nominal and indexed Treasuries, as well as the forecasts of the average inflation rates for the next ten years based on the Blue Chip Consensus forecast, and on the Survey of Professional Forecasters (SPF). Figure 4.4 shows that from 1999 to 2003, the liquidity risk premium in 10-year TIPS was, on average, 0.55-percentage-point higher than the inflation risk premium in 10-year nominal Treasuries. This may have surprised non-active fixed income market players "who tend to consider the liquidity risk premium to be of secondary importance to the inflation risk premium," the Kansas City Fed said.

Figure 4.4 – yield spread compared to inflation forecasts

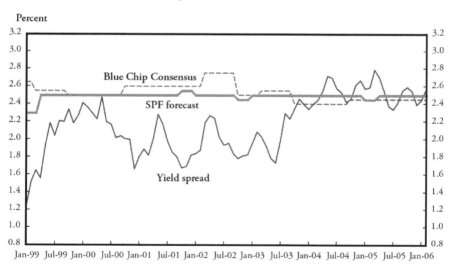

Source: **www.kansascityfed.org/Publicat/econrev/PDF/2Q06Shen%28rvd%29.pdf**

In June 2010, the Cleveland Federal Reserve[25] unveiled its own inflation expectations index. The index is updated each month on the release day of CPI.

> "The Cleveland Fed's estimate of inflation expectations is based on a model that combines information from a number of sources to address the shortcomings of other, commonly used measures, such as the 'break-even' rate derived from Treasury inflation protected securities (TIPS) or survey-based estimates. The Cleveland Fed model can produce estimates for many time horizons, and it isolates not only inflation expectations, but several other interesting variables, such as the real interest rate and the inflation risk premium."

Traders watch inflation breakevens closely too. A well bid TIPS auction would suggest that the market was worried about inflation and saw better value in the TIPS yield over Treasuries. Conversely, a well offered TIPS auction would suggest that the market had less concern about inflation and did not see better value in the TIPS yield over Treasuries. The past few years offer a good example of how far investors will go to protect themselves against inflation.

In a 20 April 2011 research piece[26], Robin L. Lumsdaine of the Center for Financial Stability (CFS) noted that "the front end of the TIPS curve has routinely seen negative yields since 2007. Currently, all maturities through January 2017 are in negative territory." This meant that an investor buying these instruments must believe that even though the instrument has a negative yield, inflation at maturity will be high enough to compensate for this.

We repeat the Treasury Department's explanation of TIPS:

> "At maturity, if inflation has occurred and increased the value of the underlying security, Treasury pays the owner the higher inflation-adjusted principal. If, however, deflation has occurred and decreased the value of the underlying security, the investor receives the original face value of the security."

The CFS's Lumsdaine noted that in order to attract TIPS buyers, who may have been put off by the negative TIPS coupon, the Treasury took action in March 2011.

"In a 1 March 2011 Federal Register notice[27], Treasury amended 'paragraph (b) of 31CFR 356.10 to state that if a Treasury note or bond auction results in a yield lower than 0.125%, the interest rate will be set at 1/8 of one percent, with the price adjusted accordingly (i.e. at a premium)' affected 1 April 2011," she said. Lumsdaine explained that "rather than compensating Treasury each period for its willingness to pay an above-market coupon, investors are being asked to pay (deposit) a premium upfront, which will then be refunded in the form of a semi-annual 1/8 coupon payment."

"While the introduction of a coupon floor guarantees positive nominal coupon cash flow over the life of the bond, it does not guarantee that, at maturity, investors will have recouped the upfront premium they will likely need to pay at auction to offset the artificially higher coupon. That ultimately depends on the realisation of inflation over the life of the bond," Lumsdaine said.

The December 2010 piece by Haubrich and Linder of the Cleveland Fed also touched on breakevens:

> "These measures may give estimates that are different from those gotten in a popular way, which is to compare the interest rate on Treasury bonds that are protected against inflation (TIPS) with ordinary, nominal Treasury bonds, which are not. The difference between those rates, often called the breakeven rate, is the estimate of expected inflation. Using inflation swaps to gauge expected inflation has an advantage over the TIPS-based way because the difference between TIPS and Treasury rates can change with liquidity differences between the two instruments. However, the breakeven rate, whether derived from TIPS or from inflation swaps, also includes an inflation risk premium, and so is not a pure measure of inflation expectations. Getting a pure measure of expected inflation is possible, but it is more difficult to update date day by day and to see high-frequency patterns."

Federal Reserve Chairman Ben Bernanke, when he was a Fed Governor, also addressed the pros and cons of using inflation breakevens[28].

> "We need to be cautious about drawing strong conclusions about the short-run behaviour of expected inflation from the data on breakeven inflation. The fact that the volatility of breakeven inflation is so much greater than that of standard survey measures of inflation expectations (such as those collected by the Federal Reserve Bank of Philadelphia for professional forecasters or by the University of Michigan for consumers) should give us pause. The responsiveness of breakeven inflation to what might be construed primarily as liquidity disturbances, such as the Russian debt crisis and recent bouts of mortgage hedging activity that roiled Treasury markets, suggests that variable liquidity premiums, together with varying inflation risk premiums, contaminate breakeven inflation as a measure of expected inflation.

> "I have emphasised some reasons to be cautious in interpreting breakeven inflation as expected inflation. Nevertheless, I expect that the usefulness of inflation-indexed securities as a tool for measuring expected inflation will increase over time. The liquidity of TIPS should continue to improve as the share of government debt issued in inflation-linked form continues to rise, particularly if the Treasury decides to expand the range of maturities of indexed bonds that it offers. Moreover, our ability to model risk and liquidity

premiums is improving, which will help us control an important source of volatility in breakeven inflation. Finally, the universe of inflation-linked financial assets seems to be increasing, which will allow for fruitful comparisons and cross-checking. For example, futures on the CPI were recently introduced on the Chicago Mercantile Exchange. Although these contracts are not yet widely traded, they may at some point provide useful measures of breakeven inflation out to the maturity of the shortest-term TIPS, thereby filling in an important portion of the term structure of breakeven inflation."

Mr. Bernanke was in for a disappointment. The Chicago Mercantile Exchange CPI futures contract that was launched in February 2004 failed to attract interest and the contract was delisted in November 2010. Traders care about *securities* they can bet on to make money and this one didn't qualify.

Bottom line, analysts and traders are so hungry for information about inflation expectations that they will follow data on TIPS despite its many inadequacies and drawbacks.

When safe-haven trumps yield

The trading action in 2011 taught the market that even low-yielding currencies have something to offer – as safe-havens. The year started out with investors slowly putting money back into developed markets after keeping a greater than usual share in emerging markets and commodities the year before. At first, global data was upbeat and there was a sense that the ECB would be raising euro zone interest rates first, probably before the summer, and that the Fed would also be able to raise rates, possibly before the end of the year.

The earthquake and tsunami that shook Japan in March 2011 created a supply chain domino effect that eventually spilled over into most major countries, as evidenced by falling purchasing manager indices. Two months later, renewed concern about Greek debt, as well as spread-widening in the peripheral bond markets of Portugal and Ireland, led to fears of contagion into the larger bond markets of Italy and Spain. As the summer wore on, the market moved from one crisis to the other, finally ending with a nail-biting eleventh hour increase in the US debt ceiling and the US rating agency Standard & Poor's lowering the United States long-term sovereign debt rating from AAA to AA+.

Traders joked about a contest between currencies and debated which was uglier, the euro or the dollar. One thing that was certain, the low-yielding yen and Swiss franc were being crowned prom queens. Initial yen and Swiss demand came from remaining carry trades, where those who were long a high-yielding Aussie dollar and short the Swiss franc or yen decided to take profit on this trade.

Beyond the carry trade, each currency had its own allure. The yen had the second largest and second most liquid bond market covering its back. The Swiss franc was the non-euro, where the market could invest in Europe, but not the euro zone. In both instances, benchmark interest rates were close to zero and longer-dated yields were lower than many other countries, although as noted above, the real return on Japanese notes is not only positive, but fairly high (over 3%). Even the Swiss National Bank lowering Swiss interest rates even closer to zero in early August 2011 did not prevent the Swiss franc from forging ahead to post new life-time highs. It took the introduction of a euro-Swiss peg at CHF1.2000 in early September to turn the table on the Swiss franc and that came at a high cost for the Swiss National Bank. In Japan, massive interventions undertaken by the Bank of Japan, estimated at $60 billion in early August 2011 and $118 billion on 31 October 2011 and the first few days of November, had initial knee-jerk reactions to weaken the yen but failed to make a major dent in pro-yen sentiment.

As the euro zone peripheral crisis wore on, countries such as France and Austria also lost their AAA label. The world's remaining AAA countries saw stepped-up inflows, with currencies such as the Canadian dollar, Aussie dollar and Norwegian kroner all gaining as a result. The lesson to be learned is that when the market is panicked and wants to buy a currency for comfort, the domestic yield of a country gets placed on the back burner.

Conclusions

Current interest rate differentials and yields are important, but need to be put into context when entering into a currency position. It's not only yields that drive currencies, but interest rate expectations built on inflation expectations that are a driver, too. Low-yielding currencies can be attractive when they offer a reward beyond yield, namely the preservation of capital. Somewhat strangely, the current real yield differential tends not to be a currency driver, but rather the combination of existing yields and inflation expectations. We see this most strongly in the Japanese yen, which has near-zero nominal yields but real yields due to deflation of 2% to 3% and thus a genuine yield advantage over both the US and Germany – and yet traders do not pile into the yen for this reason. Instead, when the yen is rising, it's because of domestic Japanese players taking their money home and out of harm's way.

Also, just because a currency has a higher yield, such as the Australian dollar, does not protect it from a sell-off if new data about the domestic economy suggests a rate cut might be called for to boost activity – even when the currency will still have a higher yield than other currencies after the cut. It may take some time for the favourable differential to reassert its power and the currency to recover.

Another difficulty is that while the euro zone has a single interest rate, it doesn't have a single yield. For the period 2009-2012, changes in the US-German 2-year yield are highly correlated with the euro/dollar, which disregards the far higher yields of other euro zone members, such as Spain and Italy.

Finally, we come to realise also that there will be times when conundrums are never solved. The US, as the issuer of the reserve currency and the largest safe-haven, is unable to manage the entire yield curve for its own policy purposes because its notes and bonds are sought in times of international financial distress, even to the extent of retaining safe-haven status after a ratings downgrade. Bottom line, FX traders and analysts cannot make a decision solely on a yield differential. The outlook for a change in the yield arising from inflation/deflation and judgments about the institutional environment can be more important than the yield number alone.

CHAPTER 5 –
FORECASTING FX

"… if there is a consensus result in the empirical literature, it has to be that nothing, but nothing, can systematically explain exchange rates between major currencies with flexible exchange rates."

Kenneth Rogoff[29]

Economists see the FX market through one lens and FX professionals see it quite differently; this is true of traders at banks, brokers and hedge funds, as well as analysts. Economic theory seems logical but doesn't work in the real world, which leaves practitioners with no solid economics underpinning and therefore the inability to forecast with any confidence.

This seems an enduring drawback, but it does have a virtue – FX professionals are free to abandon orthodoxy and ideology. A professional may choose to adopt an ideology and be able to defend it vigorously, but another professional can adopt an opposing ideology and defend it just as impressively. Off on the side, the key traders themselves tend not to adopt ideologies – ideology offers them no payoff.

This chapter covers some of the basic theories from economics that have failed to be effective in FX and emphasises that one reason these ideas fail to help forecast FX prices is that you can have two opposing factors at work at the same time, when theory says you *should* not see such things.

Another reason theory fails is that certain institutional developments are full-bore overrides, including banking sector crises, political developments and, most of all, government intervention in the FX market. The very existence of government intervention illustrates that FX market structure, whether fixed or floating, has a rocky relationship with the real economy. In a nutshell, economic theory is pretty useless in FX at the best of times and irrelevant when it comes to certain institutional events.

Traders, economists and theories

Traders with shifting worldviews

Traders track the data release schedules of the major economies and have their trigger fingers poised to buy or sell depending on the data released. As a general rule, data that meets the forecast gets little response or the opposite response of what logic would dictate. This is the *buy on the rumour, sell on the news* effect. If the data is far better than expected, the existing bias is reinforced and traders buy (or sell) in bigger amounts. If it's a disappointment, the currency will be sold, although if the bias was a negative one to begin with, the selling can turn into a real rout. A disappointing data release coming into a strong pro-currency bias may get only a fleeting response or none at all. Data always needs to be seen in the context of existing sentiment and expectations. We see this effect in all markets, not just the FX market. Equity prices move in response to discrepancies between expected and actual earnings, for example.

Just as earnings is a core concept in equity pricing, the FX world must have core concepts that drive prices. We can see traders have a finely calibrated array of responses *to certain key economic releases*, so we imagine traders have a worldview that it would be useful to know about. How does the FX market prioritise inflation, trade and budget deficits, growth rates, employment, productivity, and so on? In other words, what are the macroeconomic factors, exactly, that traders use to forecast exchange rates?

Unfortunately, you will seldom find professional traders with a systematic worldview and strong opinions on what economic variables support or trash a currency. We can say with confidence that today the top factors in the US are nonfarm payrolls and purchasing managers indices, and in Europe, the purchasing managers indices and sentiment surveys by German IFO and ZEW research institutes.

But only a few years ago, the top factors were money supply, inflation and trade balances. Core clients like hedge and sovereign funds usually have a worldview, but the traders themselves tend not to embrace an analytical point of view and certainly not an ideology. If this year we are focusing on budget deficits, then traders will turn their antennae to news about budget deficits. If an *old* factor starts getting new attention, like inflation, then that's what will be watched. In the UK from 2009 to 2011, inflation never went out of favour as a key indicator, and it remains an obsession lying just under the surface in other countries.

The misalignment of exchange rates

At any one time, professional traders do have a hierarchy of economic and institutional factors they are watching, but it's a constantly evolving and shifting hierarchy, and its relationship to a theory or worldview is tenuous at best. There's a good reason for this: most of the trading in the FX market is speculative in nature. It's the trader's job to make a profit from trades lasting seconds and minutes, not to engage in deep thinking about economies or be analytically correct about the true meaning of some economic development.

How, then, do exchange rates move more or less in line with the big economic themes of the day? Well, they don't. Exchange rates are *always* misaligned with what an economist would deem *equilibrium* value or what a financial analysis would consider *fair value*. If it seems that the dollar is depreciating because of the trade deficit or budget deficit, consider all the occasions when it was announced those deficits were rising and the dollar failed to fall.

The correspondence of exchange rates with economic variables is worse than spotty – it's often downright perverse. Exchange rates do not move the way theory says they should move. FX moves are maddeningly inconsistent and unmoored from what seems like economic reality, and they can stay unmoored from reality for very long periods of time.

The problem lies not with the exchange rates, but with the theories, or rather, with what professional and armchair economists alike think economic theory says. In practice, we lack a single coherent and universally accepted theory of how exchange rates are determined.

Economic theories on FX

Theory, in FX, is a sorry thing – despite strenuous work over many decades by very smart and capable economists.

Here's a summary of what economists theorise on FX:

If you are a plain-vanilla economist, you like purchasing power parity, the idea that the exchange rate will adjust so that the same product will cost the same in two countries sharing free trade with one another. You can draw a chart showing how exchange rates track the trade balance.

If you are a monetarist, you add money supply and demand as the key driver to the price changes that determine inflation and thus purchasing power, which in turn affects the trade account. Monetarists come in several flavours but one chart that can be drawn shows how an x% increase in money supply changes the exchange rate by y% with a lag of z periods.

If you acknowledge that trade flows are only part of the total of what goes on between two countries, you add capital flows to the mix and will focus on the balance of payments. The basic framework of most exchange rate determination models starts here, with the Mundell-Fleming model. You can't read anything about exchange rate theory without running into this model. In a nutshell, Mundell-Fleming says a currency reaches equilibrium when the outflow from net trade matches capital inflow, or vice versa. One drawback of the Mundell-Fleming model, of many drawbacks, is that it assumes a small, open economy. All the same, even for big economies you can draw a nifty chart showing strong correlation between a trade-weighted currency and the current account balance.

If you want to combine the current account and the capital account, you embrace the real interest rate differential as the dominant factor. In this version, it's not the supply of money itself or the relative interest rate that counts, but rather the expectation of inflation baked into the interest rate. You can draw a chart showing how exchange rates track the relative real interest rate differential, as done in Chapter 4.

If you are from the equity and/or fixed income side of the universe, you are interested not only in relative real return, but also asset value and expected asset value – the so-called balanced portfolio approach. Expected asset values are influenced by factors like depth, variety and liquidity of assets on offer, plus other factors that can be hard to measure or evaluate, such as sovereign and country risk, demographic changes, education and productivity, inventiveness, confidence in the fiscal probity of governments, and political stability.

Reviews of the various economists' theories and models can be found elsewhere.[30] Suffice it to say that no single theory or model covers all the bases.

The absence of a single, tell-all theory

All the theories mentioned above are true, at least to some extent and for some time periods, but this also means that none of them is completely right all of the time. That means you will see a chart showing a near-perfect correlation of an exchange rate with some economic variable and become convinced that this is the holy grail for forecasting purposes, only to have it fall apart the next month, quarter or year when the next factor *du jour* becomes the fashion.

Take, for example, the issue of inflation. Many observers believe that over 2009-2012, the massive stimulative spending and injections of liquidity into the US economy by the Fed are by their very nature inflationary. Under normal conditions this would likely be true. But bank lending, the vector by which a rise in money supply multiplies into economic activity, continues to contract. Money supply, by one definition, is up 9% but commercial bank lending is down by 9%. What the Fed was worrying about in this period was deflation, not inflation. If inflation is inevitable, longer run, then the dollar *should fall*. But at the same time, the drop in economic activity back to near recession levels resulted in two countervailing effects – an improvement in the trade balance and high capital inflows seeking a safe haven, because troubles elsewhere are worse. These factors *should* cause the dollar to *rise. So which is it to be?*

Get used to situations like this. It would be comforting to think that exchange rates are determined by relative economic performance and capital flows. In theory, a country's exchange rate is an equilibrating factor of economic activity. If a country has a trade surplus for a prolonged period, for example, its currency must be undervalued and the FX market will eventually adjust the exchange rate to make exports more expensive and dissolve the surplus. If a country has a higher rate of inflation than its trading partners, it should also have rising interest rates to keep the real rate stable, and if not, capital will flow out.

Alas, exchange rate adjustments based on those sensible and logical ideas take an exceptionally long time to affect activity – and sometimes fail to affect it at all. This is the *disconnect puzzle*. Since 1976 the US has run large, persistent trade deficits and Japan has run large, persistent surpluses. That's over three decades of imbalance. Exchange rates have failed to do the equilibration job. Everyone in FX is aware of the disconnect puzzle and, as far as we know, it's unique to the FX market.

The disconnect puzzle

The *disconnect puzzle* states that exchange rates far overshoot levels where fundamental economics dictates they should go. In addition, they overshoot with far greater volatility than warranted or expected.

Not long after the dollar was floated in 1973, economists started trying to build FX models that could incorporate flexible exchange rates. By this time, price modelling was advanced and sophisticated. Price theory guru Milton Friedman had said floating rates would swiftly and efficiently reflect international inflation differentials. But it wasn't so. Prices of goods lagged and were sticky, and wages were even more sticky (and certainly sticky downwards). Exchange rates were overshooting any reasonable comparison of prices between the two countries.

The overshooting paper – Dornbusch's solution

In 1976 Massachusetts Institute of Technology (MIT) economist Rudi Dornbusch published a paper titled 'Expectations and Exchange Rate Dynamics', informally called the "overshooting paper," that is still the starting point of much FX analysis today. No book or paper from the academic sphere neglects to name the overshooting paper.

Dornbusch starts with the uncovered interest parity equation that says the home interest rate on bonds is always equal to the foreign interest rate plus the expected rate of depreciation or appreciation of the exchange rate. This concept implicitly incorporates rational expectations, an important point because later we will see that experienced FX market players loudly and rudely reject the concept of rational expectations.

Now introduce an unexpected permanent increase in money supply. Remember, prices are sticky and slow to respond, mostly because changes in real output and wages are slow to respond and information is not instantly transmitted everywhere simultaneously. The first effect of a change in money supply, while prices are stalled in the short run, is for interest rates to fall.

But the interest rate can fall vis-à-vis other foreign interest rates only if we expect the exchange rate to appreciate – that's the uncovered interest parity assumption. And yet we know that an unexpected rise in money supply will have the long-run effect of raising inflation, causing the currency to depreciate – the opposite of what is actually happening. Dornbusch argued that the *initial* depreciation of the exchange rate on the money supply news will be bigger than the *eventual* depreciation caused by the real economic effect of the money supply increase, and be followed by an appreciation in between the first depreciation and the second depreciation. In other words, any unexpected increase in money supply must cause the FX rate to overshoot downward and then, perversely, rise, before falling again. This explanation is followed logically by the deduction that if prices could, in fact, adjust immediately to changes in money supply, no other price (the price of money or the exchange rate) would need to overshoot.

Believe it or not, academics quarrelled bitterly for decades over whether prices are sticky. This calmed down a bit after Fed Chairman Volcker engineered a contraction of US money supply in 1979-1980. In those days, everyone involved in finance of any sort, including every last foreign exchange trader, watched the money supply releases, especially M3, like hawks. Forecasters specialised in money supply the way they specialise in forecasting GDP today. M3, by the way, was discontinued in 2006, although some diehards continue to create their own versions. In any case, the sticky prices argument was more or less set aside, at least outside of academic circles.

Notice that no one disputes the uncovered interest parity assumption – that interest rates will be the same everywhere except for embedded expectations of upcoming exchange rate changes. This is a classic chicken-and-egg problem, and economists resolve it by refusing to change the core assumption. They brush off empirical evidence, including sentiment surveys and behavioural studies of things like liquidity preference, as temporary aberrations away from the universal truth that interest rates are the same everywhere. In real life, interest rates are hardly ever the same everywhere and if they are, it's an accident. Another thing that is missing is realistic interactivity. The model is not exactly static, but it doesn't account for a change in the exchange rate arising from some other variable and that change affecting interest rates. A one-way causality is almost never correct in finance. We do have feedback.

The Dornbusch solution to the disconnect puzzle has some interesting consequences. If overshooting is caused by a one-time money supply shock, the spot rate should move farther than the forward rate. But empirically, this tends not to occur. In addition, investing on the basis of uncovered interest rates fails to achieve profits from the embedded exchange rate forecast – over all holding periods. Instead of trading on that basis, we have the latest staple of FX trading, the carry trade.

The Dornbusch model may have proved less than useful in day-to-day trading, but Dornbusch did everyone a big favour by repudiating the concept of equilibrium, which basically holds that market volatility is abnormal and temporary, caused by friction, imperfect information, communications problems or some external hindrance, including the disincentive of taxes and fees. The Dornbusch argument incorporates volatility as a fundamental of the market pricing process, and this is more in keeping with what real traders observe.

Pragmatic acceptance of disequilibrium

We no longer slavishly follow money supply numbers to forecast exchange rates, but we do have two cases in which this kind of ivory tower economic modelling lives on. The first is the ECB's acceptance that changes in money supply are invariably the cause of changes in inflation. And yet the ECB reported money supply growth at high levels (such as 7% to 9%) for most of the 2000-2010 decade without panicking about impending inflation. Eventually the ECB started publishing staff articles on how and why money supply, while exceeding target levels for years on end, does not necessarily affect its inflation targeting. Reasons include credit conditions, lending to various sectors, actual output and inflation expectations.

The ECB never fails to let an opportunity pass by to congratulate itself for managing inflation and has published numerous advanced economic studies demonstrating that optimum monetary policy can view monetary aggregates as only one component of the overall policy mix, if not sometimes outright irrelevant. More central to good policy is interest rate targeting, and so today that's what traders watch.[31] As a result, both the users of money in the euro zone and their observers, FX traders, are almost indifferent to euro zone money supply. And yet no one doubts that if euro zone money supply were to start rising to high levels again, the old orthodoxy of money supply creating inflation would re-assert itself among the public and in the press, exactly as it has done in the US, leading the ECB to defend belief in an economic mechanism but also asserting the need for real-world modification.

Another example is from the Japanese Ministry of Finance and Bank of Japan. When they want to alert the trading world that they are thinking about FX market intervention, they speak of "excessive volatility." The MoF and BoJ never actually define what they mean by excessive volatility and it would be easy to argue that the dollar/yen is not actually excessively volatile by any standard statistical definition (varying too far both ways from a central trendline). The yen is just moving too far, too fast in a single undesirable direction.

The point, however, is that a major country implicitly accepts volatility as a norm and has some idea of when that norm has been violated. Economists do not build exchange rate volatility into their models except as noise and yet as a practical matter, exchange rates overshoot with great regularity and real-world central bank and ministry of finance officials have to deal with complaints from exporters and other economic players effected by exchange rates.

Purchasing power parity

Purchasing power parity is another theory based on the concept of equilibrium. PPP states that if trade is free of transportation costs and trade barriers, the same basket of goods will have the same price in two different markets. PPP is based on the law of one price. The logic is pretty good: if German screwdrivers are cheap relative to French screwdrivers, the pragmatic and thrifty French will buy German screwdrivers until either the French manufacturer lowers his price or goes out of business. At some equilibrium point, the cost of screwdrivers will be the same in both countries.

Unfortunately, the number of things that are wrong with this theory is almost endless. Transportation is not free. The French screwdriver-maker may have a friend in the tariff office. The quality of the German screwdriver may be better. The German screwdriver may have a prestigious brand for which buyers will pay a premium whether it's actually better or not. The screwdriver may have a different relative value to the French workman in his basket of tools than to the German workman. German inflation may be rising faster than French inflation and pretty soon the advantage will vanish.

Most of all, the basket of goods of the average consumer in each country differs wildly – there is no average basket that is valid worldwide. The Japanese basket contains more rice than the American basket. But the Japanese believe that Japanese-grown rice has special qualities, so you can't compare the price of rice in the US with the price of rice in Japan. In short, rice is not an internationally tradeable good in Japan, but you can't exclude rice from a Japanese basket of goods. Finally, the price level in a country is set by more than internationally traded goods. Services like haircuts, restaurant meals and lawn-mowing are always purely domestic.

These are big reasons to be wary of purchasing power parity but for lack of better measures, important organisations like the United Nations, World Bank and, most prominently, the IMF use PPP anyway, if in a much modified and more nuanced way. The use of PPP is pervasive at the IMF and appears in many reports, including the influential semi-annual World Economic Outlook.[32] The Organisation for Cooperation and Economic Development (OECD) is another user of PPP and publishes a monthly report available to the public. The IMF and the OECD use PPP for a multitude of purposes, including setting quotas (IMF) and evaluating competitiveness and other economic measures. Beware of searching the internet for the IMF or OECD PPP data and expecting to find an instantly readable table, though – the statistical gyrations they go through will make your head spin.

One of the main reasons not to consult the PPP tables of the supranational organisations is that few FX professionals are consulting them. The formation of sentiment is always a group exercise; a factor may be true, but it's not useful for forecasting and trading purposes unless the broader market is looking at it, too.

Recently Bloomberg News Service started publishing the OECD monthly PPP data in a highly readable format. As far as we know, traders still view PPP as a curiosity, although one not to be missed. In Table 5.1, every currency except the euro is overvalued against the US dollar as of June 2012. We do not know whether, or by how much, such a judgment affects market sentiment toward the dollar.

Table 5.1 – OECD purchasing power parities against the US dollar

Undervaluation (%)	Currency	Overvaluation (%)
	Australian Dollar	33.98
	Norwegian Krone	26.86
	Swiss Franc	21.84
	Danish Krone	21.70
	Canadian Dollar	17.40
	New Zealand Dollar	16.81
	British Pound	2.12
3.03	Euro	

Source: Bloomberg

Those who observe fair value – PPP forecasts

Even given the above, the concept of PPP-based fair value does lurk in the bushes, presumably contributing to overall sentiment, even if it's doubtful anyone ever places a big bet on PPP alone. Some banks (and possibly some hedge or sovereign risk funds) create PPP tables and those are occasionally quoted in the financial press.

Credit Suisse, for example, calculates PPP using not only traded goods but also market-relevant factors such as investor demand for portfolio investments and direct investment. Direct investment, for example, is derived from long-term productivity trends, a splendid deduction, whereas portfolio investments are influenced by interest rates. The Credit Suisse model takes into account other factors, including trade deficits/surpluses. Its goal is to derive fair value for a currency pair, chiefly the euro/US dollar. Wisely, the bank offers a range based on standard deviation and not just a single number.

UBS is another of the banks that adds to PPP by estimating the amount of time a worker must expend in each country to earn enough to buy a Big Mac from McDonalds, an add-on to *The Economist's* Big Mac Index.

The Big Mac Index

The Big Mac Index, published every year since 1986, judges whether a currency is undervalued or overvalued, and by how much, based solely on the cost of a single item – a Big Mac – instead of a basket of goods. The index has had a surprisingly accurate track record for *forecasting* currency moves, albeit with varying time lags. *The Economist* now tweaks PPP by adjusting for GDP per person, since the price of a Big Mac has to have some relationship to affordability.

The measurement starts with the cost of a Big Mac in the US as the benchmark, against which is measured the cost in other countries. The implied purchasing power parity cost in other countries is deduced by how much more or less the Big Mac actually costs. The difference is attributed to the exchange rate. If the exchange rate were to change to the implied PPP cost, it would equilibrate the costs perfectly and everyone in the world would pay the same amount for a Big Mac.

Looking at Table 5.2, in July 2011 *The Economist* implied PPP exchange rate for the Australian dollar was $1.12 when the actual exchange rate was $0.92. Sure enough, a year later, the Australian dollar had appreciated to $1.0313, closer to the implied rate.

The euro should have been $1.18 on the implied PPP basis when it was actually $1.43 in July 2011, and again the euro moved in the correct direction and a year later was closer to the PPP forecast, $1.2154 from $1.43. The UK pound, however, went the wrong way. In 2011, the implied PPP exchange rate was $1.70 when the pound was actually $1.63. The pound should have risen but, instead, a year later it was lower at $1.5498. Obviously the FX market considers many factors other than relative purchasing power.

Table 5.2 – forecast outcomes from the Big Mac Index

	Actual Exchange Rate (25 July 2011)	Economist implied PPP exchange rate (25 July 2011)	Actual exchange rate (25 July 2012)
Australia	0.92	1.12	1.0313
Euro zone	1.43	1.18	1.2154
United Kingdom	1.63	1.70	1.5498

Eurostat purchasing power parity and advance applications of PPP

Eurostat, the statistics arm of the European Union, doesn't have a use for a dollar-based purchasing power measure but does have a use for one based on its own members. Only 17 of the 27 European Union members belong to the European Monetary Union and therefore use the euro. The other ten use their own currencies.

Since a primary goal of the EU is to facilitate regional cross-border trade and price convergence, Eurostat wants to display the range of price levels using its own European currency base. It achieves this aim by creating a purchasing power standard (PPS) in which the combined currencies of the EU-27 equals 100. Every other measure is in reference to this standard.

For example, as of June 2012 for June 2011, the price levels of the EU-27 vary from 51% of the standard (Bulgaria) to 142% (Denmark). The GDP per capita of the 27 EU members ranges from 45% to 274% of the standard. The comparison among countries shows that after prices are standardised to the EU-27 benchmark, the EMU countries have GDP that is 8% higher than the standard (as shown in Table 5.3).

Table 5.3 – GDP per capita at the EU purchasing power standard (June 2011)

European Union (27 countries)	100
European Monetary Union (17 countries)	108
Germany	120
United Kingdom	108
Norway	189
Switzerland	151
United States	148
Japan	105

Source: epp.eurostat.ec.europa.eu/portal/page/portal/purchasing_power_parities/introduction

In other Eurostat data, you can find relative price comparisons. By comparing any price in a country to the EU-27 purchasing power standard, you can tell whether a good or service is expensive or cheap relative to the group. A 2010 study found that overall prices in the UK (for food, clothing, electronics and other items) were exactly 100, or equal to the EU-27 standard. Ireland was relatively expensive at 118 and Albania was the least expensive at 50.[33]

One of the most interesting applications of the purchasing power parity concept is Eurostat's measurement of private household consumption (including indirect taxes) over time, since a goal of a currency union is to get price convergence. Eurostat calculates a coefficient of variation away from the EU-27 purchasing power standard. Increasingly lower numbers mean convergence of prices and this is what the EU and EMU have achieved. From 1995 to 2011, the EU-27 had decreasing coefficients, from 42.6 to 25. The EMU-17 also had price convergence, from 28.3 to 15.5.[34]

The Taylor Rule

Economists and traders watch inflation very carefully – inflation is the source of currency devaluation now that coin-clipping and counterfeiting of metal coins are irrelevant. A key cause of inflation is money supply outstripping production capacity, and so we also care about GDP and the so-called output gap, referring to spare capacity or its absence. A rise in input prices will be passed through to the buyer if demand is high and capacity is tight, but producers will let higher input prices eat into their profit margins if demand is weak and there is a lot of spare capacity.

Central banks strive to make monetary policy that keeps the output gap small but not zero, meaning production capacity needs to increase, assuming rising population and thus rising demand for goods and services. How do you get investment in production? You have a real (after inflation) rate of return that rewards savers and investors. If the real rate of return is zero or negative, nobody will invest and your manufacturing base (or housing stock) goes to wrack and ruin. Central banks face the question of how to balance the mix of money supply, the inflation rate (inflation targeting) and the interest rate to obtain the optimum non-inflationary growth rate.

Since standard economics fails to inform us how to make effective monetary policy, in 1993 a Stanford University economist named John B. Taylor devised the Taylor rule in which he observed that central banks make the best and most effective policy when they raise or lower short-term interest rates when inflation is rising too fast or output growth endangers closing the output gap. As a practical matter, you can use the unemployment rate as a proxy for the output gap. The Taylor rule incorporates the principle that to keep savers/investors involved, a rate increase needs to be bigger than any inflation increase. If inflation is going up at a pace of 1%, the rate increase needs to be more than 1%.

The Taylor rule is far more useful than other formulations because it shows the trade-off between inflation and growth. In the original, most simple version, the Taylor rule said the short-term interest rate should be a direct function of the divergence of inflation from the desired rate of inflation, plus the assumed equilibrium real interest rate, plus the difference between GDP and potential output.[35]

A problem immediately surfaces – which inflation rate? Core inflation, controversially, excludes volatile prices like energy and food. Taylor uses the GDP deflator, which is closer to core inflation than to headline inflation. Another issue is how you treat negative growth in GDP. A negative number makes everything else in the equation negative but you can't have a negative nominal interest rate (although you can have a negative real interest rate). In May 2009, for example, Taylor applied his own rule and concluded that Fed funds should be 0.50% (the rate was 0% to 0.25% at the time). The FX market deduced that the Fed had over-loosened and this would be a dollar-negative because inflation must follow – helping the euro in its recovery off the March low at 1.2457 caused by the Greek bailout to the high in November that year at 1.5142.

By June 2009, according to an article on the Bloomberg News Service, Dr. Taylor said the data suggested a rate of negative 0.955% (when the Fed funds rate was the same 0% to 0.25%). This was harder for the FX market to digest. Observers who thought the Fed had gone too easy were confused. Pimco, the biggest bond fund in the world, had reduced holdings of long-term government debt on the inflation scare early in 2009 and added more on the equities side. That same spring, Pimco made a splash with "the new normal," a roadmap for post-crash conditions that explicitly called for much slower growth – permanently slower growth – but accompanied by higher inflation, or stagflation. The anti-inflationary (if not downright deflationary) effects of slower growth were not recognised at Pimco for several more years – in 2011, Pimco admitted it was wrong about the yield trajectory of longer notes and bonds. Pimco may end up being right about ultra-low interest rates leading eventually to inflation, but that assumes policy-makers are not following Taylor rules.

The ECB and Fed do not officially and explicitly follow the Taylor rule, although you can find research papers from Fed economists that go into excruciating detail suggesting that they do.[36] Overall, the Taylor rule is an effective, if simple, policy guide.[37] It should go without saying that economists and market players alike enjoy debating the finer points of the Taylor rule, now expanded to the plural – Taylor rules. European economists apply the rules to the ECB, with both historical data and on currently evolving data, to judge the central bank, including many who work for the central bank. It's safe to say that the Taylor rule ideas have taken over whatever theoretical debate is still going on in the field of FX determination. If you Google 'Mundell-Fleming', you get 318,000 hits, but if you Google 'Taylor rule', you get 18.9 million.

Notice that the Taylor rules do not address the determination of FX rates directly. Instead we care about the Taylor rule as a way to judge a central bank's ability to measure the most important variables affecting exchange rates – inflation and growth. From this we can easily see why traders view as the most important indicators those that pertain to inflation (or pending inflation) and growth expansion or contraction, featuring most prominently the purchasing managers indices in all countries and sentiment indicators like the IFO index in Germany. In fact, in the oversimplified trader's world where decisions have to be made in a fraction of a second, the top indicators all pertain to inflation or the output gap, even if the output gap is not the economics concept most traders would say out loud.

Institutional overrides

Events with an upper-case E affect exchange rates in a predictable way, generally because they contain the seeds of a plausible forecast. We can think of dozens of events over the past 20 years that have moved the market like a herd, including central bank announcements, the Shanghai Surprise, the invasion of Kuwait and Iraq, the US Secretary of the Treasury denouncing China's exchange rate policy, and Europe's sovereign debt and banking sector crises that started in 2009 and have not yet ended.

Events can come from any direction, let's look at some examples.

Markets for other assets

Moves in *other markets*, especially very large downward stock market or commodity price moves, affect currencies. On the whole, routs and crashes in other markets tend to send traders to the dollar as a safe haven, unwinding months and years of diversification into equities, especially emerging market equities, and commodities. We talk about this in more detail in Chapter 6.

Central banks

Central banks are often the source of Events. As everyone in finance knows, central banks use code words to alert markets to their upcoming actions. The ECB favours phrases like "second round effects" (meaning wages are moving up and threatening inflation). One of the most interesting cases was ECB chief Jean-Claude Trichet using a single word – "brutal" – to describe the overvalued euro on 12 January 2004. It worked – the euro fell over 500 points in response in subsequent days. He tried it again in November that year and failed to get the same effect, at least not right away. But by December 2004, analysts at Goldman Sachs were writing of the overvalued euro and predicting a drop. The euro obediently fell from a close of $1.3558 at end-December 2004 to $1.1638 by 15 November 2005.

At the Kansas City Fed's annual international conference in Jackson Hole, Wyoming, in 2010, Fed chief Bernanke tactfully mentioned a second round of quantitative easing. Traders didn't need to be hit over the head – they knew instantly it meant the dollar would fall. Sure enough, the EUR/USD rose from a close of $1.2762 on the date of the speech (27 August 2010) to a high of $1.4281 by 4 November when QE was actually announced.

Political events

Political events like elections tend to get short shrift among FX market players – Japan has booted out more than one prime minister, including for corruption in office, without causing the yen to twitch. When the US was nearing official default during the Clinton Administration because of opposition party pique, the dollar remained in a narrow range around 1.1550 against the Swiss franc for the entire crisis period (October to December 1995). When the US was nearing default in the spring of 2011, however, more than pique was at play. The political environment was poisonous and the S&P ratings agency downgraded US sovereign paper on the basis of political dysfunction as well as the ratio of debt to GDP. This time, the dollar fell and the euro rose, from $1.4055 on the downgrade date (5 August 2011) to a high of $1.4517 by 17 August. The dollar index fell from a high of 75.383 on 5 August to a low of 73.452 on 17 August over the same period. Many other things were happening at the time, of course, but it's not unfair to attribute the dollar's drop to the downgrade.

In Europe, many political developments during 2011 were euro-negative, such as the announcement by Bundesbank chief Weber that he would resign from the BBK and withdraw his candidacy for the top job at the ECB. In September, the German representative on the ECB's policy-making board, Juergen Stark, resigned. In each case the euro was already falling when the news was released and it fell another 50 to 100 points on the news.

War

Military skirmishes and events during wars tend not to move the FX market, but declaration of war does. When the US moved to the aid of Kuwait in early 1991 – something in the works ever since the Iraqi invasion on 2 August 1990 – the dollar/DM ended a lengthy downtrend by rising from $1.4535 (7 February 1991) to $1.8386 on 6 July 1991. The same thing happened again when the second President Bush invaded Iraq in March 2003. Against the euro, the dollar rose from the euro high at $1.1084 on 11 March to 1.0498 at the low on 21 March 2003 – in the midst of a major euro upmove. This time the dollar's gains were short-lived but the point is made – the rising dollar was a vote of confidence in the US, perhaps somewhat puzzling in the context of much of the world disapproving of the US' action.

International conferences

The Group of seven or G7 hardly ever delivers thrilling news, but an exception was US Treasury Secretary Snow announcing, ahead of the 15 April 2005 meeting, that it was time for China to "fix" its financial system "and increase FX market flexibility." At the same time, John B. Taylor, US Treasury Undersecretary for International Affairs (the same Taylor of the Taylor rule) urged China to revalue the yuan, saying China had been in preparation long enough. These comments caused a tremendous stir, not least because the G7 tends to be decorous to the point of stupor. And yet a few months later, in July, China did indeed end the yuan's peg to the US dollar and initiate a float.

At the G20 summit in Seoul, South Korea, in 2010, Brazilian Finance Minister Mantega spoke passionately about the developed countries ruining emerging market financial plans by selfishly keeping interest rates abnormally low for the sake of their domestic economies. He said this was inspiring excessive capital inflows to emerging markets and currency appreciation to the point of harming exports. The emerging market response had to be FX market intervention, capital controls and other unpleasant policy choices.

The phrase "currency war" was the hot ticket for many weeks and while superseded shortly after by the European sovereign debt crisis and debate over the future of the euro, it has not completely gone away. In fact, James Rickards published *Currency Wars, The Making of the Next Global Crisis* in 2011, postulating that currency wars are historically not uncommon and public policy makers persist in failing to see how currencies interact with other financial affairs as well as national security and other non-financial matters. Currency wars always end badly, he says.[38]

The G7 (or G8 with China) have now largely been replaced by the G20, which consists of 19 countries along with the European Union. In September 2009 at the G20 Summit in Pittsburgh, President Barack Obama said "We can no longer meet the challenges of the 21st century economy with 20th century approaches. And that's why the G20 will take the lead in building a new approach to cooperation. To make our institutions reflect the reality of our times, we will shift more responsibility to emerging economies within the International Monetary Fund, and give them a greater voice."[39]

It remains to be seen whether giving emerging markets like Brazil, Russia, India and China a bigger voice in actual decisions is even remotely possible. For example, they disapprove of the Fed cutting interest rates to the bone because it means yield-seekers arrive on their shores, driving up asset prices and causing currency overvaluation, which in turn harms export-driven growth. The Fed's rate cuts are targeted to the US economy without regard for others' economies. Should the Fed not do the best job it can to promote US growth in order to provide succour to emerging markets? The mind boggles.

***

While these Events were going on, they captured the attention of the trading world almost entirely. Economic data was being released on schedule, as usual, but the standard responses to the data were heavily influenced by the Events, sometimes to the point of being excluded as determining factors altogether. That is certainly the case when governments intervene.

Government intervention in the FX Market

The uniqueness of FX intervention

FX is the only market in which governments regularly intervene directly, buying or selling their own currency to influence its price. We see government interference in other markets in other forms, including subsidies and taxes, limits on short sales in equities, and adding or releasing strategic commodities like oil. For example, during the Asian crisis of 1997, the Hong Kong Monetary Authority intervened in the equity market as a means of defending the HK dollar peg to the US dollar, and at various times, Japan has directed government entities to buy Japanese equities as an offset to falling equity prices triggered by a too-strong yen. Even so, government intervention in FX is unique among financial markets.

Unlike the official pro-intervention policy of the late 1970s, the current US stance is that intervention should be a rare thing and should become ever-rarer:

> "Since the breakdown of the Bretton Woods system in 1971, the United States has used FX intervention both to slow rapid exchange rate moves and to signal the US monetary authorities' view that the exchange rate did not reflect fundamental economic conditions. US FX intervention became much less frequent in the late 1990s. The United States intervened in the FX market on eight different days in 1995, but only twice from August 1995 through December 2006."[40]

But in practice, the US has intervened in FX every few years in one context or another. Just after the March 2011 earthquake/tsunami/nuclear meltdown in Japan, the US joined the other members of G7 to intervene, at Japan's request. Japan went on to intervene on its own, spending $58 billion in August 2011 alone.

Intervention in practice

Even a partial list of interventions by the major countries would run for dozens of pages. A full list would include numerous interventions by emerging market central banks, including South Korea, Taiwan and China as well as others, and also run for many pages. During the period 1985-95, the Fed intervened in the dollar/DM 237 times and in the dollar/yen 213 times. During the same period, the Bundesbank intervened on 326 days and the Bank of Japan, 380 days.[41] One of the most sentiment-affecting interventions was on 22 September 2000, when the Fed, ECB and BoJ jointly intervened to drive the euro up after it fell below 85¢ for two days in a row, a loss of almost 30% from inception in January 1999. It was the first-ever intervention by the ECB.

Another remarkable instance was the massive intervention undertaken by the Bank of Japan during 2003 and ending in March 2004. During 2003 alone, the amount spent was ¥20.2 trillion, or $177 billion, and in the first quarter of 2004, it spent another ¥14.8 trillion, or $139 billion. This was the biggest intervention before or since. During this period, the yen still appreciated from ¥119 to the dollar to ¥104, although of course nobody knows how much further the yen might have gone in the absence of intervention. After all, in an earlier incident, the yen had reached ¥79.75 in April 1995. If you are a Japanese exporter, ¥104 is still preferable to ¥79.75.

Japan is the biggest serial intervener among countries, not only for the size of the commitment but also the frequency. Before the stunning 2003 blow-out, the BoJ had been actively intervening from 17 September to 28 June 2002, with the US joining on 27 September 2001. And before that, the BoJ sold yen a total of 18 times between January 1999 to April 2000, with coordination with the Fed and ECB on a few occasions.

We often do not know the exact amounts governments are spending in intervention forays, although traders try to judge from the price effect. Japan is the only country that publishes data from which intervention can be deduced. The Bank of Japan (and the Federal Reserve) announce intervention or having refrained from intervention in the monthly central bank reports.

In July 2012, the Swiss National Bank reported a rise in official reserves, attributed to FX market intervention, to over 60% of GDP and the press extrapolated that to 100% by year-end. Nobody knows what this means or what action the Swiss can or should take. Is 100% too much? In what way does it matter? As long as the central bank sterilises the money supply so it does not leak into the domestic banking system to promote inflation, it's not clear that intervention has any effect on the real economy.

Sterilisation

Note that when a central bank intervenes to prevent its own currency from getting too strong or too weak, it pumps more money into the money supply or siphons it out by buying/selling FX reserves, generally dollars and euro. Altering monetary aggregates like this can really mess up other policy goals. Raising money supply risks inflation, for example. Central banks sterilise the FX operation by withdrawing or adding to money supply in some other manner.[42]

Note also that sometimes central banks have to borrow FX reserves to intervene, which is one stated purpose of various swap line arrangements. Unlike the Asian crisis when emerging market central banks had low foreign exchange reserves, in recent years, with reserve holdings beefed up, EM central banks are better fortified to intervene when their currency is weakening.

Sterilisation is vitally important in any discussion of intervention, including intervention in bond markets as well as foreign exchange. This is because failure to sterilise results in a surge in the domestic monetary base and therefore the intervention can become self-defeating as the central bank feels compelled to raise rates alongside rising inflationary expectations, resulting in the very capital inflows the intervention is trying to ease. Then the intervening country can end up with debt to the other country that has lent it the reserves with which to intervene and no respite from rising capital inflows. The immediate currency effect may be as desired but, longer run, the country has shot itself in the foot.[43]

Therefore, FX traders are always on the lookout to discover whether an intervening country is also sterilising, regardless of whether the intervener is an advanced country or an emerging market country. As the ECB intervened in the peripheral sovereign bond market in recent years, for example, analysts were careful to stipulate the amount of sterilisation it also undertook – nearly 100%, as it happens. If the ECB had not sterilised, FX traders would have deduced the ECB was flirting with inflation and the ECB would have lost some of its hard-won chops as a dedicated inflation-fighter.

Why governments intervene

The chief reason governments give for FX intervention is to combat "disorderly market conditions." The Versailles intervention study added "to reduce short-term volatility" and "on occasion to express an attitude toward exchange markets."[44] Another idea is to *signal* to the market what the government believes is true fundamental value. The official BIS and G7 stance is that intervention is effective only when other policies support and complement it, especially monetary policy. During the late 1970s, for example, Fed economist Edwin Truman reports, US thinking ran along the lines that inflation was not so bad that interest rates needed to be goosed upward and intervention could take care of the dollar devaluation resulting from rising inflation expectations. Equally counterproductive is to intervene to resist a currency rising while the central bank is tightening. This is exactly what happened during 1989-90, when the US Treasury intervened for a record 97 days (to the dismay of the Fed).

Few countries specify their ideal exchange rate, at least not out loud. In fact, some academics who studied interventions come to the conclusion that governments are more effective when they do not specify a target exchange rate when intervening, although traders always try to guess the "line in the sand," the FX rate that will trigger intervention. Exceptions include currencies managed to a basket of other currencies and the influential dollar/yen forecasts of the Japanese business association Keidanren, technically not a government agency.

Instead, as a general rule the goal of free market economic management is to get the fastest growth and highest employment rate possible without inflation. The level of the currency (and the trade or current account balance) doesn't enter into it and can conflict with the high growth or low inflation goals. If monetary policy remains higher for longer to be sure of having stamped out inflation, as in the early 1980s in the US, you get a strong dollar and damage to the export sector. In other words, often the goals of a government for its domestic economy are wildly different from its goals for external sectors (trade and current account balances). In two major countries, the US and Japan, the agency tasked with managing the currency is the Treasury and Ministry of Finance, while the agency responsible for monetary policy and domestic sectors is the central bank (even though in both countries it is the central bank that actually executes the intervention trades at the direction of the Treasury or Ministry of Finance).

The efficacy of intervention

A fair amount of government and academic ink has been expended to evaluate whether intervention works, including studies covering a few hours to those covering the longer term, or three months.

Academics tend to be sceptical about the efficacy of sterilisation. It seems to work in the short run, but Hutchinson writes:

> "The evidence is not clear on how long the effects of intervention last. Moreover, large-scale sterilised intervention, coordinated intervention and substantial currency swap arrangements may not be enough to stabilise an exchange rate parity in the face of a speculative attack in the absence of a strong and credible political commitment by the affected central banks and, ultimately, coordinated monetary policy. A strong political commitment, in turn, is usually more easily sustained when economic fundamentals are broadly in line both with the desired exchange rate parity *and* other macroeconomic objectives."

Remember, though, that studies of intervention and sterilisation are written by economists for whom equilibrium is not a fiction but an actual policy goal.

In 1993, the BIS published a study saying intervention doesn't work, but it was overtaken by other studies – and by events, including the shocking, massive and successful Japanese intervention in 2003-2004. On the whole, the hammer comes down on the side of intervention working about half the time. Former Fed official Truman says intervention is effective when it incorporates:

1. a public announcement

2. others joining in (coordinated intervention)

3. policy consistency (monetary policy is going in the same direction as intervention)

The Swiss National Bank had two of the three success factors when it announced in early September 2011 that it would intervene to rein in the too-strong Swiss franc. The public announcement was strong and the SNB had already signalled near-punitive measures against hot money inflows. Judging from Figure 5.1, which illustrates the price movement around the intervention, the market was as impressed and fearful as the Swiss wanted. The EUR/CHF put in an upside channel breakout, if not to the 200-day moving average.

Figure 5.1 – EUR/CHF September 2011

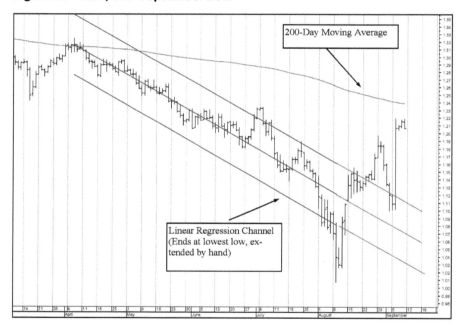

But in the wider picture, Switzerland had been intervening fitfully for many years. In June 2009, the BIS intervened on Switzerland's behalf. Switzerland intervened six to eight times during 2010 and earlier in 2011 before the September pegging announcement. If you look at the big-picture Figure 5.2 of the EUR/CHF, the chief target, you can see that the overall trend remains the same.

Figure 5.2 – EUR/CHF long-term trend unaffected by interventions

Similarly, the earlier Japanese intervention – which failed for months on end during 2003 as traders played chicken with the Bank of Japan – was abruptly ended in February 2004, on no advance notice. The dollar/yen stopped falling by the end of that year and proceeded to put in three full years of less-strong yen prices, even surpassing the 200-day moving average. This is illustrated in Figure 5.3.

Figure 5.3 – USD/JPY

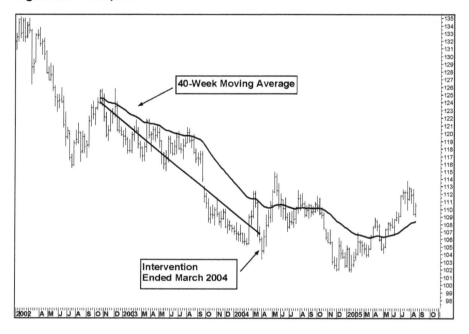

But over the longer run, can Japan claim to have won? No. But then it was not the intent of the Japanese Ministry of Finance to effect permanent change, just to provide relief for the beleaguered export sector. The dollar/yen has been on a downtrend since 1985 and in 2011 broke the lowest-low line from 1995, when the grounds of the Imperial Palace in Tokyo were notionally worth more than the entire state of California. See Figure 5.4 for the longer-term picture.

Figure 5.4 – USD/JPY longer term

Japanese financial officials have a specific constituency not shared with most other nation's officials – the Nikkei stock index, which is highly correlated with the dollar/yen. In fact, of all the purported intermarket correlations, this is the tightest and longest-lasting of them all. When the yen gets too strong, exporter shares suffer. See Figure 5.5.

Figure 5.5 – USD/JPY vs. Nikkei 225

Emerging market interventions

As noted above, emerging markets have found it necessary to intervene to slow down the rise of their currencies in recent years to avoid killing off their export markets, including China, Brazil, South Korea, and Taiwan. The assertion of a "currency war" by Brazilian Finance Minister Mantega at a G20 meeting in late 2010 continues to reverberate. The hot emerging markets (like Brazil) feel that ultra-low interest rates in the developed economies are a selfish policy and amount to "currency manipulation," since the universal and never-ending quest for yield drives investors to their markets.

Ironically, sometimes emerging market central banks have also had to intervene in the other direction – defending their currencies from excessive depreciation – when a global financial crisis sends capital to safe-havens, as occurred in September 2011. Emerging market equity markets tanked and hot money flowed out.

Summary

Economic theories of exchange rate determination are inadequate to help the FX market practitioner, especially professional traders, make good decisions. We use various bits and pieces of theory along the way, such as taking notice of a fresh estimate of purchasing power parity or responding vigorously to the payrolls report in the US (if they are too low this means the output gap is widening, there is reduced danger of inflation and thus reduced probability of a rate hike).

The important thing about economics and the trader is that where theories are not helpful, simple formulas like payrolls are adequate to the job. We disparagingly refer to stockbroker economics as inaccurate and often misguided but, in practice, following the crowd on interpretation of economic data is the pragmatic and expedient path to good trading outcomes, at least in the short run.

It is especially wise to abandon any preconceived ideas about how economics affects exchange rates when Events emerge, and most of all when governments intervene. Intervention pretty much proves the point that economics has yet to help governments adequately design policies that cover all the bases.

CHAPTER 6 –
POSITIONS AND FLOWS

"Card counting is illegal in this town."

Las Vegas Rule

Unlike equities, commodities and new bond issues, we have no information about trading volume in the professional FX market. This is because each trade in the professional market is a private contract. As a proxy for volume, traders use the weekly data from the Commodities Futures Trading Commission (CFTC). In this chapter we'll look at what exactly the CFTC data tells us about market positions and whether it is worth trading on.

The market can also gain an idea on volume by looking at positioning data from retail brokers, world central banks such as the Bank of Japan, or fund flow data from firms such as Emerging Portfolio Fund Research or **HedgeFund.net**. Studying the information on flows is laborious and time-consuming, but traders do it anyway, or hire economists to do it, because information on existing positions and flows is a substitute for data on volume and thus a barometer of sentiment.

Observing positions and flows

As in poker, the FX trader needs to assess the odds before entering into a position. In a zero-sum game – and each FX trade has a single winner and single loser – it makes sense to use all tools possible to figure out what other players are holding. Why go long the euro or yen if FX speculative positions are already at record highs? Why not wait until positions are less extended? What if Swiss risk reversals are skewing negative, do I really want to be long Swissy? Before traders enter into a new currency position they want to make sure that the trade they are looking at is not too crowded, i.e., that not everyone has the same idea. In technical analysis terms, traders seek to know whether a currency is overbought or oversold.

Positions do not always dictate FX direction but when they are extended, historically there has tended to be a reversal in trend, usually within a few weeks or a month. This was true in January 2012, when net euro short positions by speculative accounts reported by the Commodity Futures Trading Commission were at a record high number. (The other side of those short positions was held by the category of traders deemed to be *hedgers* under CFTC rules.) The euro rallied a few weeks later and continued into early March. By mid-May, however, speculative accounts had entered into another new record short euro position. This time, instead of the euro reversing course, these accounts continued to increase the size of their short position, creating a new record nearly each week. Despite extremely extended short positions over a period of several weeks, the euro did not see what was expected to be a larger short squeeze.

Traders depend on reports from wire services like Reuters, Bloomberg and Market News International about who is buying or selling what. Depending on wire service reports is a high-risk undertaking, since most reporters have never traded themselves and are often young and naïve, without the judgment to know when a big-bank trader is blowing smoke up their skirt. For example, a big-bank trader may tell a reporter that he sees "demand from the Middle East" at a specific level when in fact he is the one who wants to see that level serve as support, since his stop-loss is just below it.

In the absence of data on volume, traders have several positioning and flow reports that offer insight into what speculative accounts globally are doing in foreign exchange. Weekly reports are closely watched by bank and position traders and retail traders, and monthly, quarterly or annual reports are tracked by bigger picture players such as fund managers and carry traders. Before we talk about positioning reports, we need to look at the FX players themselves.

The players

In foreign exchange, as in other asset classes, the player with the deepest pockets has a distinct trading advantage on many levels. When you carry a big stick, you can bully other participants. Sometimes a large trade has shock value that awes other traders into action. In times of turmoil, being large and liquid allows you to take a loss and still take advantage of price dips or unexpected rallies. Size gives you directional clout and size allows you to potentially stall or stop a developing trend.

Size can be good or bad for the little guy in FX. There are times when a big name plays the range and keeps a currency pair from following its natural trend. Other times, one name may bully the market and force a breakout that might not normally have occurred, as in the case of a *short squeeze*. The names of these so-called bullies of the FX market have changed over the years but their tactics remain the same. Let's have a look at some of the big players now:

1. As of Q4 2011, global **central banks** have $10.197 trillion in total reserves,[45] of which $5.646 trillion is allocated and $4.551 trillion is unallocated. In allocated reserves, the breakdown is $3.015 trillion for the advanced economies and $2.630 trillion for emerging and developing economies.

2. **Sovereign wealth funds** are next with around $5 trillion (estimated by the Sovereign Wealth Fund Institute[46]).

3. **Pension funds, mutual funds and insurance funds** had assets under management of $79.2 trillion at the end of 2010, a new record amount for conventional assets. This was up from $64.2 trillion in 2008 as well being up

on the record $74.5 trillion seen in 2007.[47] This includes $29.9 trillion in pension assets, $24.7 trillion in mutual fund assets and $24.6 trillion in insurance funds. Adding in alternate assets, such as sovereign wealth funds, hedge funds, private equity and exchange traded funds, along with the funds of wealthy individuals, total global fund management was a whopping $117 trillion at the end of 2010. In terms of country breakdown, the US was the largest source of conventional funds in 2010 (about $35.6 trillion), with the UK in the number two slot with about $6.5 trillion. Taking out the assets of other major countries (Japan, France, Germany, the Netherlands and Switzerland) the remaining countries had about $21.9 trillion of conventional assets under management (AUM) at the end of 2010.

4. **Retail foreign exchange** is a small but growing sector. A Celent study[48] from August 2011 found that "retail FX is growing to be a $200 billion (daily) business by 2011, at an annual growth rate of 33% since 2007." More than 40% of the volume growth was seen in Asia, with growth plateauing in the US and Europe. Growth has been "heavily influenced by the regulatory control over leverage, as well as the exit of many players due to higher capital requirement demands," the study said. This is evidenced by the decline in the number of retail aggregators. In the US the number of retail aggregators with electronic platforms fell from 32 in 2007 to 17 in 2010 and in Japan from 500 in 2005 to 70 in 2010.

∗∗∗

Each player has his moment in terms of effects on the FX market. Central banks and select sovereign wealth funds with deep pockets produce a larger splash effect when they execute deals but, in the end, it is global investment flows that remain the real driver of currencies. When clients at global pension funds, mutual funds and insurance funds get nervous, fundamentals and future prospects get relegated to the back burner and safe-havens are brought to the front burner. This is evidenced by the exodus out of risk assets over the course of 2011.

In early September 2011, when Greek two-year yields rose above 50% as the market entertained fear of the country leaving the EMU, a guaranteed 2.0% yield on a US 10-year yield looked pretty good in contrast to the prospect of a negative return. The dollar, yen and Swiss francs stood out as safe-haven currencies in late 2011 and early 2012; the dollar and the yen had the two largest and deepest bond markets, and the Swiss franc represented a safe way to stay invested in Europe, but outside the euro zone. The dollar stayed in hot demand even when 10-year US Treasury yields fell to record low levels under 1.5% in June 2012.

Volume in Retail FX

How traders utilise volume data

The absence of volume information is a massive shortcoming in the FX industry. In equities, volume is an indispensible tool. If a price is making higher highs but at a decelerating pace and volume is spiking to new highs, we can easily deduce that the upmove is nearing exhaustion – it takes more and more volume to get less and less of a price rise. Volume denotes liquidity and, as a rule, the higher the liquidity, the lower the volatility and the more likely it is that a price move can be named a trend. An orderly trend tracks its trendline with low variability.

Several important technical indicators are based on the comparison of price with its associated volume, including Joe Granville's *on-balance volume* and Marc Chaikin's later refinements. In the on-balance volume indicator, you cumulatively add volume on days when the close is higher than the day before and subtract it when the close is lower. Rising volume on a rising price trend confirms that the price rise is not an aberration or error, and declining volume means a trend is weakening. Volume spikes mark the beginning and end of many trends. The theory is that the trader should derive confidence from volume moving in the same direction as the price trend. In contrast, a divergence between price and volume is a warning. It may seem counter-intuitive, but if prices are falling and volume is also declining, a bottom (and buying opportunity) is getting close.

Volume data

Only in retail FX do we get information on trading volume. Some retail FX brokers that cater to the individual trader display volume from their own order flow and assert that it's valid to extrapolate that volume (which accounts for a fraction of 1% of total daily volume) to the total FX market. We say the assertion strains credulity. If small retail traders are of so little importance that the Commodity Futures Trading Commission doesn't bother to add their trades to the Commitment of Traders Report (see below), and further, if it's true that a very high percentage of retail traders fail after only a short while, as often charged, why would anyone want to know what they are doing?

Having said that, the 2012 Greenwich Associates annual flow report, which we will discuss later in this chapter, notes that retail aggregators generated 18% of FX trading volume worldwide in 2011, up from 10% in 2010. Overall Japanese retail trading volumes were up about 70% last year.

And the evidence is in the data. On 2 May 2011, one of the bigger retail spot brokers, Oanda, published its open positions for the major currency pairs showing the market was 76.09% long the USD against the yen.

The next day, the USD/JPY fell from 80.64 at the open to a low of 79.56 – but in subsequent trading sessions, dollar-yen fell from 81.27 to 79.55 on 5 May. We would say this is a case of the Oanda data correctly identifying an overbought condition. Similarly, the 2 May Oanda report on euro/dollar positions had the market 61.46% short. Two days later the euro peaked at 1.4940 and proceeded to a low of $1.3968 by 23 May.[49] Again, the Oanda position ratio correctly identified an impending change in direction. Perhaps we (and the CFTC) underestimate the small retail trader.

In the US futures market, the Chicago Mercantile Exchange publishes volume data, but not until after the trading day has ended. We also have a metric named tick volume, which is a change in price that is recorded as a tick regardless of how many contracts were actually traded. A change in tick volume associated with a move from $1.6500 to $1.6501 in sterling could be one contract or 1000 contracts. It's obvious that tick volume is not actual volume and to use it as a substitute for true volume is questionable, and yet tick volume may be useful when prices are moving quickly, from which we can safely deduce that there is real volume behind the ticks.

Traders can compare the number of ticks in each hour of the trading day to the number in the first hour, say, to determine whether activity is robust or languishing. Since the open will typically see a surge in activity, it's not clear whether the first-hour benchmark is all that useful, although we see three occasions when tick volume might come in handy:

1. The end of the day, when traders normally pare positions. The end-of-day tick volume, if high and associated with the usual end-of-day pullback, may mean fewer traders willing to hold positions overnight. It they do not pare positions, and tick volume is low while the price is closing at or near the high or low of the day, the price can be expected to keep going in the trend direction during the next session.

2. The divergence between tick volume and price can be a useful – traders could look out for cases where tick volume is moribund during big price moves or where tick volume is very high at a time when prices are moribund. We consider it noise when tick volume is lacklustre while prices are moving a lot, or price moves are lacklustre when tick volume is moving a lot. A divergence between price and tick volume marks a stalemate, and low volatility in either measure almost always precedes a directional breakout.

3. We expect to see higher volume (and more ticks) as prices approach important benchmark levels like support and resistance lines, previous highs/lows, or a Fibonacci level. These are used as levels to place stop-loss and take-profit orders, and if tick volume does not rise near them the market may have the bit between its teeth and be running away. Once a key level is broken, you would expect to see tick volume rise, just like regular volume.

Some spot analysts will go to the trouble of consulting spot retail broker volume, or futures volume – even if a day late and not the exact market they are trading – or tick volume, in a nearly desperate search for information on market sentiment. Why? One case is that volume can indicate traders are positioned so long (or short) that the next move pretty much has to be a reversal. Except in Event Shock conditions, traders want to make sure that the trade they are looking at is not too crowded. There are a number of sources traders consult to get the information they desire on volume.

Where FX traders can find information on positions and flows

There are a number of sources FX traders consult to get information on positions and flows to use as a proxy for volume data.

Report 1: Commodity Futures Trading Commission (CFTC)

The US Commodity Futures Trading Commission's Commitments of Traders report, released weekly, is by far the most popular positioning report followed by the currency market. The report is currently issued every Friday for data as of the previous Tuesday.

The COT report is broken up into commercial and non-commercial positions. Non-commercial is a semantically neutral way of saying *speculator*. To qualify as a commercial trader, the trader has to apply for that status and claim that his trades are for hedging, such as an importer buying goods priced in a foreign currency. The classic example of a hedge is the farmer who sells wheat and the bakery that buys it – both are hedgers. A trader may be classified as a commercial trader in some commodities and as a non-commercial trader in other commodities but has to pick one designation or the other in a single commodity.

Market players typically look at the number of non-commercial contracts (ex-options) that are outstanding in a given currency as a good indication of the consensus view held by the speculative community. If the market is net long or net short a record number of contracts or is getting close to a record long or short position, such extended positions may prompt a trader to rethink his outlook.

The dividing line between commercial trader and speculator is a wavy one, not only because commercials usually receive preferential margin conditions and so participants strive to get that designation, but also because day-to-day trading decisions are a blend of both activities. Many trades that are really speculative are labelled as hedges because of the trader's designation, and thus the volume attributed to speculators is inaccurate. This doesn't make the information less useful, however, because what we are interested in seeing is the *change* in positions. The mislabelling of some trades doesn't affect this change as long as the mislabelling is consistent across time periods.

For example, here's a case where a commercial trader is executing a transaction:

> Bank A has a client who wants do to a swap, i.e. to sell and buy €10 million from spot to 19 September at +15 forward points.

> Bank A's forward trader then does the other side of the FX swap and he buys €10 million from the client in the spot date at $1.2300 and then sells €10 million to the client on the forward outright date of September 19 at $1.2315.

In a perfect world, the forward trader would go into the forward market and get a price to do the opposite trade, i.e. sell and buy €10 million spot to 19 September with another bank, hopefully at a profit (less than 15 points).

At times, however, the forward trader will realise that 19 September is also the expiration of the September contract (always the Wednesday following the third Monday of March, June, September and December). If he does the spot deal to sell euro at $1.2300 and then buys them back on the futures exchange at an outright price of $1.2313, he will be up two points.

The portion of the artificial swap (spot deal plus futures deal) that is done on the futures exchange would be included in the commercial section of the CFTC report – because it is effectively part of a hedge of the original swap done with the corporate client of Bank A – and yet it has a speculative component.

Now let's consider an example of a non-commercial trader, say a hedge fund, that buys 20,000 Swiss franc contracts (or CHF2.5 million) as a pure speculative bet. Meanwhile, a commodities trading advisor may decide to sell 15,000 Swiss franc contracts as a hedge against one of its other currency positions. The CFTC would look at this trade as just another speculative punt, even though one leg of it is a true hedge.

If these two deals were the only transactions completed that week, then Friday's CFTC data, for positions as of Tuesday, would be that speculative accounts had a net Swiss long of 5000 contracts. Any trader looking at the Swiss CFTC data would not be swayed one way or the other by the position, since it's small. But in many instances, extended CFTC positions of over 100,000 contracts quickly lead to a sharp reversal. This is what FX analysts are looking for – extreme positioning.

A textbook-perfect case was the euro in early 2010, which began to show ever-bigger net short positions in the Commitment of Traders as euro zone peripheral debt jitters began to cause nail-biting about holding the euro. By early February 2010, a new record short euro position was reported and it kept getting bigger, to over 85,000 contracts in March. By 11 May 2010, the new record euro short was nearly 114,000 contracts. In this instance, the euro bottomed on 6 June 2010, right after this most bearish of reports.

However, from late December 2011 onward into February, new net record euro short positions were posted nearly each week, with net euro shorts rising to well over 200,000 contracts in early June 2012. That these positions were deemed *extended* had no effect on the market's willingness to maintain them. It would take a larger change in risk appetite sentiment to prompt players to pare these positions more substantially. This was an abnormal response to the euro being oversold and even if you had not been following the news behind the sell-off in euros, the continuation and extension of the oversold condition would have told you something big and historically aberrant was going on.

2. Japanese flow data

Spot and short-term traders like to keep an eye on yen flows that may set the tone for other currencies. Starting in the mid-2000s, Japanese retail investors began to look abroad for higher yields. While there is still a clear home bias on the part of Japanese investors, the small percentage that does find its way abroad has had a distinct effect on the yen.

Hedge funds and others quickly discovered this *carry trade*, which involves going short a low-yield currency like the yen and long a high-yield currency like the Australian dollar. When Japanese yen carry-trade players are in a risk-seeking mood, the yen dips on sales conducted for the carry trade, and when they are feeling fearful and risk-averse, the yen gets so-called repatriation inflows.

Market players keep tabs on overall Japanese flows by looking at three main reports:

1. The weekly Ministry of Finance (MOF) report on fixed income and equity inflows and outflows
2. Reports released by the Tokyo Financial Exchange (TFX)
3. Equity flow data released the Tokyo Stock Exchange (TSE)

The Ministry of Finance report is called 'International Transactions in Securities' and breaks down the net purchases/sales by residents into Equity Securities, Bonds and Notes, and Money Market Instruments. In a true carry trade, the proceeds of yen sales are actually invested in foreign securities, most often the Money Market Instrument category. At the same time, the MOF reports the same breakdown of purchases and sales by non-residents or foreigners. Sizable inflows or outflows by either domestic or foreign accounts are taken as a red flag that may signal a larger trend.

The TFX releases daily data on foreign exchange pairs such as euro-yen futures that offer insight into what Japanese retail traders – who account for hundreds of billions of FX trades per month – are doing. The TFX report includes both trading volume and open interest on euro-yen and select other yen crosses. The TFX also releases a more comprehensive report monthly and yearly that includes data on option and interest rate product demand. The report includes open interest and volume for margin accounts in dollar-yen, euro-yen, Aussie-yen, sterling-yen, Canada-yen, and many other yen crosses.

Market players looking to gauge yen direction also keep an eye on monthly data from the Tokyo Stock Exchange, which offers data on retail margin account trading in equities. The TSE's daily report provides price and volume data for stocks, bonds and derivatives.

Active Japan/yen watchers closely scrutinise all data from the MOF, TFX and TSE, hoping to see a pattern developing that can translate into a foreign exchange trading idea.

3. EPFR weekly data

Other flow data comes from weekly data released by Emerging Portfolio Fund Research or EPFR Global, a subsidiary of Informa, a subscription service. EPFR began to release fund flow data on a monthly basis in 1995 and switched to a weekly basis in 2000. Their current report tracks daily, weekly and monthly equity and fixed income fund flows, and monthly fund allocations by country sector and security. Each Thursday, EPFR releases the flows seen over the past week, with the data including flows up until the prior business day (Wednesday). Emerging Portfolio Fund Research tracks traditional and alternative funds domiciled globally with $16 trillion in total assets under management.

EPFR's full line-up includes: Equity Funds, Bond Funds, Money Market Funds, Balanced Funds and Alternative Funds. Each category is comprehensive and has multiple sub-categories.

"It is our geographically focused fund groups, in particular country funds, that are most used by our FX strategist and FX investor clients," explained Brad Durham, managing director at EPFR Global, adding, "And it is actually not our fund flows, but our Country Flows data that is the most used by FX clients."

"EPFR Country Flows data combines our fund flows data and country allocations data to estimate the total distribution of flows by country for all funds (both equity and bond) that we track. So it picks up the flows into a country for the geographically diversified funds (Global equity, GEM equity, Europe regional equity, etc.)," he said.

For currency traders these flows are all important. Larger outflows from Money Market Funds into Global Emerging Markets, for example, can explain recent trends and positioning and suggest a new, more risk-friendly FX trend. Similarly, a widespread exodus out of Global Emerging Markets into Money Markets would suggest risk aversion, with currency implications also.

Any larger outflow from one group into another gives the FX trader insight into what fund managers are thinking and doing, and therefore what kind of outstanding positions the currency community as a whole may hold. Similarly, a rush into the Commodities sector often can go hand in hand with a rush to buy currencies such as the Canadian and Aussie dollars.

4. BofA Merrill Lynch Monthly Fund Manager Survey

In addition to weekly flow data, market players can get an idea about current risk sentiment toward stocks, bonds and currencies by looking at the BofA Merrill Lynch Monthly Fund Manager Survey of global fund managers. The detailed report is available only for Bank of America or Merrill clients, but an overview, taken the first week of a given month, is released to the public about a week after the final survey day. The global survey polls 200 or more global portfolio managers with at least $500 billion in assets under management. The BofA/Merrill survey asks fund managers whether they are overweight or underweight in fixed income and equities.

The survey includes questions about US interest rate direction, inflation, and the health of the global economy. Fund managers are asked their sector and regional view also. In currencies, portfolio managers are asked whether select currencies (euro, yen, sterling) are overvalued or undervalued currently and on a 12-month basis.

5. TICS Data

The Treasury International Capital System (TICS) report is released by the US Treasury around the 15th of each month, but refers to transactions done two months before, so the June report is about actions taken in April. While clearly backward-looking, the data is examined to see whether US investors are buying or selling fixed income/equity instruments overseas and whether foreign private and official accounts (especially central banks) are buying or selling US Treasury bonds and notes, government agency bonds, corporate bonds and equities.

Figure 6.1 shows the total net TICS inflow (or outflow) for each month, including all capital market transactions, against the dollar index for the period 1985 to 2012. It might seem better to match up the report release date with the FX price action, since the TICS report lags FX prices by two months. But remember, the big banks that are moving prices already know the underlying capital flows that are going to be reported in two months' time, because the parties behind the capital flows are their customers. Thus the key players don't need to wait for the TICS release – they already have the information in-house. Also, be aware that the net total flow doesn't change when a foreign manager switches from (say) Treasuries to equities by the same amount.

Figure 6.1 – TICS Capital Inflow (dark line) and Dollar Index (monthly)

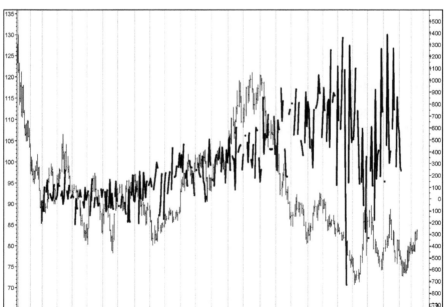

One thing this chart does tell us is that over 2003-2007, capital flows to the US continued to rise while the dollar index was falling. In the most recent period, from 2007 to the present, capital flows vary wildly from month to month, which is a function of intermittent panics causing safe-haven inflows, regardless of what direction the dollar index is taking.

Sometimes both the dollar and US Treasury market reacts negatively if the TICS flows suggest that the United States' current account and trade deficits are underfunded, especially when it appears that the largest reserve holders, China or Japan, are not buying US assets. When the trade deficit is (say) $45 billion and the long-term capital inflow is a smaller amount, traders get worried that international creditors could withhold funding. Strictly speaking, it is not long-term portfolio flows that finance trade, but rather commercial banks via short-term letters of credit and open accounts, and yet the TICS incoming balance is always named in the context of the outgoing current account balance on the assumption that they should roughly balance and too big a discrepancy would imply a loss of confidence in the US.

6. IMF COFER report

The International Monetary Fund's Currency Composition of Foreign Exchange Reserves (COFER), released quarterly, is also tracked by the market. The COFER data shows which currencies the major world central banks are holding as reserves, with the breakdown into US dollars, the euro, sterling, yen, Swiss francs and 'other currencies'. Unfortunately, some countries (such as China) do not report their reserve holdings to the IMF, leaving a black hole in the data that has to be filled in by educated guesses.

The FX reserves in the COFER report contain world central bank holdings of foreign banknotes, bank deposits, treasury bills, short-term and long-term government securities and "other claims usable in the balance of payments." COFER data includes only foreign currencies held, not the home currency (which by definition is not reserves).

Using the COFER data to assess reserve diversification

In recent years, the market has kept a close eye on the IMF COFER data to see if stories of reserve diversification are valid, especially diversification from US dollars into euro.

Many of those who observe the data mistakenly look at just a year or two and fail to include the entire sweep of dollar history. This is an error because it's critical to note that the US share of reserves has been as low as under 55% in the late 1960s and it has been as high as nearly 80% in the mid-1970s. The US share fell to just over 45% in 1990, and has returned to 60% to 65% in the first decade of the new millennia – about where it was in 1970.

They also assume, wrongly, that once a share starts dropping, it continues to drop in a straight line. The US share of reserves exhibits a surprising amount of variation for a factor we might think should be more of a constant, and explains why just about anything you want to say about the dollar (or the euro) as a reserve currency is both true and false at the same time. We can say the dollar's share of reserves is up 50% (from 1970) or down 20% (from the mid-1970s), and both statements are true.

Traders understand that the data is difficult to work with and can be confusing. Still, they have begun to pay more attention to the claims in *other* currencies, or currencies other than dollar, sterling, yen, Swiss franc and euro. In the final quarter of 2011, claims in other currencies rose to $290 billion or 5.1% of allocated reserves, with the increase in reserves spit between advanced and emerging/developed economies. In Q1 2009, as global equity markets plummeted, claims in other currencies totalled $87 billion or 2.1% of total allocated reserves. What might be viewed as a small 3% FX adjustment in total allocated reserves of $5 trillion could mean the equivalent of $150 billion being bought or sold on the currency market, and if done in a short time period, could be capable of moving the market.

As for the euro share, this can be tricky too. Global reserves have more than quadrupled since the turn of the century and at the same time, market share of euro holdings has increased steadily since the advent of the euro in January 1999. At the end of the fourth quarter of 2000, total world FX reserves stood at $1.936 trillion. Of the $1.518 trillion in allocated reserves, $1.079 trillion or 71% was in dollars and $278 billion or 18.3% was in euro. A mere $23 billion or 1.5% was in other currencies.

By Q4 2005, total world FX reserves had risen to $4.32 trillion and of the $2.844 in allocated reserves, $1.903 trillion or 66.9% was in dollars and $6 684 billion or 24.1% was in euro. The *other currency* total rose to $49 billion, or 1.8% of total allocated assets. The percentage shifts reflect exchange rate fluctuations as well as central bank reserve diversification.

For example, from Q2 2010 to Q3 2010, the euro share of allocated reserves rose from 26.2% ($1.257 trillion) to 26.6% ($1.362 trillion). On the surface, it would appear that global central banks were buying euro during this period in order to diversify. However, from Q2 to Q3 the euro rose 11%, which means that if central banks did nothing, total Q3 euro reserves would be worth a bit over $1.55 trillion. That this was not the case suggests that global central bankers were in fact net sellers of euro in Q3, not buyers.

Analysts dissect the COFER data when it is released each quarter to see if a trend is emerging. They especially want to know whether China, with its $3.3 trillion in FX reserves, is diversifying out of dollars into the euro and other currencies. While China does not report the breakdown of its reserve holdings, the trend of other countries offers insight into what the People's Bank of China may be doing.

7. Sovereign wealth funds

Central banks are the most important of FX market participants, but sovereign wealth funds are close behind. A sovereign wealth fund (SWF) gets initial seed money from a country's government, typically when official reserve coffers get too full. Oil and commodity-rich countries tend to attract investor inflows and their central banks often end up with more reserves than they feel it is prudent to have. So the central banks allocate funds to a SWF in the hope of higher returns than is normally achieved by allocations to government notes and bonds.

The SWF can then invest its capital stake in stocks, bonds, commodities or other financial instruments. Some SWFs have the ability to buy shares of companies or even a whole company, depending on their mandate. SWFs have become a major player in just a few years and can have a powerful announcement effect when they declare re-allocations and other decisions.

The oldest SWF is the Kuwait Investment Authority, created in 1953. The biggest single one is the Abu Dhabi Investment Authority, although if you added up the several owned by China, China's may be bigger. Two US states (Alaska and New Mexico) and two Canadian provinces (Quebec and Alberta) have SWFs. Libya's sovereign wealth fund lost hundreds of billions in ill-advised investments, it was disclosed in mid-2010.

One of the first SWFs, and among the most aggressive, is the South Korean fund. Nigeria's Excess Crude Account SWF is surprisingly small (under $1 billion), given its oil producer status. The Norwegian fund, which used to be named a petroleum fund and is now called a pension fund, is the biggest SWF outside of the Middle East and generally considered to be the best run and most transparent. As of 2009, it owned 1% of the world's equities. It also has oversight by a Council of Ethics.

The Sovereign Wealth Institute or SWI (**www.swfinstitute.org**) is a subscription service that offers information about current and expected SWF asset allocation. It puts total assets under management at world sovereign wealth funds at $5 trillion as at May 2012. Reserves related to gas and oil stood at $2.8816 trillion and total other reserves stood at $2.1478 trillion.

8. BIS triennial report

The Bank for International Settlement's triennial report on foreign exchange and derivatives market activity is considered the bible for foreign exchange and is quoted frequently by analysts and economists. The triennial report was designed from inception "to yield comprehensive and internationally consistent information on the size and structure of foreign exchange (FX) and over-the-counter (OTC) derivatives markets."

Traders, analysts and economists pick apart the report to glean information on what currencies and instruments are being actively traded. While not a help in day-to-day trading, the survey helps bigger picture players assess how the FX market is evolving in terms of currency choice and vehicle. The 2010 survey, released in September 2010, showed that global foreign exchange turnover rose 20% to $4 trillion in April 2010 from $3.3 trillion in April 2007. And the 2007 survey had been a shocker, reporting traditional FX turnover up by an unprecedented 60% from April 2004.

At 85% of all global FX transactions in April 2010, the dollar remained the currency of choice, although this was down from the 90% peak seen in the 2001 survey. The dollar share of average daily turnover was 85.6% in 2007 and 88% in 2004. "This decline benefited the euro, which gained two percentage points in market share since the last survey and accounts for 39% of all transactions," the BIS survey said. Traders assume that when the 2013 BIS survey is released, the euro share is likely to have declined in light of the euro zone crisis. Once bitten, twice shy, this will make investors reluctant to own euro until it is crystal clear that peripheral country problems will be addressed.

A surprise in the 2010 survey was commercial banks doing fewer FX trades, for the first drop ever. In terms of trading counterparties, the BIS noted that the higher global turnover was associated with "increased trading activity of 'other financial institutions' a category that includes non-reporting banks, hedge funds, pension funds, mutual funds, insurance companies, and central banks, among others." The turnover in this category increased to $1.9 trillion in April 2010, up 42% from the $1.3 trillion seen in April 2007 and dwarfed the $1.5 trillion in turnover of transactions between reporting dealers. "For the first time, activity of reporting dealers with other financial institutions surpassed inter-dealer transactions (i.e., transactions between reporting dealers)," the BIS said.

In December 2010, the BIS released an in-depth study to explain the move away from trading with commercial banks. Because there was no mechanism in the Triennial survey to get a breakdown of what trades were being done where, the BIS used other tactics, including "discussions with market participants, data from regional FX surveys and an analysis of the currency composition and location of trading activity." The BIS said "Taken together, they suggest the increased turnover is driven by: (i) greater activity of high-frequency traders; (ii) more trading by smaller banks that are increasingly becoming clients of the top dealers for the major currency pairs; and (iii) the emergence of retail investors (both individuals and smaller institutions) as a significant category of FX market participants."

A key driver for these heightened trading flows is the spread of electronic execution methods. "Electronic trading and electronic brokering are transforming FX markets by reducing transaction costs and increasing market liquidity. These changes, in turn, are encouraging greater participation across different customer types," the BIS said.

9. Corporate/Institutional/Retail FX/Hedge funds

Traders always like to know what other market players are thinking and doing, if only to let them feel more comfortable with their own position. Unlike a central bank or a sovereign wealth fund, where the sheer size of the deal may sway FX direction, when corporates and hedge funds trade, the effect on the market can be a shock or mere ripple, depending upon the liquidity and the time of day as well as the currency pair involved. Retail accounts, while insignificant individually, can be a larger FX driver collectively, so traders like to know what retail is up to also, if only to gauge currency sentiment. Traders look also at the volumes involved. If volumes are down, they may be more mistrustful of a move; conversely if volumes are rising, traders would be more inclined to believe that the move "has legs."

Greenwich Associates conducts an annual study on global foreign exchange flows that is helpful in tracking developing trends of corporate, institutional and retail customers, as well as hedge funds. From September to November 2011, Greenwich Associates conducted in-person interviews with 1,632 top-tier users of FX at large corporations and financial institutions in North America, Latin America, Europe, Asia and Japan. "To be considered top-tiered, a firm must be a central bank, a government agency, a hedge fund, a fund manager, a FT 100 global firm, a firm with reported trading volume of more than $1 billion, or a firm with reported sales of more than $5 billion," GA explains.

The Greenwich Associates report, released in April 2012, showed that global FX activity, including short-dated swaps and rollovers, increased by 15% in 2011. Overall global short-dated swap and rollover trading volumes, including tom-next trades and extending to one-week swaps, were up 21% from 2010, with the spike most evident in Japan (volumes doubled to about 60%).

As might be expected, given the euro zone crisis and ensuing safe-haven demand, the largest growth in global FX demand in 2011 took place in the North and South America. US FX trading volumes for ex-short-dated transactions were up 34% in 2011, with, albeit much smaller, Canadian FX trading volumes for longer-dated transactions up 60% and Latin American FX longer-dated trading volumes up 45%.

In terms of breakdown, Greenwich noted that retail aggregators globally generated 18% of worldwide FX trading volume in 2011, up from 10% in 2010. In contrast, bank trading decreased to 30% of overall trading volumes globally in 2011, from 39% in 2010. Hedge fund trading volumes shrank to 11% in 2011 from 15% in 2010 and now rank behind retail aggregators in terms of global trading volumes.

While not considered a driving force, retail foreign exchange traders have multiplied explosively in recent years. In the latest triennial survey, the BIS noted that "trading by households and small non-bank institutions has grown enormously, with market participants reporting that it now accounts for an estimated 8% to 10% of spot FX turnover globally." Japanese retail investors are deemed the most active, with market estimates suggesting that this segment accounts for about 30% (or more than $20 billion per day) of spot Japanese yen trading.

In recent years, financial regulators globally have taken steps to make sure that retail investors are not biting off more than they can chew. In 2009, regulators in Japan implemented measures to reduce the leverage of foreign exchange margin transactions. They lowered the maximum allowable leverage for Japanese retail FX investors to 50:1 starting in August 2010. Beginning in August 2011, the leverage would be lowered further to 25:1.

In the United States, the Commodity Futures Trading Commission implemented similar measures in August 2010. The CFTC's proposed 10-1 leverage limit for all retail foreign exchange clients drew widespread criticism among traders, who warned that FX flows would move to overseas platforms. The CFTC decided instead on a compromise mechanism, whereby major currency pairs will have a minimum required margin of 2% of notional value of each trade, which corresponds to a maximum allowable leverage of 50:1. Minor currency pairs will have a minimum required margin of 5% of notional value, which corresponds to a maximum allowable leverage of 20:1. Prior to the CFTC rulings, leverage on FX trading platforms was typically around 100:1, but in some cases ran as high as 400:1.

Other flow reports

In addition to official flow reports, many banks now offer a breakdown of the flows actually executed by their traders on behalf of clients. Custody banks, such as State Street and Bank of New York Mellon, currently offer daily, weekly and monthly updates on transactions executed for clients in stocks, bonds and currencies. These capture only a small portion of the daily $4 trillion in FX turnover, but are considered accurate reports of real money transactions. Not all of the data is publically available, with some flow reports released solely to clients and bank personnel.

Conclusion

The amount of information on FX positioning is overwhelming and yet, at the same time, it arrives too late and is often too big-picture for day-to-day trading. Of all these reports, the one that carries the most weight in day-to-day trading is the CFTC Commitments of Traders Report, which is almost a week late, hard to read and covers futures instead of spot. Still, you will often see major newspapers like the *Financial Times* cherry-pick a bit of data from the COT report, like the number of long contracts at or near a record high, that offers the opportunity to multiply by the contract amount and come up with a shocking *bet* in favour of one currency or another. Stories like this are not exactly wrong or misleading, but they are incomplete. In any case, they contribute to setting the tone.

Reports like the BIS Triennial survey offer a look into the big picture changes going on in the background of currency trading. That the bulk of trading continues to be concentrated in the major FX pairs serves as a reminder not to go overboard in a less liquid currency, although some hedge funds rejoice in exotic crosses like the South African rand against the Turkish lira, and claim to have no liquidity problems. Weekly reports like the CFTC report can tell a trader if speculative accounts are overly long or short a currency in comparison to their historical pattern. Because traders can't know the exact size of all existing positions, they use any and all available reports to gauge whether the market is overbought or oversold.

CHAPTER 7 –
INTERMARKET ANALYSIS

"It ain't necessarily so."

Sportin' Life, *Porgy and Bess* by George and Ira Gershwin

TV announcers, securities analysts and the man on the street all glibly assert that the dollar is up because oil is down, or oil is down because the dollar is up. They also say the stock market and the dollar have an inverse correlation, or that asset classes follow a cycle of boom and bust that starts with commodities, then equities, then bonds and then currencies, or maybe it's the other way around. *Data doesn't confirm?* Gee, there must be a lag. We do not mean to say intermarket analysis doesn't have usefulness, but much of it is nonsense.

In this chapter, we propose that risk appetite and risk aversion, as the vector or medium of transmission of information, is often a pretty good explanation of these effects but does not cover all the bases. At bottom, supply and demand in each of these markets is the real driving force and cannot be short-changed or dismissed in favour of more distantly related factors. In other words, correlation is not causation and appetite for risk is the underlying driver, rather than a direct and measurable relationship among commodities, currencies or indicators.

Overview of big-picture intermarket ideas

Origins of intermarket analysis

John Murphy wrote the first book titled *Intermarket Analysis*,[50] but the core idea arose with Charles Dow's observation that stock market trends follow economic activity. Dow first published the Dow index in 1896 (containing 12 companies) and a year later, the railroad stock index. Dow proposed that if the railroad index and the Dow index were both rising to new highs, it was a bull market and investors could have more confidence investing in equities. A turndown in the railroads, assuming it was based on declining railroad revenues and not some other factor, implied that the Dow index may decline on falling revenues, too – an early warning signal. Dow himself advised against putting too much stock in the relationship because many other influences are at work.

Note the parallel a century later when the Baltic Dry index, a compilation of international shipping costs, became popular as a purported leading indicator of global economic growth. Whether transportation cost is a valid measure of all economic activity is debatable, and yet the Baltic Dry has a pretty good track record.

Murphy's 1991 book tried to explain how the four major market sectors – stocks, bonds, commodities and currencies – reflect the business cycle. Commodities come first, as robust economic activity results in higher commodity prices.

Equities then fall as money flows to commodities, but rising inflation caused by rising commodities also attracts the attention of central banks, which raise interest rates in response and cause bond yields to rise. Rising yields draw investors from equities and commodities. Currencies rise alongside interest rates.

The commodity bubble burst in 1980 ushered in major bull markets in stocks and bonds that reversed as commodity prices started rising again in the first half of 1987, leading to the stock market crash later that year (19 October 1987, Black Monday). Building on this evidence, Murphy asserted that falling commodity prices usually produce higher bond prices and thus, by definition, lower yields. He also said the correlation between stock prices and interest rates is inverse – stocks go up when interest rates go down, except when they don't.

In the revised edition of his book,[51] Murphy pointed out that in the deflationary environment that started in 1998, falling interest rates did not help stocks. Of course, we could always postulate that the effect was there, just overwhelmed by the stock price crash. Perhaps an absence of falling interest rates would have made the drop in stocks all the greater. As for commodities leading stocks, during 1999 and 2000 they rose together in tandem instead of the usual inverse relationship. Earlier, in 1993 and again in 2011, the CRB index and the 30-year bond rallied at the same time, even though they are supposedly negatively correlated. In the first half of 2012, it was the euro that was inversely correlated with gold, not the dollar, and Brent oil was positively correlated with the FTSE 100.

We could name literally thousands of cases in which the purported relationships are the opposite of what they should be. In short, intermarket relationships vary so much over time and are so often decoupled that you have to wonder if they deserve to be named relationships at all. It is also possible that the bivariate relationships are disguised because they are a subset of a greater multivariate model where the other variables mask the impact of the two items for a while.

Where intermarket analysis falls flat

Intermarket analysis is like an infant that is failing to thrive. What it lacks most of all is a theoretical foundation. Economists agree that there is such a thing as a business cycle, but the problem is that at any one time there are half a dozen cycles simultaneously at work. In the US, the National Bureau of Economic Research (NBER) is the arbiter of business cycles, and it uses measures of aggregate activity like output (GDP) and employment to determine expansion or contraction. These are economic activities, not financial prices, and since even the most crudely defined business cycle varies from one to twelve years, they are only distantly relevant to current supply and demand for financial assets.

Note also that inflation and deflation are not central to the identification and measurement of business cycles, although they are certainly relevant to financial prices, not to mention the central banks that consider information about business conditions when determining the extent of their response to inflation or deflation. There is always a large element of the chicken-and-egg problem in any discussion of business cycles and their effect on asset prices. Is it good enough to say falling interest rates are highly correlated with rising equity prices except under deflationary conditions? You decide.

Another problem with intermarket analysis is that central banks famously decline to consider anything other than core prices, i.e., excluding food and energy prices, when making interest rate decisions. The decision to use only core prices, while annoying to the average citizen, has its justification in the perfectly accurate observation that a central bank's interest rate policy is powerless to affect food and energy prices. Central banks also decline to consider irrational exuberance in equity markets as something in which they can or should intervene to restrain. In addition, in the US and other developed countries, central banks do not target specific exchange rates; to the Federal Reserve, the level of the dollar is a residual of policy that targets other activities and other prices. So, if interest rates are the central driver of intermarket relationships but the agent in charge of interest rates ignores three of the four asset sectors, how strong can the relationship be among the four sectors?

Finally, correlation is a statistics term that the scientifically-minded find much abused in financial market commentary. For a correlation to be valid, it has to persist over some minimum time period, and it has to be both strong and consistent. It's not good enough to say that a 70% correlation over three months or even three years can be extrapolated to a permanent relationship, or that a 55% correlation over any number of periods is worth talking about at all. Therefore, traders have to stay on their toes to identify when an intermarket relationship is an active factor in sentiment and when its day in the sun has faded. An intermarket relationship may be observed to exist strongly for a short period of time, but that doesn't mean it is always strong or that it's always there.

Where intermarket analysis comes good

You don't need to buy into a grand theory of intermarket relationships to observe that some markets do have effects on other markets, at least sometimes, and to an increasing extent as information flows improve with every passing day. We must also acknowledge that the four big asset sectors are all related in that they constitute the universe of possible investment targets of those seeking both diversification and yield, and it is certainly true that the professional and amateur investor alike have become increasingly willing to entertain so-called alternative investments.

In the FX market, we observe that exchange rates are strongly correlated with interest rates, although which interest rate is the relevant one changes over time and under varying conditions. We talk about this in Chapter 4. Stock markets, on the other hand, are the most distantly related to currencies. We have two true economic influences at work, earnings and repatriated earnings of multinational corporations, and diversification. Diversification became the watchword of the late 1990s and was eagerly embraced by one and all, although as crises develop, such as the maturing of the European sovereign debt crisis in 2011, we see capital flee high-yielding emerging market stock markets in droves. We might note that foreign inflows into the US equity market are markedly independent of the level of the dollar, whereas US outflows to foreign equity markets are reversed very quickly when crises appear.

Changing correlations

The thing about correlations is that just when you think you have figured one out, something happens to make the correlation no longer hold true. A June 2009 Federal Reserve International Financial Discussion paper[52] addressed the reasons for the Mexican peso tending to be more closely correlated with the US dollar than the euro and other currencies. The paper, based on a study of 29 currencies, found that the bulk of cross country variations in currency correlations between the dollar and euro could be explained "by just a few variables."

> "First, a country's currency is more likely to rise against the dollar as the dollar rises against the euro, the closer it is to the United States and the farther it is from the euro area. In this result, distance likely proxies for the role of economic integration in affecting exchange rate correlations. Second, and perhaps more surprisingly, a country's currency is more likely to exhibit this unusual pattern when its sovereign credit rating is more risky. This may reflect that currencies of riskier countries are less substitutable in investor portfolios than those of better-rated countries," the paper said.

On one hand it makes sense, given the close trade ties between Mexico and the US, that the peso would track the dollar rather than another currency. However, Canada also has a close trading relationship with the US and yet the Canadian dollar does not always suffer when the greenback is under pressure.

For many years, Mexico's sovereign credit rating and history of default overshadowed other potential positives. Once Mexico received investment grade status in the early 2000s (from Moody's in 2000, and Fitch and Standard & Poor's in 2002), investors were more willing to buy Mexican bonds and stocks. The peso started to trade inversely with the US dollar, like the Canadian dollar and other majors.

Just as the supposed correlation of the peso and dollar was reversed from positive to negative because of the ratings agency change, a new development could break down the new relationship, such as a major policy change in either the US or Mexico that affects their respective ratings. We might think that because it was ratings that caused the correlation reversal last time, it will be ratings that most threaten the new relationship, but for all we know, it could be some other as-yet unknown factor. A one-time change in correlation doesn't mean the end of correlation changes and it doesn't mean the factor that caused the correlation change will cause a correlation change next time.

Considering notable 'correlated' markets

We will now look at two of the notable areas where there are supposed correlations, namely between the dollar and oil, and the dollar and gold.

The dollar and oil

The commodity markets provide the deepest and most lasting relationship with currencies, especially gold and oil. Since everyone knows, or thinks he knows, about these relationships, we have ended up with entirely circular reasoning on this subject. This takes the form of explaining that a rise in oil or gold is due solely to a drop in the dollar, but at the same time currency analysts are blaming the falling dollar entirely on rising oil or gold. Circular reasoning like this assumes what it is attempting to demonstrate and thus can't lose. It is a particularly pernicious form of fallacy that acquires authority and becomes a self-fulfilling prophecy.

Some people find the inverse relationship of the dollar and oil to be intuitively obvious, but it's not obvious by a long shot. If oil and other commodities are rising in price, commodity buyers have to buy more dollars to pay for them. By any measure, this is demand for dollars and should support a rising, not falling, dollar price. It would be silly to say that FX traders are somehow in cahoots with commodity buyers to drive the price of the dollar down so the price of oil in (say) euro is constant.

In fact, the inverse correlation of the price of oil and the dollar is a myth. Before the late 1990s, the price of oil and the dollar/Deutsche Mark exchange rate were positively correlated; from 1985 to 1996, it was the Deutsche Mark that was inversely correlated with the price of oil. When oil went up, so did the dollar. We used to write that higher oil prices harmed European economies with higher costs whereas the UK (and Norway) had its own oil supply and the US, while a big importer, had its own oil supply, too.

In a demonstration that partial self-sufficiency in oil has nothing to do with currency levels, consider the Japanese yen and oil – they display no consistent relationship at all. Japan, which has no domestic oil production, is the most import-dependent of all the big industrialised countries, and one might expect the yen to fall when the price of oil goes up as a direct reflection of worsening economic conditions. Instead, you cannot force the two sets of data, oil and the yen, to show a relationship. One mitigating factor is the remarkable advances Japan made in becoming more energy-efficient since the second oil crisis in 1978-79; its oil imports as a percentage of GDP fell by five times from 1980 to 1990.[53] The unhappy fact remains, though, that if oil and currencies are inherently correlated, they should all be correlated and we should be able to find the economic mechanisms that make such correlation easy to understand.

Figure 7.1 shows the inverted dollar index vs. the price of oil over a long time period (1986 to end-September 2011). Until 2002, there is no obvious inverse correlation that jumps out at you. In fact, in 1999 and 2000, the dollar index was rising while oil was falling. It's only after 2002 that the correlation looks pretty good. But not always. Figure 7.2 shows the same data on a shorter timeframe. In 2005 and 2006, we have the same outcome as in 1999-2000 – oil is rising and so is the dollar index.

Figure 7.1 – Dollar Index (inverted) vs. WTI Crude Oil (weekly)

Figure 7.2 – Dollar Index (inverted) vs. WTI Crude Oil (weekly) (shorter term)

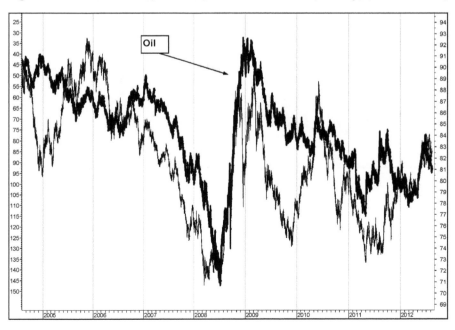

As for the price of oil in euro terms, it is not remaining constant, i.e., the euro has not risen enough against the dollar to offset the rise in the price of oil. See Figures 7.3 and 7.4. In the first figure, it looks like the euro is rising in tandem with the price of oil in a strong correlation. But then see Figure 7.4. From a low in September 2001 to the peak in 2008, the price of oil in euro terms rose by 360% (€20.02 to €92.90) while the price of oil in dollar terms rose by more, 760% ($17.15 to $147.27) – but oil did rise in price for Europeans, more or less in lockstep with the price of oil in dollars. Europeans may be able to pay less of a price increase than the US, but the euro is offsetting only about a third to a half of the price increase.

Figure 7.3 – oil (dark) vs. Euro/USD

Figure 7.4 – oil in euro terms (heavy line) vs. oil in USD terms

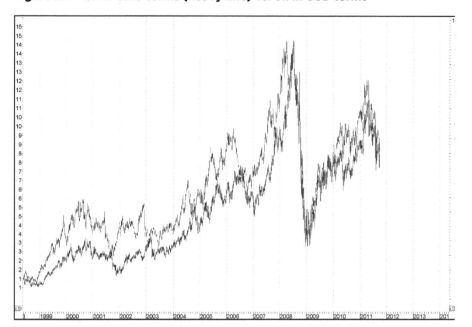

When the dollar and oil are correlated

Historically, the periods of highest correlation of the dollar and oil are during oil price peaks and lows. In other words, risk appetite and risk aversion come more into play in the oil-dollar relationship when conditions are tense and geopolitical relationships are rocky, as during the 1973 and 1978 oil embargoes, the US invasion of Kuwait and then Iraq, and other big events of the last 40 years. Economists specialising in the oil industry point out that producers have a real need to maintain high amounts of cash in their treasuries to pay for their generous social spending, and this is an implicit agenda item at OPEC meetings.

Oil producers tend, on the whole, not to have available to them the escape hatch of temporarily borrowing in the international capital markets to make up for an oil revenue shortfall. The financial crisis of 2008 that culminated in the price of oil falling to $33 and €24.45 in January 2009 posed a threat to those domestic subsidies, and incentivised producers to help their advanced economy customers as much as possible in the form of steady supplies. Similarly, as Libyan supplies went off the market for several months during the uprising in 2011, other producers rushed to commit higher output, lest rising prices derail the US and other advanced country recoveries. Leading up to the US and European Union embargo on Iranian oil on 1 July 2012, Saudi Arabia promised as much make-up supply as would be needed to maintain prices at stable levels. It worked. Risk aversion and rising oil prices were prevented. The price of oil fell from $100.43 on 1 May 2012 to $77.28 on 28 June 2012. The price experience from the Libyan and Iranian episodes suggests that oil producers themselves are breaking the inverse correlation of oil and the dollar by managing supply and thus price expectations.

A separate issue is that we do not know what effect is caused by falling oil import dependency in the US during the same period. US dependence on imported oil fell from 60% of total consumption in 2005 to 45% by end-2011.[54] We can speculate that if US dependence on foreign oil had been rising instead of falling, breaking the oil-dollar inverse correlation might have been more difficult. Does this imply that if US dependence on imported oil were to rise again, the correlation will come back? Nobody knows. We see that dependence on imported oil tends to result in no long-lasting or consistent relationship between oil and the Japanese yen, but the dollar is different – it's the world's reserve currency. Still, while we can recognise that the dollar holds a unique place among currencies, it's probably a good bet that the degree of dependence on oil imports is far less important than overall risk appetite and risk aversion.

Flawed analysis of the dollar-oil relationship

Oil economist Jim Williams says that "Until late 2002, the best short-term indicator of the oil price was the level of total petroleum stocks in OECD countries relative to the 5-year average for the same time of year. As more US data came onstream with the publication of weekly data from the US Energy Department, oil traders used US inventories relative to the 5-year average as a proxy for all of the OECD. Oddly, when you chart the oil price against OPEC spare capacity, spikes in spare capacity are due to cutbacks because of low prices, not actual increases in true capacity. A spike because of increased capacity almost never happens because of the long lead time between price, exploration and production." In other words, information that oil traders use to estimate supply (OPEC capacity) is itself heavily influenced by price, meaning you are trying to forecast price using something based on price, which is clearly not the most rational process.

Similarly, to attribute demand to all of OECD from US data is lacking in analytical rigor – demand from China and other big emerging markets (Brazil, India) must have a big impact. The International Energy Agency does its best to track demand, but estimates are derived from growth rates, not hard numbers. China does not release official oil demand statistics nor inventory reports, and reports on various aspects of oil from different state agencies cannot be reconciled. A subscription service named Platt's estimates demand for oil based on refiners' crude throughput and net oil product imports, and from this Platt's derives demand rising at 10% to 12% p.a. in 2009-2010. Platt's also reports that some analysts say China will overtake Europe as the world's second largest consumer of oil before 2020 and catch up with the US by 2030.

Finally, demand for oil comes from speculators, who discovered black gold not long after the first Gulf War (1990-91). Demand for futures contracts in oil tracks the oil price with frightening correspondence. It's hard not to conclude that the demand for futures positions may be a factor in oil prices as well as the fundamental demand for oil. See Figure 7.5. As noted in the chapter on technical analysis, at one point there were more oil contracts traded for delivery at Cushing, Oklahoma than there were barrels of deliverable oil.

Figure 7.5 – Demand for futures contracts in oil vs. oil price

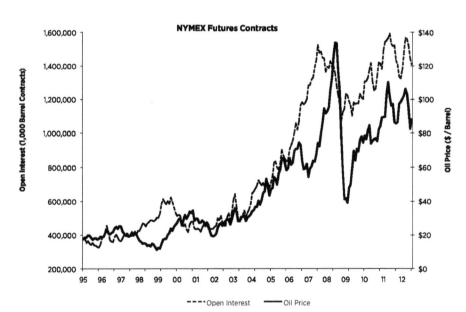

Williams points out that with everyone having the same massive computing power today, oil traders are all likely modifying their forecasts based on the same data, and then as the new prices, including intermarket data, provide feedback to new correlation studies, before long the original supply/demand factors are overridden. Note also that some players, such as Goldman Sachs, own oil companies, refineries, utilities, and so on, at the same time as they are issuing forecasts on the price of oil, evidently without any loss of credibility.

***

In the end, though, it doesn't matter whether the seeming correlation of the dollar and oil is true. It matters only that traders think it's true and act accordingly. And it is our experience that they are most likely to do that – trade the dollar according to what they see oil doing – at times of stress in financial markets. When a major party like OPEC or Saudi Arabia reduces stress by promising supply, the correlation is far weaker, may disappear altogether, or may someday reverse, so that expected price rises induce a rise in the dollar.

A digression on commodities

Conventional wisdom used to be that unless you get lucky on price, investment in physical commodities is not by itself the most lucrative of investments and takes a lot of specialised knowledge, like crop yields, diseases, and weather patterns – but you can earn interest on the collateral you put up, usually US or other government notes, and you might make a gain on rolling over futures contracts if there is backwardation, i.e, farther out contracts are cheaper than the current expiring contract.

Two major developments changed all that. The first was a slew of academic papers proving that you want commodities in your portfolio not for their own intrinsic return but rather to get the same or a better return while also reducing the risk of the other components. These papers started showing up in the 1970s and were cited far and wide by portfolio managers newly enchanted with modern portfolio theory and portfolio optimisation.

One study in particular[55] demonstrated that adding an equal dose of commodity futures to a conventional stock and bond portfolio resulted in a nicely stable return of 10.3% p.a. from July 1959 to December 2004, all due to commodities having an inverse correlation with stocks and bonds. The authors noted that "The negative correlation between commodity futures and the other asset classes is due, in significant part, to different behaviour over the business cycle. In addition, commodity futures are positively correlated with inflation, unexpected inflation, and changes in expected inflation."

The second big development was the publication of a book on the virtues of commodities over all other asset classes by Jim Rogers in 2007.[56] Against war stories of the poor guy who lost his shirt in soybeans or forgot to close out a futures trade and got a load of wheat on his front lawn, Rogers asserted that hard assets would replace paper financial assets, and the rise of China and other emerging markets in Asia would shift power from financiers in London and New York to producers of real goods – miners and other lifters of natural resources. It's curious that an arch-capitalist like Rogers would promote a point of view that harkens so strongly to Marx's first musings on how value is created in the form of commodities.

All the same, currency analysts were quick to slot this perspective into their already existing worldview of Australia and Canada as key providers of natural resources to emerging markets, and thus the AUD and CAD as commodity currencies. In these instances, we do have strong, nearly one-for-one and nearly immediate currency effects from changes in commodity prices – but still subject to big-picture crisis overrides. When the euro fell in the spring and summer of 2011, for example, the CRB and Australian dollar fell by the same relative amount and in the same pattern. We don't say the AUD was dragged lower by the euro or even by the CRB index, but rather that all were on a downmove because of rising risk aversion.

As usually happens when everyone rushes to the same conclusion, a falling tide lowers all boats. An investor newly terrified of a bubble bursting or fearful of global recession is likely to flee to pure cash, whether he was in the S&P, the Shanghai Composite, or silver. Today, more than ever, we see wildly different securities moving in tandem but only under crisis conditions.

Gold – the third rail of currency analysis

No subject arouses more emotion than gold, as least in the form of gold vs. the dollar. Armchair analysts are certain that gold is the only valid alternative to mere paper money, since it is outside the control of governments. Rational arguments – that gold has not actually kept up with inflation and is not therefore a hedge, gold is not money and has no inherent rate of return (and in fact has high costs for storage and insurance), and so on – fall on deaf ears. As the Fed frets about the possibility of deflation rather than inflation, gold aficionados persist.

When gold took off as an alternative investment in 2005-2006, complete with exchange-traded funds holding bullion or mining company stocks, the gold crowd seemed vindicated. Suddenly the correlation with the dollar did, indeed, seem straightforward. But look again. In Figure 7.6 we have two upward spikes in the dollar index while gold is rising steadily. A truly inverse relationship would have gold falling when the dollar is rising. Now look at the dollar spikes up close, in Figure 7.7. The first spike is the dollar gaining as the financial crisis hit other countries, including Iceland and Ireland, harder than the US. The second dollar index spike is associated with the European peripheral debt crisis. And all the while, gold goes upward. Clearly, factors other than the dollar are at work, including fresh demand from a newly wealthy middle class in India, China and elsewhere in Asia, barely dented by new supplies inspired by the higher prices, causing old mines to be re-opened, even in the UK.

Figure 7.6 – Dollar Index vs. gold

Figure 7.7 – Dollar Index vs. gold

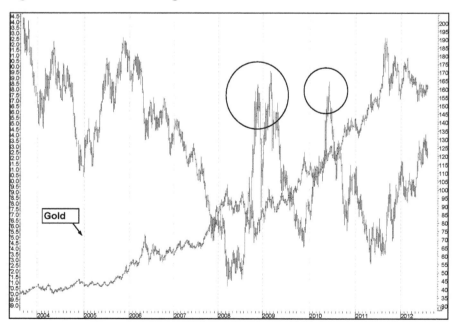

Market guru Mark Hulbert wrote in the *Wall Street Journal* (27 April 2011) that in testing the correlation of the dollar and gold over a five-year timeframe, he did indeed find the expected inverse correlation, but the dollar's moves explained only about 25% of the change in gold. To be precise, "the r-squared for the correlation was never higher than 0.26," regardless of whether the data was analysed on a daily, weekly or monthly basis. Hulbert cites work done by Ned Davis Research that indicates only about a third of the change in the S&P GSCI Commodity Index can be explained by the change in the US dollar.

So this correlation does not really exist either, or rather it is far weaker than some imagine.

Conclusion

Intermarket analysis is not a scam. We see many occasions when assumed correlations work out exactly as the current conventional wisdom suggests they should, such as the inverse correlation of oil and the dollar, and gold and the dollar. When the correlations are not working out as assumed, we see press reports of "de-coupling" and "segmentation," so that we need to look at the risk implication of changes in less prominent assets (copper, coffee, corn) instead of the primaries, oil and gold.

Plenty of honest and earnest analysts try to winnow out the wheat from the chaff. Websites offer the retail trader the chance to name two securities from any asset class and see whether there is some hitherto unknown valuable correlation. It is conceivable that a FX trader can use today's massive computational firepower to find a correlation that works to forecast profitable trades.

But on the whole, it is unwise to accept conventional wisdom about correlations without a grain of salt. They are weaker than we think and susceptible to change, including outright reversal. Moreover, the laws of economics – supply and demand – are not suspended by fancy computations. It is always better to have a logical reason why two securities *should* be correlated. What is the economic machinery by which a price in one market can be seen to affect prices in a seemingly unrelated market?

We say that risk appetite and risk aversion suffice to link any asset price to any other, but that is a short-term phenomenon and not a reliable trading guide over longer periods of time. In the end, the price of oil will always ultimately have something to do with the demand and supply of oil, in turn influenced by producer budgets and technological advances in alternative energy – and not the level of the dollar alone. The same thing holds for gold or any other commodity or security.

CHAPTER 8 – TECHNICAL ANALYSIS IN FOREIGN EXCHANGE

"I am shocked, shocked, to find that gambling is going on in here!"

Claude Rains in *Casablanca*

The foreign exchange market was the first market to adopt technical analysis wholesale, even though the ideas arose first in equities. A vast majority of professional FX traders now use technical analysis in one form or another. It is a logical development because foreign exchange prices tend to be highly trended due to the cyclical nature of underlying economic conditions and their associated interest rates. It is our observation that technicals are a more powerful influence in FX than in other markets.

In part because of the pervasive use of technical analysis, FX trading practices are different from equity market trading. In the absence of a benchmark or fair value concepts, FX trading is rule-based and geared to gain or loss alone. Nearly all trading is short term – minutes and hours, not weeks and months – and therefore the FX trader is more acutely conscious at all times of whether a position is winning or losing. The equity trader may make a buy or sell decision on a specific issue only once a month when recalibrating allocations or once a quarter when earnings are released, whereas the FX trader will make a buy or sell decision on the same security several times a day.

Meanwhile, those who are buying and selling FX as an asset class or who are hedging equity or bond positions do have a longer timeframe, like the equity investor, but their only benchmark is still the gain or loss on their specific positions. Fortunately, technical analysis serves both the short-term trader and the longer-term investor, because prices exhibit what is called a "fractal" characteristic – in the absence of a label, you cannot tell the difference between a chart of one-minute prices and a chart of daily prices. Most techniques work on all timeframes.

It is fair, however, to name expectation-based trading *speculation*. Speculation is a dirty word in some societies, but this is because speculators are blamed for unpopular outcomes even when the critics have to confess that the trading decisions were perfectly rational. Most financial market participants are taught that speculators provide an essential service to the market by providing liquidity, the grease in the wheels of price-setting. But speculators provide more essential services, too. The topmost one is being the front-runner in detecting securities that deserve to be sold, either because of fundamental reasons or because the chart shows support is wavering and weak. As the long-time head of FX at a major US bank said, "We do not speculate. We anticipate price actions based on rational observation."

The prevalence of TA in FX

Technical analysis is a tool for telling us whether a price is moving up, down or sideways and at what pace. It therefore helps a trader decide whether to buy or sell and where to place a stop and profit target. Some folks go overboard and make it into a religion, which is a pity, because applied systematically over long periods of time, technical analysis is capable of producing a better profit/loss profile than human judgment alone.

Technical analysis is empirical – it is the study of price movements themselves without regard for the reasons behind the price movements. It is therefore free of ideological baggage and doesn't require the study of economic fundamentals. The core idea is credited to Charles Dow, the founder of the *Wall Street Journal*, in the first decade of the 20th century. Dow Theory can be summed up in a near-Newtonian way: a price that is rising will continue to rise until some news comes along to make traders stop buying it. Then traders cut or eliminate positions, and may go short.

At least three-quarters of FX market participants, and probably more than 95%, use technical analysis in some form to determine their trades; an astonishingly high proportion. Even traders who publicly disown technical analysis will use a 100-day or 200-day moving average as a benchmark, not appreciating that all moving averages are technical analysis. While most FX active traders embrace technical analysis, fund managers may take a different stance, distancing themselves from technical analysis because they want to avoid association with ideas still considered crackpot by some. Many FX managers are coy about using technical analysis because their customers are crossover customers from equities, where the Graham and Dodd concept of value investing has retained its grip on a majority of market players since the 1934 publication of their book, *Security Analysis*.

While technical analysis doesn't use fundamentals or value concepts, practitioners are free to add as much economics or value input as they wish. Contrary to common opinion, the two techniques for analysing securities prices are not antithetical. Both technical and fundamental analysis have virtues and shortcomings.

For example, during the summer of 2011, the Swiss franc rose to extreme high levels against the euro and dollar. The rise was due to safe-haven flows to the franc as the euro zone sovereign risk and banking crisis evolved. Commentators noted that a can of Coca-Cola cost the equivalent of $6 in a Geneva supermarket when it cost $1 in the US, implying that the franc was overvalued by a multiple of six. But this is a situation where relative purchasing power was not the correct guiding principle for judging an exchange rate and certainly not for trading it. If you were trading on purchasing power, you would sell the Swiss franc at the extreme high levels in anticipation of a drop – exactly the wrong trade, as the can of Coke proceeded to $9. Technical analysis would have rescued you from the bad trade by displaying that the Swiss franc was still rising. What the chart will not tell you is how long the Swiss franc will continue to rise or what will be the peak. But then of course fundamental analysis won't tell you those levels, either.

Why technical analysis is pervasive in FX

Technical analysis burst on to the FX scene less than a decade after the dollar was floated in 1973. When Citibank offered the first big-institution technical system to multinational corporate clients in 1981, it garnered several hundred subscribers in the first few months, including many of the top 50. Multinational corporations were first to adopt technical analysis, with big bank traders lagging far behind by a decade or more. In a way, multinationals were mystified, as were most economists, by the seemingly illogical price action in the FX market, and technical analysis was a method of cutting through the clutter of what economics seemed to say prices should be doing and what prices, set by big bank traders, were actually doing. As the usefulness of technical analysis became apparent to the big bank traders, they too accepted it.

The embrace of technical analysis was due to seven factors, some of which we explore further below and some in other chapters:

1. **Economics failed**. Economic theories of exchange rate determination led to bad exchange rate forecasts and thus to suboptimal trading, hedging and investment decisions. In a nutshell, economics fails to factor in the human element of crowd behaviour, including that FX rates tend to overshoot. At Amazon.com, you will find only about 300 books on forecasting FX, compared to 33,000 on technical analysis.

2. **Technical analysis offers a methodology for measuring market sentiment** arising from economic and other factors (such as intermarket relationships). The trader may know that an economic release or central bank policy decision should, in theory, influence exchange rates but he also knows that effects vary over time. Technical analysis offers a way to evaluate various factors by looking at how and by how much prices respond to news about the factors. Sentiment is the consensus of many different players interpreting the same data, and technical analysis reveals the consensus. In the absence of a universally agreed-upon economics framework for forecasting FX, we know how much weight to give to a fundamentals announcement only by how the market responds to it as revealed on the chart.

3. **Timing matters**. Technical analysis tools vastly improve the odds that you are not buying at the top or selling at the bottom. Managers in trading rooms and managers in strategic planning alike appreciate the contribution of technical analysis to better decision making.

4. **Technical analysis is empirical.** Technical analysis entails no ideology. You don't have to grasp any fancy theories using unrealistic assumptions, such as the efficient market hypothesis. Technical analysis uses visual and statistical evidence to identify trends.

5. **Technical analysis is easy.** Anyone can draw support and resistance lines and calculate moving averages. At more advanced levels, technical analysis is complex and nuanced, but as a practical matter, the most basic technical analysis is better than the most advanced financial theory for decision-making purposes.

6. **Technical analysis works**. The foreign exchange market is highly trended and we can identify trends with a reasonable degree of confidence.

7. **Computers are available to everyone**. Technical analysis was accepted early by professionals with access to mainframes, but until the PC and the internet became widely used, the cost of the data alone was prohibitive and manual chart work was laborious. The first PC-based program for non-professionals, Equis' Metastock, was released in 1982. The first book on technical analysis since Edwards and Magee in 1948 was published in 1978.[57] Today you can find hundreds of software packages and thousands of books (as noted above, 33,000 at **Amazon.com**).

Timing matters

It should be too obvious to mention, but it's absolutely better to have bought a security when it was priced at $5 than when it was priced at $10 if you are selling the security when it's priced at $20. If you bought at $5 and sold at $20, you quadrupled your capital stake. If you bought at $10 and sold at $20, you doubled it. Both are nice outcomes but four times the stake is better than two times. Assuming you can do it repeatedly, you have the opportunity to increase your capital exponentially.

The purpose of using technical analysis is to buy at $5 rather than $10 and to sell at $20 rather than any lesser number. Technical practitioners admit that their tools will not get them in at the exact low and out at the exact high, but they will do better than not using any timing tools at all.

No benchmark

It's critical to acknowledge that the great preponderance of trades executed in the FX market are speculative in nature. The single goal of the FX trader is to make a profit. To the FX trader, the only reason to buy a security is to sell it for a gain. No professional FX trader buys a security solely for the joy of owning a security. Investors and investment managers in other asset classes are different.

The equity trader is more concerned with having high *fair value* securities and the correct portfolio mix than with having bought near the low and sold near the high. They may buy a security to get an embedded return, like a coupon or dividend, or because the rules of their firm require that they match a benchmark like an equity index. He has far less need for tracking prices on a chart or even knowing the current price trend than the FX trader. In fact, the equity trader may have a hard time dumping a security that starts to go south if his mandate requires he hold the biggest five names in a sector, giving him no incentive to follow trends.

In FX, there is no benchmark that dictates what currencies a manager should hold. FX traders are blissfully free of the benchmark problem by which an equity manager must hold Security X because it's the biggest name in his sector, even if it's a real dog. In fact, equity managers with some latitude in portfolio selection can claim to be successful if they lost only 20% while their benchmark index lost 30%, and this is a source of pride. FX traders who lose 20% are out on their ear.

The equity trader also cannot, in most circumstances, go short a security that is going south – that would not be *investing*, but rather speculation. But the FX trader seeking only price gain will dump any security going south and short it, to boot. And his top tool for detecting an explosive rise or catastrophic drop is technical analysis. In other words, the management criteria for excellence in equity investing – benchmarks – inhibit the use of technical analysis, while the management criteria for excellence in FX trading – pure cash profit – make technical analysis the topmost tool.

Technical analysis is empirical

The technical trader looks at what other traders are *doing* rather than what they are *saying*. He deduces market sentiment from the price action.

As an example, let's look at Figure 8.1, displaying the rise of the EUR/USD from the low on 01/10/11 at $1.2860 to the high on 05/04/11 at $1.4940. Early in the upmove, the price moved above the 20-day moving average and the 20-day moving average crossed above the 55-day moving average. At the same time, we could draw a support line connecting lows. Then on 05/05/11, the euro put in a big-bar close that broke support. Anyone following the simple rule of buying when the price crossed above the 20-day and holding until hand-drawn support was broken would have made a gain of 1,165 points, or about 60% of the total move.

Figure 8.1 – important moving averages, EUR/USD

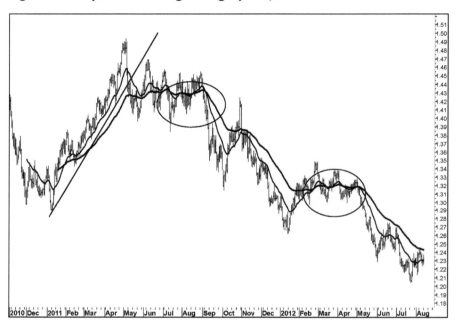

Note that what follows in the circle is a period of sideways moves named congestion, described below, from May to September. The 20-day crosses the 55-day to the downside definitively on 6 September 2011 and stays in a *sell* mode until February 2012. A trader selling the euro at $1.4295 on 6 September and holding the short position until the opposite moving average crossover on 22 February 2012 at $1.3151 would have made a net gain of 3164 points, or about $60,854 on a starting capital base of $1 million, or 6% over five months. A trader could have improved this result by re-entering after the moving average crossover after the congestive period to early May, when the downmove resumes. Clearly, during congestions, the moving average crossover technique is not useful – it works only when prices are trending (i.e., have a steeper slope off the horizontal).

In practice, few professional traders would have made only a single trade over such a long time span and on so few indicators, but the point is that by using technical tools, it was possible here to capture a high proportion of the move and have confidence that a breakout below the support line would serve to signal an exit that would result in a net gain. In fact, most professionals would have made thousands of trades over this time period, including trades in which the EUR/USD was sold on pullbacks, but always keeping in mind the core concept of confirmed primary uptrend or confirmed primary downtrend and thus a known market sentiment bias toward buying or selling the euro. Hedgers can use moving averages like these to decide the timing of remitting a dividend or making a new capital investment. Investors can use moving averages like these to determine whether they will get an extra return from an investment in euro or whether the drop in the euro will strip their returns.

Traders, investors and hedgers all assume that market sentiment is pro-euro or anti-euro because they know that everyone else in the market is looking at similar charts and indicators. Trends arise and persist because traders interpret prices as containing the embedded net sentiment of all the traders in the security. Sentiment may be based on solid economic analysis, inside information about big-player flows, or throwing darts – it doesn't matter. When sentiment is favourable, the price rises. Rising prices attract other buyers. This is the so-called *bandwagon effect*. For more on this, see 'A Riff on Sentiment' later in the chapter and what Georges Soros has to say about sentiment.

As more and more traders pile into the same security, eventually there are no more buyers to be found. The price starts showing lower lows and closes under the open, indicating the uptrend is ending. When a major *primary* trend pulls back, you never know whether it will be a temporary *secondary* trend in the opposite direction or a full-bore reversal. The technical analyst has tools to judge what's a pullback and what's a reversal, including consulting the economic and institutional reasons behind the pullback.

This is why the post-trend periods on the chart marked by circles are especially difficult. After the downside breakout, the 20-day moving average remains over the 55-day until July, or over two months, even as the price oscillates above and below the 20-day. The market is in a congestion phase, just like pedestrians milling around on a sidewalk. We literally do not know the direction of the next breakout. Even after the 6 September moving average crossover, the euro spikes for three days starting 27 October. This is a particularly severe pullback from the downtrend but never forms a congestive phase or delivers a new moving average crossover in the opposite direction. Still, at the time, a strong corrective move like this can be very confusing. Often we are not sure of market sentiment and just have to wait for the next event to become current to see the effect on the chart.

No fight between technicals and fundamentals in FX

In equities, fundamentalists say the price of a security should be based on value and if the chart of a high-value security shows a downtrend, the chart is temporarily wrong and should be disregarded. But in FX, a falling price is never ignored. Some market player is selling and has a reason to be selling. We can seldom find out who it is and why he is taking the short side, but the FX trader has to heed the price move anyway, because if the move gets big enough and lasts long enough, he has to trade in that direction.

Trading success in the FX market is directly tied to grasping the directional bias of the big players' prime customers, not fundamental values that are often unreliable. A good example during 2008-2011 was the euro's ability to recover strongly – twice – from major downmoves inspired by the perception of impending sovereign default by Greece. History teaches us that the currency of a defaulting country always devalues – look at the Icelandic kronur. But the big players – hedge funds and sovereign wealth funds – persisted in buying the euro at lows, making that fundamental less than a verity. If the prime customers chose to disregard that defaulting currencies historically devalue, the professionals reckon there's no point in arguing – the wise move is to go with the flow.

This is why we so often get what is called the fundamental disconnect – order flows that we can deduce from price action that are at odds with any conventional interpretation of the actual news and data releases. Going with the flow also explains otherwise mysterious bouts of volatility that are out of scale with the supposedly underlying fundamentals.

How to go with the flow – technical analysis in action

Today technical analysts use sophisticated techniques, but if you are new to the subject, you must begin with moving averages, the workhorse of technical analysis.

Moving averages

At times of crisis, when a currency is on the cusp of a big move, moving averages re-emerge as a factor that everyone talks about. From May to September 2011, for example, the euro/dollar gyrated around the 55-day moving average in a sideways move without forming a real trend. Traders were forced to trade on a shorter timeframe because a sideways move embodies a high level of uncertainty.

Anyone can construct a moving average – add up ten prices and divide by ten. The next day, drop the first day's price, add today's, and divide by ten again. Voila, you have a 10-day moving average. Due to their being based on previous days of price action, moving averages are by definition lagging indicators and as such they are used more for benchmarking than for active trading.

The virtue of a moving average is that it smoothes out spikes and aberrations, and reveals a trend direction. A moving average crossover, wherein a shorter-term moving average crosses above a longer one, is a tried-and-true trading technique. We have to note that these big-number moving averages came into vogue as long ago as 1910 in equity markets. The 20-day moving average is a month worth of trading days. The 50-day is 10 weeks and the 55-day is 11 weeks. The 100-day is 20 weeks, and the 200-day is 40 weeks. The longest, the 200-day, has no meaning other than to denote a long time. Why these specific numbers gained acceptance and how that acceptance was transferred to the FX market is not known.

We do know that at the shorter end of the timeframe, the 10-day (two weeks) and 20-day (one month) are powerful indicators. As a general rule, the 10-day crossing above the 20-day is a reliable indicator. It doesn't always work this way, of course. Moving average crossovers can generate losses like any other mechanical technique.

In practice, very few professional traders hold positions as long as 10, 20 or 55 days, let alone 100 days or 200 days, although institutional investors, hedge funds and multinational corporate hedgers do see things in such a long timeframe. Among active pros, though, moving averages are useful; Figure 8.1 should demonstrate the allure of technical analysis generally and show that currencies are often trended, or trended enough to make profits using simple techniques. In addition, there is a bit of market lore that many traders will observe: if a price breaks the 10-day moving average, it more often than not goes on to test the 20-day. The price may not break the 20-day, but the trader has a directional clue.

Combining fundamentals and MAs

Consider again the euro collapse in the second circle of Figure 8.1. The euro closed under the 20-day moving average, which on its own might not inspire an exit from a long euro position. But when we consult the news of the day, we see that we don't have to wait for the two moving average crossover. That day brought multiple Events, each sufficient in its own right to trigger a reversal. These included a change in the pre-existing pro-euro bias within minutes of European Central Bank (ECB) chief Trichet signalling in his press conference following the policy board meeting that the bank would not be raising rates the following month, contrary to popular belief. Not only did he decline to use the code phrase strong vigilance, he quoted the US Treasury Secretary who had said the US wants a strong dollar.

In addition, the Commodity Research Bureau index fell 4.9% on the day, with oil down 8.6% in the biggest one-day drop in over two years, and panic selling spreading to equities. Safe-haven dollar buying ensued. Some analysts noted that the commodity *flash crash* came on the same date (5 May) as the US equity flash crash two years earlier (indicating that sophisticated traders are attracted by silly superstition as much as the next guy).

This is an example of news trumping the technicals. Technical trading is, on the whole, trend-following, but even the most devoted chart-reader would rush to exit a long euro position on the Trichet and commodity stories. If we look at euro/dollar on that date on a one-hour chart, we see that response to the Trichet story was immediate. The euro fell 141 points in the first hour – and 140 points is the normal high-low range for a full 24-hour period. By mid-afternoon in New York, the total drop was 338 points, or more than double the usual daily range in far less than a full trading day (which is 24 hours, starting in the Far East at about 6 pm New York time and ending in New York at 5:59 pm).

Breakouts and support and resistance

The 10-day moving average crossing the 20-day is a form of breakout. A breakout is any price move that surpasses some concept of what is the normal or expected next move. A breakout below hand-drawn support, a previous low, a band or channel (see below) and sometimes just a round number (like 1.2500) are also breakouts. Breakouts announce a change in direction, including a change from a sideways or trendless move, or acceleration of an existing trend.

When the Trichet breakout arrived, not only did the price break the 20-period moving average and support line, it also broke the previous low that had temporarily established itself as an ad hoc benchmark. Previous intermediate highs and lows on both the hourly and daily charts are something that traders remember and watch. If a trader had not heard the Trichet and commodity stories that day, it wouldn't matter – breaking the old low would suffice as a trading rule to trigger an exit from a long position or to initiate a short one. Old highs and lows seem to matter more in FX than in equity trading.

Moving average convergence divergence (MACD)

One of the most reliable indicators in FX is the moving average convergence divergence indicator. When you subtract a longer-term moving average (26 periods) from a shorter one (12 periods) and the resulting line on the chart is rising, the two moving averages are converging and you have an uptrend. When the line levels out and starts falling, it means the shorter moving average is losing steam while the longer one is still rising and you have divergence. Something is happening. You put another line on the chart that is a moving average of the first line, and when the first line crosses the second one to the downside, you have a sell trigger.

Bands and channels

A Bollinger band is formed by taking two standard deviations of a simple 20-period moving average and adding and subtracting that amount from the moving average to form the band. See Figure 8.2. The magic properties of the 20-period moving average existed long before Bollinger bands came on the scene but may account for its continuing usefulness, since many traders look at Bollinger bands as a key measure of volatility.

Figure 8.2 – Bollinger bands, EUR/USD

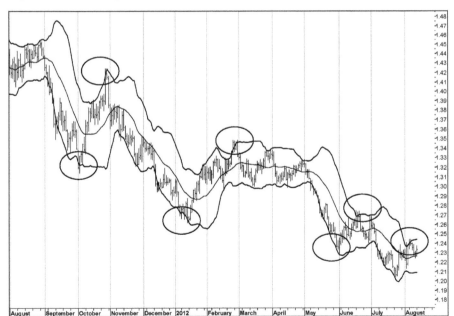

The Bollinger band rule articulated by John Bollinger is that a breakout of the top or bottom band accurately predicts a continuation of the price move in the same direction as the breakout. In FX, this is not the case. In fact, a breakout of the top band in FX reliably predicts a pullback to the centre (the 20-period moving average), and often to the other band. What was designed as a confirmation of a change in direction is, in FX, a contrarian indicator. We seldom find the Bollinger band broken for longer than three days, as the circles show.

Another channel is the standard error channel, which is the same concept as the standard deviation except the standard error is calculated off the straight-line linear regression. Figure 8.3 illustrates the use of this technique. This time we really are looking for a breakout. The linear regression identifies trendedness, although it can be tricky to draw it correctly. Obviously you need to start a linear regression from a significant high or low, and sometimes what is significant is down to personal judgment.

Figure 8.3 – linear regression channel and relative strength, EUR/USD

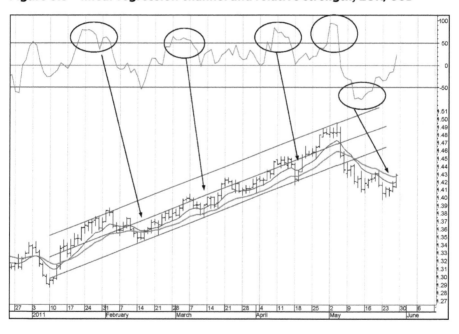

In this chart, it's not hard – we start at the most recent low and continue to the most recent high. By drawing a dotted line out from the linear regression and its channel lines, we can project the normal upcoming high-low range. These estimates of potential gains and losses can be helpful in allocating capital to a trade and in setting a stop-loss limit. Once a price breaks a channel line, conditions are no longer normal. We don't necessarily know that the breakout will continue, but we do know that risk just went much, much higher and the wise trader will exit.

Overbought and oversold

It can be frustrating to be a newcomer to FX trading and ask an old-timer why a price has reversed direction, only to be told "more sellers than buyers" or "it had gone too far." Both responses express the same phenomenon, today more universally named *overbought* or *oversold*. These phrases refer to the not-uncommon development of most big players in the market adopting the same bias and holding the same positions, so that there are no buyers or sellers left to propel prices further. Technical analysts have devised a number of tools to identify this condition, which offers the savvy pro a really good shot at making outsized profits, since once the overbought or oversold condition has been recognised by a sufficient number of traders, the slightest shove will set off a cascade of trades in the opposite direction as stops get hit and those on the losing side exit in haste.

In Figure 8.3, the indicator at the top of the chart is a relative strength indicator and its purpose is to identify overbought and oversold conditions. It performs this function by comparing where the close is relative to the high-low range in an upmove and where the low is relative to the high-low range in a downmove. By fixing this information to a specific period of time, say 14 days, we know whether the close-near-high is gaining or losing strength relative to that lookback period.

In this case, we see three circles in which the euro is overbought, and sure enough, the same day or within a few days, the euro dips. In the fourth circle, the degree to which the euro is overbought is extreme on 2 May, three days before the Trichet and commodity flash crash. *The euro was going to dip in a day or two no matter what the news would bring.* The dip might have been mild, but this time, the news justified more than a dip – an outright breakout. Notice that after the giant move down, the relative strength indicator shows an oversold condition, and the euro bounces upward obediently. That doesn't mean the downmove is over, though. It means some sellers have exited short positions.

Cyclicality and waves

This development, the corrective upmove after a breakout, brings up a delicate subject. Actually, it brings up two. The first is whether FX prices are mean-reverting or fully trending. The second is whether we can reliably identify a specific sequence of move and countermove in the pattern of FX trends.

Mean reversion

The mean-reverting model implies that FX prices tend to return to some central rate that represents a form of equilibrium. The UK pound, for example, has averaged 1.6312 from November 1982 to May 2011, or roughly 38 and a half years. The only years where sterling prices actually clustered near the average were 1997-99, as shown in Figure 8.4.

Figure 8.4 – GBP cluster around long-term average

It may seem a little silly to choose such a long timeframe, but what is the correct timeframe? As with all statistical studies, deductions can never be announced as gospel truth without naming the statistical timeframe. A shorter timeframe for mean reversion is almost certainly to be preferred, but how many data points should it cover and would it be okay to cherry-pick certain periods? How about using a moving average instead of a fixed one? Clearly building a trading strategy on mean reversion is trickier than it looks at first and only gives the appearance of being a scientific methodology. That doesn't mean plenty of traders, particularly high-frequency – algorithmic – traders, do not use mean reversion as one of the variables in the formula dictating their trades. In very short timeframes, like a series of rapid-fire trades over 15 minutes, mean reversion may be an effective guide.

The core problem with the concept of mean reversion is not whether it's true (and over what timeframe it's true), but whether a sufficient number of traders believe it to be true and thus cause a self-fulfilling prophecy. We like to think that technical analysis is empirical and we start our observations with an open mind, but to a certain extent what you see on the chart is what you expect to see and what you expect to see is informed by preconception and ideological bias.

Moves and countermoves

Analysts have laboured, for example, to explain pullbacks as following a pre-set pattern that somehow reflects a form of natural law. An early technical analyst named W.D. Gann wrote that pullbacks tend to end at 25%, 50%, and 75% of the original primary trend, or some fraction (like 12.5%). Say your security has risen from $50 to $100 and now it starts to pull back, or correct. The gain is $50, so a 50% pullback will stop at $75 and then the price will not only start rising again, but surpass the original high at $100. The Gann 50% pullback is the best of all possible pullbacks and one should bet the ranch when it appears. Needless to say, plenty of pullbacks end at numbers far removed from the Gann model.

Another idea is that human nature follows a Fibonacci sequence. A retracement should end at 38% or 62% of the original move, based on the 13th century mathematician Fibonacci's self-replicating series (1, 1, 2, 3, 5, 8, 13, 21, 34, 55, 89, etc.). Add each number to the one before it to get the next number; the ratio of any two consecutive numbers approximates 1.618 or its inverse. The Fibonacci ratio appears in nature (daisy petals, atomic particles) and the ratio 1.618 is the golden ratio of the pyramids and Parthenon, which is cool but it is inherent in securities prices only if you choose to see it that way.

One theory based on the Fibonacci sequence is the Elliott Wave theory, named for a trader named Ralph Elliott and expounded and popularised by Robert Prechter. Elliott Wave postulates that prices proceed in five waves, a first impulse wave followed by a corrective pullback, then another impulse wave in the original direction followed by a second correction, and a third impulse wave in the original direction. The pattern is two upward thrusts followed by three smaller pullbacks, and these can have internal thrusts and pullbacks that are numbered and lettered to keep them straight. The corrections are supposed to match Fibonacci numbers – and sometimes they do, given the widespread acceptance of both Fibonacci numbers and the Wave theory in FX. Every technical analysis software program, and every FX brokerage platform, offers Gann and Fibonacci retracement capability.

Whether the brains of all traders are hard-wired to the Fibonacci sequence is unlikely in the extreme. In fact, we have no evidence that the human mind is hard-wired to any number sequence, including other magic numbers (like pi) or other sequences (like prime numbers). But in FX, so many traders believe in these ideas that they become self-fulfilling. Usually when a retracement begins, you can put so many possible Gann and Fibonacci retracement levels on a chart that the actual retracement is sure to hit one of them. Many proponents chose to display the retracements that qualify and neglect to mention the ones that do not. But even sceptics are forced to look at the bigger retracement percentages, just in case this is the time the theory works.

Manipulating bars

All technical formulas involve manipulating the components of the bar – open, high, low, and close – in some manner to formulate a forecast of the next price action. Most indicators use the closing price over a series of periods but many, such as relative strength indicators, use the position of the close relative to the high or the position of the close relative to the high-low range. The logic is easy – when a price is closing near the high or near the high end of the high-low range, you have a buy signal, and when upward momentum fades and the close starts creeping away from the high or toward the lower end of the high-low range, your trend is weakening and possibly reversing. When the market flips and starts selling, you see the reverse pattern – closes near the low.

Reversals are often accompanied by ambiguous bars, such as the dreaded inside day, wherein the high is lower than the period before and low is less low than the day before. Another ambiguous bar is the candlestick named the doji, where the open and close are the same or nearly the same. By themselves, inside days and doji bars have no meaning and other tools have to be invoked.

Some bars have real meaning on their own. When the Swiss National Bank announced (in September 2011) it was taking action to slow the pace of the euro's decline against the franc, the market took it very seriously indeed. Looking at Figure 8.5 we can see the bars immediately after the announcement are far bigger than the normal bar, and the move was prolonged without a corrective pullback. Then we had a period of tiny bars, far smaller than the norm. A set of abnormally small bars is the same thing as low volatility and they are a warning sign of a breakout – but they don't forecast in which direction the breakout will go! Then, as the euro began to creep down again, the SNB announced it wanted to peg the Swiss franc to the euro at around 1.20 and would take all measures necessary to achieve the level. Again, traders took the SNB very seriously. The euro put in another abnormally big bar followed by a series of tiny ones. The implication is that if the euro slips back again, the SNB will act again.

Figure 8.5 – EUR/CHF and intervention

The timeframe problem

Technical analysis means different things to different users depending on their timeframe. The professional bank trader has a horizon of a few minutes to a few hours, while the investor and hedger think in terms of months and years. We have a caveat here – one of the great virtues of technical analysis is that it works in all timeframes. Securities prices are fractal, meaning that we see the same patterns on a 15-minute chart as on a weekly chart, and many of the same technical tools can be used with equal facility on charts of wildly differing duration.

Someone with a big-picture view of how the global economy works may easily find confirmation of his views on long-term charts that are contradicted on shorter-term charts. Which is right, the long-term chart or the short-term one? A strategist will say there is less risk in sticking to the long-term worldview and its chart, while the short-term trader will quote Keynes ("In the long run, we are all dead") and prefer to make profits on both the upside and the downside, with no need for a worldview.

The long-term strategist has to be able to suffer bigger losses as prices move into corrections against the primary trend, and the short-term trader has far higher transaction costs. Bottom line, both long-term worldview managers and short-term traders in FX employ technical analysis to buttress their decisions or to design them in the first place. You never hear among FX market participants – as you often do among equity mangers – that technical analysis is voodoo nonsense or without value.

Fads and fashions

Technical analysis is just like any other human endeavour – subject to fads and fashions. In the early 1990s, the top indicator was the MACD described above. When the relative strength indicator named the *stochastic oscillator* was in fashion in the late 1990s, you got better trading results in your own book if you charted that indicator – because everyone was looking at it. Elliott Wave and Fibonacci never really went out of fashion, and moving averages seem to come back into prominence when the market is beset by two strong but opposing forces.

Ichimoku clouds

One of the current fashions is a Japanese candlestick charting technique named the *Ichimoku Kinko Hyo* cloud formation. On the chart, it resembles the swarm concept mentioned later in the chapter. See Figure 8.6 for an illustration of this. Ichimoku is based on moving averages but plotted using the halfway point of the high-low range (instead of the close), which has the effect of forming minor and major support and resistance areas (instead of lines). In some versions Ichimoku also projects the data back a certain number of days to confirm the formation of the support/resistance regions. When the price is above the support cloud, you buy.

Figure 8.6 – Ichimoku Cloud, EUR/USD

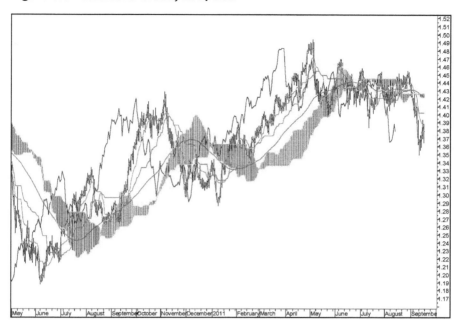

One of the great virtues of Ichimoku is that is can be applied to a chart comprised of one-minute bars as well as 15-minute bars, one-hour bars, or daily bars. This is not the case with every indicator. Some indicators do well on shorter timeframe charts (like relative strength) and some on longer timeframe charts (like MACD and indeed most moving averages). The best of all possible worlds is when you get the same buy or sell signal from three or more charts of different timeframes.

Systematic, rule-based trading

You cannot participate in the FX market or even read about the FX market without accepting that technical analysis is a central part of the industry. In fact, some technical events are on a par with the fundamentals in terms of reforming sentiment, like the Swiss threat of intervention shown in Figure 8.5. The upside breakout was caused in the first place by an institutional policy decision and then buttressed by a second policy announcement effect, but the move took on a technical life, too. The retracement of the first move off the early-August low to the end-August high was almost exactly 50% in the first week of September. As expected under Gann/Fibonacci rules, the recovery to the higher high did surpass the original high before fizzling out (where the chart ends).

Technicals do not exactly supersede fundamentals but they cannot be ignored, especially when benchmark levels are involved, such as the 20-day, 55-day, 100-day or 200-day moving averages, historical highs and lows, and breakouts of long-standing support and resistance. The speed of a move adds or subtracts power to the importance of a move and its underlying cause, and the size of the bars themselves contains information. These are factors that professional traders watch like hawks and everyone else has to watch them, too, including (presumably) some policy-makers.

One important aspect of technical trading in FX is that decisions tend to be more systematic and rule-based than in other markets. When the technical trader gets a sell signal, he obeys it because not to obey is to risk a job-threatening loss. Many others in the market are getting the same sell signal from the same or other indicators. In contrast, when a technical trader in equities gets a sell signal, he may not obey it because (1) he must hold that particular issue as part of a portfolio or (2) he is committed to the name or (3) the issue has an intrinsic fair value and the market is wrong to be selling it. You see the problem, of course – the market is never wrong. It may be analytically wrong or in an unreasoning panic, but the falling price is never wrong.

The rule-based aspect of technical trading in FX is useful. Technical traders place stop-loss orders and often profit targets, usually based on a trend extension, formal or intuitive. The widespread use of stop-loss orders means that when we see key levels get breached, we expect a cascade of stop-losses getting hit and a corrective move. When the currency becomes oversold and there is no one left to get square, the move will start up again. This is the natural rhythm of the FX market and once you get used to it, it makes perfect sense, even if the actual prices are straying quite far from what any economist would consider fair.

A riff on sentiment

The equity trader is lucky – he has to follow the news only about a specific company and its industry in order to deduce sentiment toward the company, and he has to judge whether and by how much a change in sentiment toward the equity market overall will affect his specific security. He has an indicator named beta that calculates the degree of correlation of the security to the benchmark. A beta of 1 means the security marches in lockstep with the index to which it belongs, a beta of -1 means they move inversely, and a beta of zero means they move independently of one another.

Understanding sentiment in the FX market is vastly more complicated. Sentiment covers a far wider and deeper range of factors, and because FX traders also use technical analysis, understanding sentiment means decoding the interaction between fundamental and institutional news and what is happening on the chart.

We might say that technical indicators measure market sentiment in several different ways, and market sentiment is formed at least in part on the fundamentals. But sentiment is also formed at least in part on what traders see on the chart. This can become confusing. We sometimes hear, usually from inexperienced reporters, that a particular price move was caused by a particular data release, when in fact the movement was dictated by chart developments. Traders interpreted the data to fit their already existing bias in sentiment, or they ignored the data altogether in favour of some other factor, and the other factor was a big, important chart indicator. In other words, chart events can be as important as fundamental events to the professional trader.

For example, the German research institute IFO's sentiment release is a closely watched data point that usually influences the euro/dollar rate. If the IFO index is lower than forecast, the euro should fall in response. But if the euro is already on a technically confirmed upswing, the market may choose to ignore the IFO release. The chart wins over data. When sentiment is negative, any rise will meet the bias to *sell on rallies*. When sentiment is favourable, any drop will be met with *buy on dips*.

The bandwagon effect

Market sentiment is a complex and delicate phenomenon. Traders want to buy if they perceive that other traders will be buying, too, offering them an opportunity to sell later at a profit. The market in any security is comprised of individuals all watching one another and that watchfulness takes the form of measuring actual supply and demand of the security at various prices. In an oversimplified way, this is George Soros' theory of reflexivity, in which a circular relationship of cause and effect becomes self-reinforcing. A trader buys a security because he thinks, for whatever reason, that a price should rise. Other traders observe the price rising and themselves buy, which is a form of positive feedback for the original trader, who then buys more.

This is called, sometimes somewhat dismissively, the *bandwagon effect*. It's a mistake to denigrate the phenomenon as herd behaviour. A crowd is more than the sum of the individuals participating. A crowd behaves differently from an individual. Crowd behaviour is studied by sociologists and political scientists, mostly in the context of law and order, and public safety, but the group of traders all concentrating on a single currency at the same time constitute a crowd, too.

And a crowd with a twist, in that while the individuals converge to trade with one another in a cooperative and collegial way, they are also rivals. So while it benefits everyone in the crowd to agree on many things, it benefits some individuals to game their cohorts, such as driving a price to a support level with the intention of spooking weaker hands into selling, so that they themselves can buy more cheaply. In recent years, the application of game theory has been joined by the study of swarm intelligence, which looks to the collective behaviour of decentralised and self-selected members of a group that seem to act as a single mind. Swarm ideas are modelled on things like fish schools all avoiding the shark or a flock of birds all mysteriously changing direction at once (and back again). Today we have the math, but the swarm concept as applied to securities traders is over 170 years old – Charles MacKay wrote about it in 1841 in *Extraordinary Popular Delusions and the Madness of Crowds*.

The important thing to take away from perceiving the FX market as a crowd is that its behaviour is not irrational. At price extremes during manias and panics, some members may be acting irrationally, but each member of the crowd has a single, rational goal – achieving a profit from the other members of the crowd by buying low and selling high, or buying high and selling higher. Persons who exhibit persistent irrationality in trading decisions get the Darwinian chop.

Self-fulfilling prophecies

Reflexivity is more intricate than the simple feedback loop. It also touches on how a completely false assumption can be made to seem true by outcomes that are predicated on the assumption. Logicians rightly call it a fallacy but the foreign exchange market is chock-full of events based on *post hoc, ergo propter hoc* (after this, because of this).

Here's how it works.

So many participants believe the false assumption that they act in such a way as to make the deduction from the assumption appear to validate the assumption. An example is the euro falling by an abnormally large amount when the rumour first appeared (in February 2011) that Bundesbank chief Weber would not seek a second term as BBK Chairman and also remove himself from consideration for the chairmanship of the ECB upon Trichet's retirement in October 2011. Over the three days from first rumour to the naming of Weber's replacement, the euro fell by more than the usual daily amount.

But everyone knew the assumption was false that only Weber would fight inflation in the strict manner that is the core of Bundesbank policy; also false was the assumption that only a German from the Bundesbank would make a suitable replacement for Trichet. Any number of other qualified central bankers, German or not, would serve well. And even as traders were smart enough to acknowledge that selling the euro on the Weber resignation news was silly because it was unlikely in the extreme that policy would change at either the BBK or ECB, the traders observed others selling the euro for those reasons. It would be foolhardy to be right on the policy assumption but to trade against the crowd and take a loss. In the end, it was announced that Bank of Italy's Mario Draghi would replace Trichet – and the euro did not move at all on the announcement. To the FX trader, this is a perfectly rational and normal price behaviour.

Market extremes

Another valuable contribution to the trading world by Soros was to highlight the persistent market extremes that reflexivity causes. FX rates almost always overshoot, and then price extremes themselves influence the fundamentals that are thought to be the basis of informed trading in the first place. An example is the big drop in sterling from November 2007 at $2.1161 to the low of $1.3549 in January 2009. A big exchange rate decline like this is widely thought to create inflation in the form of higher import prices.

Sure enough, market chatter and consumer and business surveys became increasingly focused on impending inflation and the higher inflation expectations that in turn influenced inflation itself. The Bank of England admitted that they were monitoring inflation expectations because expectations can so easily and quickly create the behaviours that actually cause inflation. Consumers accelerate big-ticket purchases to get ahead of rising prices, for instance, and businesses believe they can raise prices because everyone knows inflation is impending. As 2010 and early 2011 progressed, higher inflation did emerge, along with the expectation that the Bank of England would be forced to raise interest rates earlier than otherwise expected. Sterling rose on the prospect of an end to quantitative easing and outright rate hikes. By the time inflation rates started to fall back, three of nine Monetary Policy Committee members had told the press they favoured anti-inflation policy changes. Thus an extreme price influences perception of the fundamentals and often the fundamentals themselves, resulting in another cycle of self-reinforcing market prices and fundamentals.

Equilibrium is hokum

An important implication of Soros' reflexivity thesis is that the mainstream economist's concept of equilibrium is hokum in the context of free markets. Equilibrium is a useful concept that allows economists to model prices but we must never forget that it is a theoretical fiction. In a market for goods and services, higher prices incentivise new suppliers to come into existence, and higher new supply drives prices downward. Meanwhile, demand follows the familiar downward sloping curve – i.e., demand falls at ever-higher prices. Markets for regular goods and services are self-regulating in that each round of price changes affects the mix of supply and demand. For long stretches of time, equilibrium prevails during which one incremental unit of supply brings out exactly one unit of demand and the price is, therefore, stable and in equilibrium.

This is demonstrably not true in financial markets. While technically the absolute number of shares outstanding is the limit of supply in an equity market, for example, in most financial securities, including foreign exchange, new contracts can be created out of thin air. At one point during the summer of 2008, for example, when oil was trading at $144.32 (2 July 2008) there were more contracts for barrels of oil being traded on the New York Mercantile Exchange than there were barrels of oil in existence at the delivery depot in Cushing, Oklahoma. This is a possible outcome because of a high ratio of speculators to actual oil companies that would want to take physical delivery at Cushing, Oklahoma. In the foreign exchange market, only a tiny fraction of all the trades done daily ever go to actual delivery in the checking accounts of the players. The size of the FX market is infinitely elastic; anyone with a checking account and a FX line of credit at a trading bank can create a trade as long as a counterparty can be found.

Thus there is little or no supply constraint in many financial markets and especially in the FX market. Demand that goes to an extreme on self-reinforcing assumptions results not in price equilibrium, however fleeting, but in disequilibrium. In fact, it is Soros' position that it is the very nature of financial markets to tend toward disequilibrium. Soros deserves credit for explaining this origin of financial boom-bust crises.[58] Not always so welcome is his observation that the FX market is inherently unstable.

Market leaders and positional bias

The FX market readily accepted the concept of reflexivity, since it is so obviously what is at work. In a world where money has a price but no value anchor, traders are free to overshoot to their heart's content. One factor that Soros is discreet about mentioning is that as a market leader, his reasoning and actions are the subject of intense scrutiny. More than once Soros has been falsely named as behind some move or another, and sometimes Soros takes the trouble to respond. Once a rumour begins that Soros is backing a particular move, traders pile in to the same trade on the strength of the Soros name, even if they do not know or understand the reasoning behind it.

Today, market leaders are hedge funds and sovereign wealth funds. During 2010 and 2011, as the euro came under repeated pressure because of the European peripheral debt problem, we could read that sovereign wealth funds were buying euro on dips, often during the Asian or early London session. This is useful information because the level at which big players are buying can become a floor. Later, in 2012, the Chinese sovereign wealth fund announced its dissatisfaction with the pace of institutional reform and political responsiveness, and declared it would not add any more European sovereign debt to its portfolio. The euro weakened noticeably for a few days, and gradually sentiment changed from *buy on dips* creating a floor to one of traders preferring to *sell on bounces*, creating a ceiling.

The biggest player of all is the small group of very large banks that execute trades for hedge funds and sovereign wealth funds, as well as corporate hedgers. The sole goal of the interbank trader is to make a profit for his employer, whether by adding a tiny spread to trades for other big players or by taking the same or similar trades to those of market leaders. We all read the same newswires, but the big players get information about customer order flow that the rest of us seldom hear about and can only deduce. A somewhat strange outcome is that professional bank FX traders do not try to guess what economic and financial data means, but rather how their big customers will trade just before and just after the releases. Note that the professional newswires offer, for a fee, breaking news a few seconds earlier to some big players like hedge funds and sovereign wealth funds.

All the attention paid to the behaviour of the first responders, the big players, implies there is no single correct way to interpret the effect of data on exchange rates. Professional FX traders do not make trades based on a theory of the fundamentals, *but their prime customers do*. A great deal depends on the sentiment already existing in the market as important data releases come out. Professional traders have to know that sentiment and thus can guess the effect that any particular release is likely to have on customer behaviour. If the market has a pre-existing bias in favour of the dollar, a bad news release may get brushed off, whereas when the bias is dollar-negative, a bad release gets an exaggerated effect.

Therefore, the *number one* inefficiency in foreign exchange is the dependency of the interpretation of information on pre-existing sentiment. The efficient market theory that captured the imagination of equity traders never got much traction in the FX market. FX traders know from harsh experience that the FX market is not efficient – exploiting inefficiencies is how they make a living. The efficient market theory postulates that all equity market participants have equal access to the relevant information about each equity and therefore each equity price is perfect, or at least it's as good as it can be. To the many criticisms of the efficient market theory, for foreign exchange we need to add the subjective sentiment bias of the big players to whom the big banks cater. This is why traders may not be copying big players on the basis of their ideas, but they trade that way.

This is not to say that some important market sectors do not use big-picture fundamentals to take positions in the FX market, including top hedge funds. Indeed, one of the most famous American investors for the past three decades, Warren Buffett, embraces value investing for equities and made a $12 million bet against the dollar in 2002 on the basis of fundamentals – that the US trade and budget deficits would push the dollar ever lower. Buffett raised the amount to $20 billion as of January 2005 but cut back to $16.5 billion in June 2005 (after losing nearly $1 billion in the first half). He closed the account in August 2008. Since Buffett made the FX trades in the name of his publicly-traded company, Berkshire Hathaway, FX gains and losses were reported quarterly. Sometimes the quarterly outcome was a giant gain ($2.96 billion in Q2 2004) and sometimes it was a loss ($926 million in the first half of 2005).

Another case of trading on the Big Picture is George Soros' $10 billion bet against the pound in 1992, inspired by a judgment that an institutional arrangement (UK membership in the European Rate Mechanism) had been done at an unsustainable rate. Soros purportedly made over $1 billion on this series of trades and is said to have "broken the Bank of England." The word 'broken' is a misnomer, of course; the Bank of England survived. The sterling rout, however, did motivate the Bank to intervene in the FX market and to spend £1.33 billion of the national reserves, to no avail. In the end, the pound fell 10.1% against the Deutsche Mark and 6.8% against the dollar. Early in sterling's downward trend, the bandwagon effect took over and other traders piled into the short sterling trade, making the Soros forecast a self-fulfilling prophecy.

Buffett and Soros are rare birds – most big FX market players keep their opinions close to their chest. Ray Dalio of the Bridgewater hedge fund was profiled in the *New Yorker* magazine in 2011 and was characteristically cagey about the mix of fundamental and technical tools he uses. Today one of the main purveyors of big-picture FX market forecasting is the less-shy commodities trader Jim Rogers.

In the wider market, surveys of FX managed account funds split them into technical model-driven and discretionary, meaning the managers apply judgment based on fundamental analysis. Discretionary managers are secretive but it's hard to imagine any fund manager surviving for long by applying theory or ideology that dictates trades against the prevailing trend for the simple reason that those who take massive short-term losses tend to lose their jobs no matter how compelling their argument. After all, the job of a manager is to make money for the clients, not to be analytically correct.

Secret technicals at work

Buffett was not shy about his negative view of the US twin deficits and his embrace of the idea that they would inevitably lead the dollar lower. But even if he had said nothing about using technical analysis, we could replicate much of the Buffett anti-dollar trade using simple moving averages. For all we know, Buffett was advised by someone using these exact tools.

Here's the set-up: buy when the 55-day moving average moves over the 100-day moving average and/or the 100-day moving average moves over the 200-day moving average.

This is what we have done in Table 8.1. Here we used weekly data, with the 55-day becoming the 11-week, the 100-day becoming the 20-week and the 200-day becoming the 40-week moving average. The buy/sell signals line up almost exactly to the public information about Buffett's trades.

Table 8.1 – exponential moving average crossovers during Buffett trade

	Upside crossover	Downside crossover	Upside crossover	Downside crossover
4/19/2002	11-week > 20-week			
4/19/2002	20-week > 40-week			
5/27/2005		11-week < 40-week		
06/10/2005		20-week < 40-week		
4/29/2006			11-week > 20-week	
5/25/2006			20-week > 40-week	
8/15/2008				11-week < 20-week
9/26/2008				20-week < 40-week

Buffett has never disclosed whether there was any technical component to the timing of his trades, but the key point here is that you don't need to go to all the trouble of understanding the effect of deficits on exchange rates, or engage in lengthy, complex and expensive fundamental analysis. All you really need to duplicate a Buffett track record is a handful of moving averages – a sobering thought.

Conclusion

The factors that traders observe in order to determine their trades – which direction, how much, how long a holding period – are a vast universe. As described in Chapter 1 on the FX matrix, the factors include economic data, central bank philosophy and rate decisions, institutional adequacy, politics, and so on. Technical indicators are, collectively, on a par with these fundamentals.

We know how much weight to give to a fundamentals announcement only by how the market responds to it as revealed on the chart. No economic indicator, like the IFO sentiment index or US non-farm payrolls, has a certain effect on the euro or the dollar. When the dollar is on the upswing, a bad payrolls number is disregarded and the dollar's upward trend continues in spite of it.

To complicate matters further, traders know that other traders are watching specific technical levels and try to trick them, such as driving a price just past a resistance level to squeeze out the shorts. This gaming behaviour occurs in equity and other markets, too, but it is endemic to FX and technicals-dependent to a far greater degree. Anyone who tries to transfer skills from another market to FX will dismiss and disregard technical analysis at his great peril.

CHAPTER 9 –
THE FX FILES OF TRADING

As part of the assessment of FX risk, it is important to understand the trader psyche as well as the effect of the seismic changes that have taken place in the trading world in the past 20 years.

In terms of psyche, or what makes a trader tick, not much has changed over the years. A trader wants to make money; he wants to make money for himself, for his bank or fund, and for his sense of wellbeing.

While the basic trading instinct, to make money, remains the same, in the past two decades traders have had to adapt to a changing world, one where computers, rather than humans, play an ever increasing role.

This chapter explores these changes.

FX roots

While currencies have been traded for thousands of years, mostly by importers and exporters with the help of bankers, the FX market as we know it today took roots in the 1970s. In 1972, the Chicago Mercantile Exchange (CME) introduced currency futures. This move came less than a year after the "Nixon shock" of August 1971, whereby then President Richard Nixon delinked the dollar from gold and effectively ended the Bretton Woods agreement of fixed exchange rates.

The CME's intention was to provide non-bank players with the ability to trade currencies, whether for speculation or as a hedge. At this point, inter-bank players had a monopoly on the currency market. Anyone needing to buy or sell currencies was restricted to dealing with these institutions, and had to pay whatever the price, if they could get a price at all.

This began to change in May 1971, when the CME's International Money Market (IMM) launched seven currency futures contracts. The contracts were in British pounds, Canadian dollars, Deutsche Marks, French francs, Japanese yen, Mexican pesos and Swiss francs. Economist Milton Friedman, an advocate of the futures exchange, explained why a new currency trading platform was needed:

> "At the time the Bretton Woods agreement was in existence. And currencies, foreign currencies, were traded at pegged exchange rates. Exchange rates were changed sometimes by large amounts but only at long intervals. There was none of that day-to-day price movement and fluctuations which is the very life blood of futures markets which is necessary in order to have a volume of trading that will enable hedgers to hedge and speculators to speculate."[59]

There was no shortage of banks to make prices, and in New York, London, Frankfurt and Tokyo, the global banking industry blossomed in the 1970s, 1980s and 1990s. Just as US banks opened branches abroad, foreign banks increasingly began to have a presence overseas as well, with new branches opened in New York, London, Singapore, Hong Kong and Tokyo. Most of these branches had their own Treasury department, which typically housed an FX dealing room designed to serve clients and speculate. A typical trading/dealing room contained a chief dealer, various other senior and junior dealers, corporate sales people, and position keepers and back office staff.

Even with new players in the FX arena, the currency market remained cloistered, with a handful of key traders setting the prices, especially for larger currency deals. Trading between banks was via telephone, either interbank or via a voice broker, while a bank's customer trading was done via the phone or occasionally via telex. From the 1970s into the early 1990s it was largely business as usual until the advent of the electronic dealing machines.

Enter the electronic dealing platforms

In the early 1980s, Reuters introduced Reuters Market Data Service (RMDS), which was the precursor of the current Reuters dealing system. The RMDS allowed parties to show their interest to buy or sell a currency, and then later a price would be agreed upon over the telephone. In 1987, Reuters introduced Reuters-Dealing 2000-1 which, although a system for electronic trading, did not revolutionise the market. The D2000-1 was more like an advanced telephone and made the direct trading that used to take place over the telephone more efficient.[60]

Reuters Dealing 2000-2 was introduced in April 1992 and this time competitors soon followed, with Minex launched by Japanese banks in April 1993 and EBS (Electronic Brokering Services) launched by a consortium of US banks in September 1993. Minex was acquired by EBS in December 1995 and Reuters launched the current platform Reuters Dealing 3000 in 2000.

The advent of electronic dealing platforms levelled the playing field between big bank and small bank – everyone could see the prices at the same time and have a sense of the volume behind the pricing. This took away some, but certainly not all, of the trading advantage that big players had in the market.

FX gets wired

FX was bound to get *wired* at some point, but it took time in comparison to other asset classes, such as equities. A May 2011 Celent study[61]noted that "banks are leading the way" in adoption of electronic trading systems (ETS) in the FX asset class, with 92% of transactions being done through electronic trading systems in 2009. Asset management companies' and corporate entities' use of ETS for currencies was 66% and 50% respectively in 2009, according to the study.

Currency trading has become more *wired* than ever before, with everything from pricing to back office confirmations increasingly being done electronically. While the electronic trading platforms have resulted in tighter prices, increased liquidity and ease of trade, the platforms are not without their downside.

A surprise in the 2010 BIS survey was that commercial banks were doing fewer FX trades, for the first drop ever. In terms of trading counterparties, the BIS noted that the higher global turnover was associated with "increased trading activity of 'other financial institutions' a category that includes non-reporting banks, hedge funds, pension funds, mutual funds, insurance companies, and central banks, among others." The turnover in this category increased to $1.9 trillion in April 2010, up 42% from the $1.3 trillion seen in April 2007 and dwarfed the $1.5 trillion in turnover of transactions between reporting dealers. "For the first time, activity of reporting dealers with other financial institutions surpassed inter-dealer transactions (i.e., transactions between reporting dealers)," the BIS said.

In December 2010, the BIS released an in-depth study to explain the move away from trading with commercial banks. As there was no mechanism in the triennial survey to get a breakdown of what trades were being done where, the BIS used other tactics, including discussions with market participants, data from regional FX surveys and an analysis of the currency composition and location of trading activity. The findings suggested that the increased turnover was driven by: greater activity of high-frequency traders; more trading by smaller banks that are increasingly becoming clients of the top dealers for the major currency pairs; and the emergence of retail investors (both individuals and smaller institutions) as a significant category of FX market participants.

A key driver for these heightened trading flows is the spread of electronic execution methods, in that they reduced transaction costs and increased market liquidity. This, in turn, encouraged more customers to participate.

FX trading platforms have multiplied over the past ten years, growing from a handful to over 20-plus reputable (and many less-than-reputable) firms. As currency trading became its own asset class in the mid-2000s, retail traders were eager to use these platforms. The currency prices on these platforms are supplied mostly by bank traders. As one trader explained, "The money making strategy of most large banks is to get everyone trading on their platform – this is a winner 90% of the time and only loses on large trend days."

The BIS noted that a key turning point for algorithmic trading came in 2004, when electronic broker ECB launched EBS Spot Ai (Ai stood for automated interface). This provided a computer interface to banks, by which the ECB enabled algorithmic trading in spot FX markets using the real-time prices quoted on EBS. The EBS Spot Ai service was extended to major bank customers in 2005 and allowed hedge funds and other traders to gain access to inter-dealer markets – the deepest and most liquid part of the FX market – via their prime brokerage accounts with the biggest dealers.

Algomania

While the greater participation lauded by the BIS can be deemed a good thing, traders often lament the presence of the *algos*, which can make their lives miserable in several ways. Algorithmic models now make prices not only to bank traders, but also directly to corporate clients, thereby stripping away the middle man in some cases. There are predatory algos also, who try to push FX trends or arbitrage between currencies, thereby wreaking havoc and/or diminishing traders' profits.

On the plus side, FX algo models can also be designed to track client flows. "Sophisticated computers have a profile for everyone who deals them," one trader interviewed explained. So if Bank A is a custody bank or a bank that sees larger central bank or sovereign wealth fund flows, the computer will look back to see what has happened historically when Bank A sells, for example, $50 million versus the yen.

In the algo arena, it is the high frequency trading (HFT) and latency models that rile FX traders the most. In the past, there was always a trader at one bank who would look for price anomalies and try to make money from some hapless trader at another bank who wasn't fast enough to change his price on market moving events. One trader interviewed for this book observed, "Those traders were branded as pickers and you would try not to deal with them – now the geeks on the other side don't care; they don't understand the etiquette of the market place."

Traders interviewed also addressed the issue of *pinging* or *high frequency probing*. Like a submarine might use sonar to estimate distance, some high frequency models chip away at a price until they find the point where the bid or the offer side would give way. For example, if a model wants to sell €100 million, it might test the waters first by either offering out a few euro at a time or by hitting the bid.

In a September 2011 paper[i], the BIS fretted about prime brokers becoming overwhelmed with the sheer size of the bookkeeping and taking on more exposure to risky positions than they would like because they couldn't keep up. Regulators in several countries, including the UK, US and Australia, are contemplating new rules that would mandate a ratio of bid-offer requests to completed trades. This would reduce pinging but, as usual with regulations, create unintended consequences.

One of these consequences would be to restrict non-pinging "contingency" trades, such as re-entry at such-and-such a level if a stop or price target is hit. The implication is that high frequency traders would be reined in at the expense of ordinary speculators, and conventional wisdom has it that speculation injects much-needed liquidity into markets.

Bigger is better – effect of bank size on FX trading

The major banks have had in the past, and generally still have, an acute trading advantage over medium to smaller sized banks. The *big* banks have larger credit limits and a greater number and variety of clients, which allows them to see additional trading flows, which can be informative as well as profitable. Big banks also can take larger trading positions and therefore have a greater ability to influence currency prices when the market is illiquid.

Prior to the advent of 24-7 financial news coverage, big banks heard rumours and larger news events first. They often had overseas sources that would relay market-moving commentary from central bank heads or pass on information about larger order flows. By the time the news was posted on Reuters or Telerate, the two main news sources of the day in the 1980s, big banks usually had a several minute or more trading advantage. If a trader at medium to smaller sized bank did get a tidbit of information, he might choose to call the big bank trader to tell them what he had heard in order to get a more favourable price on an upcoming trade.

If a bank couldn't be *big* and the master of all currency trading, then it tried to specialise in a niche currency. Portuguese banks made the best escudo prices and Irish banks made the best Irish punt prices. The major European Union countries all had bank branches in the US, with the trading arms located in New York City and select other US cities. There were at least four or five major Italian, German and French banks in the early 1980s, all promising to offer the best prices in their home currencies.

The advent of the euro in January 1999 changed the FX landscape irrevocably. The world lost 11 currencies that day as Belgium, Germany, Spain, France, Ireland, Italy, Luxembourg, the Netherlands, Austria, Portugal and Finland gave up their currencies for the newly minted euro – the single currency that was expected to eventually rival the US dollar.

Bank consolidation was fierce after the euro made its debut, with most European banks merging or retrenching. Those who made profits solely by being a niche bank lost their cash cow and could not be competitive with major banks. Several foreign banks closed their New York offices and concentrated on domestic markets instead.

Traders who used to trade the EMU country currencies had to find something new to trade. Volumes in Aussie and Canadian dollar rose markedly. Emerging market currencies came back in vogue, although the memory of the Asia crisis of 1997/1998 made market players wary of holding larger positions in these currencies given the proven lack of liquidity. From 2000 onward, however, increased globalisation led to renewed interest in emerging market currencies. Banks that once had a single niche currency and lost this business because of advent of the euro could again specialise, this time in Latin American, Asian, or Eastern European or African currencies.

The Spanish peseta trader became a Mexican peso trader, adapting his prior skill set to a new, equally volatile trading pair. Mutual funds and pension funds, along with the ever-multiplying sovereign wealth funds, would buy the stocks and bonds of emerging market currencies, creating FX flows and the need for traders to cover these currencies.

While big banks offer an extensive menu of FX products, some clients prefer the hands-on treatment and confidentiality received from dealing with a smaller bank, especially in niche markets. If a central bank or sovereign wealth fund wants to step in covertly, using a small bank might attract a lot less attention than going through a larger bank, unless it is a sizable trade. A big bank might get the same order and let the news out that this central bank or SWF was dealing with them, to show that they were indeed a player. A smaller bank would have greater reason to want the account to be a repeat customer and would try to keep the trade off the market's radar screen.

Price discovery

Electronic trading has mostly levelled the playing field between big bank and small bank and big corporate and small corporate in terms of FX pricing. However, larger banks still have an advantage when it comes to pricing and liquidity.

Traders currently argue that today, even more than in the past, FX trading is all about *price discovery*, i.e. finding out where you can get the best real price on your amount. It is helpful to be a trader at a bank that has its own FX platform because you see order flow from clients as well as traditional corporate orders. Unlike earlier years, where prices on EBS or Reuters Matching would shape the price of an FX pair, now price discovery is within the bank.

Larger banks still see at times sizable custody and other client flow, which allows them to *hop on board* a currency trade, expecting that the sheer size of the trade will move a currency pair higher or lower. This is especially true in emerging markets, where a larger FX deal has a greater impact. The thinking is that when they see global investors piling into a certain market, they know these flows are going to move the market. If traders see them lining up one way, how hard is it to go with them? In this context, it's astonishing that regulators never accuse big banks of "front-running" the customers for their own account, possibly because the traders can say, plausibly, that they are merely anticipating a trend and therefore their clients' expected upcoming orders.

There are times where the size of the deal is too large for one trader to handle and, as in the past, he reaches out to others in the dealing room to get prices from outside the bank. Whereas in the olden days, the spot trader would stand up and say "I need calls," now when a big client deal is being executed, the spot trader effectively says "I need mouse clicks." In this case, price discovery cannot be internal, but rather is clearly outside the bank.

Last look

The hot topic of *last look* came up in several discussions with traders. One trader offered this example:

> The market for the euro is $1.42821 bid for €10 million and a bit below that is a $1.4282 bid for €50 million. A trader, wanting to sell €50 million or more, might just hit the bid at $1.4282 to get the whole amount done in one fell swoop. In the case of banks that have a *last look* feature, they have the ability, in a nanosecond, to see if they can get out of the €50 million and if not, say the deal is not done or is only partially done. The dealer on the other side sees only *trade failed* with all this action done in the blink of an eye. The bank making the price got *the last look at the market.*

Using the same example to show the sophistication of algos in getting the best price, the trader might sell his €10 million at $1.42821 and try to sell the balance of €40 million at $1.4282. In this case, the algo might see the initial €10 million trade and pull its bid – again, all in the blink of an eye.

In contrast to banks, which have seen their FX margins shrink from diminishing price spreads, hedge fund traders are happy with the perks that have been the result of stepped up algorithmic model use. Algos "provide more liquidity and tighter prices," they say. One trader reckoned that without algos, the spread between the euro bid and offer would be 3 pips wide instead of 1 pip (or less) and called it "a nice cost savings." He added, "There is more liquidity at the point of entry – when you want to trade."

Corporate clients also like that prices are tighter, which means that the cost of their FX hedges are generally reduced. Multi-national corporations also now often have trading platforms on their desk and know far better now than in the past what a fair market price looks like. The buy side, i.e. non-bank clients such as mutual, pension and hedge funds and corporations, have gotten "a whole lot smarter" in recent years, another trader said.

Price discovery can on occasion be illusive, especially in times of great volatility like that seen in the months after Lehman Brothers declared bankruptcy and as the euro zone peripheral debt crisis erupted in waves in 2011.

Stewart Hall, senior currency strategist, at the time at RBC Capital Markets, had this to say about the state of financial markets and price discovery in October 2011:

> "Euro zone policy is not crafted in a vacuum, although at times it seems to reflect a vacuum like existence. By extension, markets do not constitute the rational decision making actors and processes that the text books suggest. Indeed, price discovery has become a voyage in the last months that has certainly felt vacuous at times. In that is a recipe for exceptional pricing gyrations as is recognised in option pricing and market risk reversals."

In the September 2011 paper mentioned earlier in this chapter, the BIS addressed the sharp 300 drop in dollar-yen seen on 17 March 2011. The drop took place in a period of 25 minutes. Liquidity, or lack thereof, during this timeframe, was clearly an issue, with the electronic platforms overwhelmed by the volume of trades. "Prices, that you could see could not be dealt on by people," said one yen trader of that occasion.

> "Because of the system halts, clients were not able to post additional margins or close positions to avoid triggering automatic stop-outs. When the retail aggregators proceeded with the compulsory stop-outs, it resulted in a wave of USD selling in a relatively thin market. As a result, USD/JPY started to exhibit a free fall. Many banks withdrew from market-making. Those that continued to make markets widened their spreads so much that their bids were far below the last prevailing market price, making it difficult for counterparties to accept and transact. A vicious cycle of USD/JPY fall and

stop-losses ensued, until the pair hit ¥76.25 at around 06:20. In the next 30 minutes or so, USD/JPY recovered to ¥78.23 as hedge funds and new retail investors began to build up fresh USD/JPY long positions. Banks, having withdrawn from making prices during the most volatile period, also resumed market-making," the BIS said.

In this case, as is always the case, liquidity was, and is, only as good as the prices being made by the providers on the electronic platforms.

Algo news

Algo news feeds bear a brief mention because they put the human trader at a clear disadvantage. In the ten seconds it takes for a trader to read and digest a key data release, such as the latest monthly US nonfarm payrolls report, algorithmic models have already assessed the information and entered into trades as a result of the data. Most major news wires offer some sort of algo-data feed, that sends the news directly into the model, which can crunch the numbers and make a decision in a nanosecond. It can be argued that sometimes there are revisions or errors made in transmitting the data, but most releases run smoothly and offer those utilising algos a clear trading advantage. In addition to economic data, news stories, especially *sources* stories, can also be fed directly into the algo model, which will then parse the words and make a trading recommendation.

Conclusion

Whether traders are *talking their own book* or speaking truthfully about the downside of using electronic platforms or algorithmic models, they do not seem to fear that algos will completely take over. The AITE group advised *The Economist* magazine in February 2012 that over 25% of FX trading is algo-based, compared to 65% of trading in equities. We have no reason to suppose that algo trading in currencies will not reach equity market levels at some point in the near future. However, while algo models can't be beat in terms of speed, the human trader has contributions, too, such as detecting when a bid being hit is just a fat-finger error and knowing when to turn off the model if need be.

CHAPTER 10 –

BE CAREFUL WHAT YOU WISH FOR: RESERVE DIVERSIFICATION AND THE FUTURE OF THE DOLLAR

"We have gold because we cannot trust Governments."

Herbert Hoover to President-elect Franklin Delano Roosevelt

Introduction

The dollar is currently the single biggest reserve currency. Reserve currency status always creates policy difficulties for the issuer and for the rest of the world, chiefly because the issuer wishes to manage growth and inflation policies for its own self-interest and those policies can clash with the needs of the reserve-holders. It is inherently unfair for a single nation to have so much power over the financial fortunes of other nations, who perceive the reserve issuer is dictating their policies. Critics of the reserve currency regime in place today, including important institutions like the World Bank, call for a new regime.

More poppycock is written about the decline of the dollar and the need for a new gold standard and new reserve currencies than any other topic pertaining to foreign exchange. People unschooled in economic theory and economic history assert the principle that the dollar is on the road to perdition because the US abandoned the gold standard, first in 1933 and again in 1971. On no other FX-related subject do emotions run so high.

And yet the dollar remains the numeraire for some 75% of world trade and the dollar remains the top reserve currency among nations. What is at the heart of the persistence of the dollar as the premier reserve currency and on what basis might the euro replace it? The answers have to do with understanding the function of a reserve currency in the first place, which is intimately intertwined with concepts of sovereignty and of country risk. We live in a revolutionary time when these words are being redefined.

What is a reserve currency?

A reserve currency is the currency issued by a sovereign state that both public and private parties in other states use in commerce and finance as a *numeraire*. Throughout history, countries that trade with one another have found it most efficient to use a single currency.

On the whole, it was the merchants themselves who decided what currency they wanted to use. In the days of Byzantium, it was the gold-based bezant. From the end of the US Civil War to the 1930s, it was the UK pound. From the Bretton Woods agreement in 1944 to today, it has been the dollar. Gold coins of various issuers were, until the late 20th century, almost always acceptable in commerce once their weight was proved, and gold remains today a key component of official government reserves in every country.

Merchants seek the efficiency of a numeraire. Efficiency is the goal of governments in choosing a reserve currency, too – in the event of a sudden need for armaments or food, their reserve money must be accepted immediately by all suppliers.

You might think that the merchants could choose their own numeraire for trade and a government treasury could choose a different currency for reserves, but historically, it hasn't worked that way. A possible reason is that states acquire reserves by buying the foreign money earned by their own merchants in return for the local currency they themselves issue. Sometimes this is compulsory – merchants are not allowed to hold foreign currency.

You don't have to be a sovereign to issue a currency. Before the Federal Reserve was established in 1913, individual banks throughout the US issued their own banknotes.[62] Today we have the strange phenomenon of a new creation named the *bitcoin*, a digital currency that actually works to enable real-world transactions without the benefit of a known issuer or fixed value in other currencies.

Moreover, you can be a sovereign and not issue your own currency. Many countries have used the UK pound, pre-EMU French franc, or US dollar as their home currency, including India, Argentina and the countries of French West Africa. The Australian dollar as we know it today was created only in 1966 when the country gave up the Australian Pound, introduced in 1910 and fixed to the British pound. The introduction of the AUD came over 50 years after the Commonwealth of Australia was established in 1901 as an independent country. Australians would argue that their country is entirely its own sovereign, although no one doubts that if the Queen asked, Australia would send troops.

How to qualify for reserve currency status

To qualify as a numeraire and reserve currency, i.e., to be accepted by merchants, creditors and governments, a currency has to meet four criteria:

1. There has to be enough of it to go around, what we today call *liquidity*. You may think, for example, that the Swiss franc would make a dandy numeraire for world trade, but Swiss money supply is less than the equivalent of $1 trillion and global exports plus imports in 2010 were $28 trillion.[63] There are not enough Swiss francs to go around.

2. Its purchasing power must be stable. Nobody wants to save up a currency that is likely to fall in value. Why might we suspect a currency will fall in value? In the absence of a gold backstop – and no currency in the world today is backstopped by gold – the main source of depreciation is inflation, which literally eats away purchasing power. Therefore, the central bank of the

reserve currency issuer must command the confidence of the users that it will manage inflation.

3. The reserve currency must offer investment opportunities. Nobody wants to sit on cash in a suitcase or under the bed that is not earning interest. The institutions offering investment opportunities have to include a wide range of maturities – from overnight to 30 years, and variety – from low-risk to high-risk in a selection of forms.

4. The reserve currency issuer must promise not to expropriate currency held by foreigners, as in sovereign default, or otherwise render it unavailable for an indefinite period of time, as in the application of capital controls.

The issuer must be able to defend itself militarily against any enemy which might unravel the first four qualifications, especially the last one.

The US qualifies on all counts as a reserve currency issuer. It has size, liquidity, variety of yields and maturities, military superpower status, and equal treatment under the law guaranteeing no expropriation (except in war-time). The US has never defaulted as a sovereign. In fact, it has everything except people's full, 100% faith in the anti-inflation resolve of the central bank. More to the point, no other country qualifies on all counts, except possibly the European Monetary Union and China, someday soon.

Predictions of the dollar's fall

The World Bank predicts that by 2025, six of the emerging market countries, including China, India and Brazil, will account for over half of all global growth and they will stop accepting the dollar as the single reserve currency[64]. It has said that the most likely global currency scenario in 2025 will be a multi-currency one centred around the dollar, the euro, and the renminbi. The World Bank refers to this multi-currency scenario as multipolarity. The Bank noted that the emerging markets as a group will grow by 4.7% per annum to 2025 while the advanced economies will grow by 2.3% p.a. on average, with international financial institutions needing to adapt fast to keep up.

The distress cries about the decline and fall of the dollar wax and wane over time. In fact, they are as cyclical as the world economy and a lot has been written on the subject down the years. If you perform a web search using the phrase "decline of the dollar" you get 18 million entries; Amazon has 53 pages of books on the subject, and that's not counting the ones that have gone out of print and the acres of forest cut down to print Congressional hearings on the decline of the dollar. Setting aside the cranks and ideologues, many of the authors are clear thinkers with a coherent line of reasoning.

In the current cycle, a very large number of FX market observers believe that the accommodative monetary policy since the 2008-09 financial crisis must be inflationary, and the only way to surmount the now seemingly unsustainable US debt burden is inflation and devaluation. The logical conclusion for them is that loss of confidence in the dollar will lead to other currencies, first the euro and then the Chinese yuan, or a basket of emerging market currencies, taking over reserve currency status.

Unlikelihood of change

These distress cries, including the World Bank's warning above, are overly dramatic because historically reserve currency status was never the possession of a single nation and reserve currencies – as we will see – are destined to have just the kinds of problems that the dollar and its issuer the US does.

In 1913, sterling accounted for less than half of official reserves, with the French franc accounting for a third and the German mark, a sixth. In the interwar period of the 1920s and 1930s, reserve currency status was shared by sterling, the franc and the dollar. "The conventional wisdom that one currency dominates reserve holdings worldwide thus derives mainly from the second half of the 20th century alone, when the greenback accounted for as much as 85 percent of global foreign exchange reserves."[65]

The situation predicted by the World Bank further seems unlikely because we have no evidence that the European Monetary Union and/or China would chose to accept the high cost and responsibility of reserve currency status – including the obligation to serve as the lender of last resort to other central banks – even if others are clamouring for a dollar alternative.

Another issue is that reserve currencies are destined to persistent devaluation because global demand for the currency always outstrips the needs of the domestic economy. When the inevitable trade deficits are joined by fiscal deficits, devaluation accelerates. Most critiques of the US dollar fail to appreciate these points and the inability of any reform to overcome them – including elevating other currencies to reserve status, especially the euro and Chinese renmimbi.

Further still, a factor that most reserve currency critics do not address is the wide and deep spread of true capitalism in the two reserve currency nations of the past two centuries, the UK and the US. Capitalism is based on a legal system that allows leveraging property rights to create capital, which is more than mere money. The euro is supported by a like legal system but China is not, so far. Thus the dollar is likely to remain the top reserve currency, if not the only reserve currency, for the foreseeable future.

So, while commentators can agree on the diagnosis of an unjust system and may argue for the euro and renmimbi to become reserve currencies, the central banks of these currencies may be less keen because of the drawbacks associated with such a move – there is potentially a limit to the economic imbalances within the issuer country that reserve currency holders will accept. The US has flirted with this limit several times in the past (inflation) and is flirting with it again in the second decade of the 21st century (public overindebtedness). But people have been predicting the end of the dollar's reign as the reserve currency for over 60 years. Despite a drop in the percentage allocated to dollars by sovereigns from over 75% to 61% of total reserves over the past two decades, the dollar still retains preferred status. Many in the FX world accept the dollar's share will continue to drop – but we do not know where the capital will go or how fast.

In this chapter we will survey the unwelcome responsibilities and the criteria that must be met for reserve currency status, and reach the conclusion that the difficulties are so big and complex that regime change is unlikely over the next two decades. As a practical matter, for the US to lose its reserve currency status should be a very frightening prospect – for non-US investors. If you are a US citizen or policy-maker, losing reserve currency status would be wonderfully welcome, aside from the blow to national pride. On balance, for the dollar to lose reserve currency status belongs in the category of "be careful what you wish for."

Reserve currencies are always doomed

Economists have known the dollar was doomed from the moment the Bretton Woods agreement was signed in 1944. This is because reserve currencies are the fall-guy for conditions outside anyone's control, least of all the reserve currency issuer itself. It is the nature of the beast to fail in the end because the economic and financial consequences of taking the reserve currency role are heavy.

The inevitable decline and fall of the dollar is due to something called the Triffin Dilemma, also called the Triffin Paradox. Triffin was a Yale economics professor who identified that the reserve currency issuer has a duty to supply larger amounts of liquidity to the world market than optimum domestic policies would call for, thus running a current account deficit.[66]

This was evident during the late 1950s and 1960s, when nations and investors complained about the shortage of dollars (the dollar gap). Further, when the US Treasury decided to stop issuing the 30-year bond at end-October 2001 – because it was paying down the federal debt and didn't need to raise the funds – the investing world complained bitterly. In the end, suspension of the 30-year issuance was ended in February 2006 in part on rising deficits and an interest in diversifying liabilities, but also in acknowledgement of demand from pension funds and other large institutional investors, including reserve holders.

For foreigners, the paradox is that the issuer becomes ever more indebted to them even as the foreigners need to keep selling goods to the issuer and racking up surplus reserves. The solution for the foreign reserve holder, if it determines that the issuer has acquired an unsustainable amount of debt, is to contract its own economy. The reserve currency that was once the risk-free asset becomes ever riskier as both the reserve holder and the issuer face either severe economic contraction or default. For the issuer, the solution is to stop running trade deficits and to contract debt, thus limiting reserves, but then the world would become illiquid and risk a global contraction – exactly what happened in the Great Depression.

The dilemma for the rest of the world is accepting that the value of its reserves will almost certainly decline over time. The world has to trust and mistrust the reserve currency and its issuer at the same time. The dilemma for the issuer, in this case the US, is that policies optimum for the domestic economy tend to run counter to the best interests of reserve holders and other international investors.

Two policy issues rise to the top – all that liquidity risks inflation and all that debt creates doubt about the ability of any country to pay it back. Countries that cannot repay sovereign debt have an easy way out – devaluation. In Triffin's day, exchange rates were fixed and devaluation was an occasional thing. But in today's floating rate world, we still see a persistent tendency to devaluation of the reserve currency. See Figure 10.1, the dollar/mark from 1970 to 1999 and Figure 10.2, the euro from 1971 to the present. These charts are retrofitted (by eSignal) to the period before exchange rates were floated, with a linear regression line superimposed that clearly shows, despite pullbacks, the euro and its legacy predecessors were on a rising trajectory for over three decades.

Figure 10.1 – Dollar/Deutschemark (monthly)

Figure 10.2 – EUR/USD (1971 to July 2012, monthly)

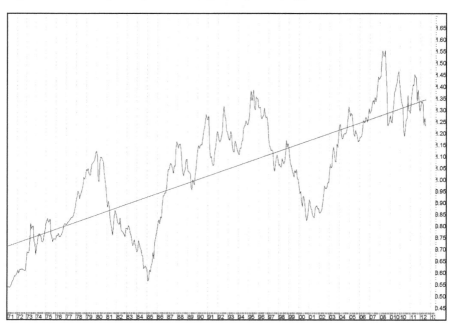

Some observers and participants decry the dollar's decline without grasping that decline is its essential nature as a reserve currency in an expanding world. Others find the dollar's decline an agreeable comeuppance for an arrogant self-appointed world leader that sometimes behaves badly on the world stage. But to colour the Triffin Dilemma with emotion from either side of the spectrum is to miss the critical point: both the reserve issuer and the reserve holders are in the same insoluble fix.

It is the very nature of a reserve currency to fall in value, whether rates are fixed or floating, because it is the reserve currency that facilitates global growth. The only way for the reserve currency not to devalue is for every international participant to embrace rates of growth and global trade far reduced from today's standards. In most countries with rising populations, this is not an acceptable choice. In a nutshell, the reserve currency issuer and reserve currency holders can have either a stable reserve currency or falling standards of living.

Somebody has to lead

The world needs a reserve currency for practical reasons, as described below, but the issuer of the reserve currency plays a far bigger role than just running the printing press – it is a leader in critical matters. It is vital that the world has a reserve currency of some kind; just look at what happens when leadership is lacking. Charles Kindelberger writes:[67]

> "The international economic system flourished, more or less, from 1870 to 1913 when Britain served as world economic leader. The public goods that it provided were a market for surplus or distress goods, a countercyclical source of capital, management of the gold standard that maintained a coherent set of exchange rates and coordinated macroeconomic policies, and the lender of last resort in crises. After 1913, Britain was unable to discharge these functions, and the United States was unwilling to do so. The Great Depression is largely ascribable to this gap."

Let's take two points from Kindelberger's statement.

First, the Great Depression may have begun in the US with the stock market crash of 1929 and the wrong monetary and fiscal policy choices, as often charged, but it's not clear that even the right policy choices in the US would have sufficed to end the crisis earlier in the absence of a properly functioning international financial system.

Second, the job of the reserve currency issuer is to lead the world economy in the sense that it provides a market for goods, is a source of capital, and acts as a lender of last resort. It is inherent in the job of reserve currency issuer that it accept imbalances in its own economy, especially a current account deficit, and that it lose control over its money supply. With vast amounts of reserve currency money in the hands of foreigners able to convert the money to gold (in the old days) or other currencies, in any amount at any time, the central bank of the reserve currency issuer cannot be said to control money supply in any meaningful way.

The chief risk of a shift from the dollar to other currencies as reserve currencies is exactly the same as the shift from the gold standard to the fiat-currency standard – an insufficiency of supply.

Miners do not produce new gold supplies at the same pace as world growth, and so investors substitute the reserve currency. That means the reserve currency issuer is vulnerable to any crisis of confidence in which holders want to exchange reserves for physical gold or some other currency.

This is the sense in which the Bretton Woods agreement that put the dollar at the centre of the financial system was flawed from the very beginning, and the US going off the gold standard in 1971 was inevitable. Before the dollar faced this problem, the UK faced it – and lost. In the interwar period 1918-1939, the UK was forced to go off the gold standard in September 1931, accompanied by a 30% devaluation of sterling (from $4.86 to $3.25 in three months). The US succumbed to the same influences in August 1971, the second year the US trade balance turned negative (for the first time since 1894), taking the dollar off the gold standard and floating the dollar two years later.

At the very centre of the Triffin Dilemma is that global money supply growth, both reflecting and enabling economic growth, is bigger and faster than the growth of gold supplies. In parallel, at the centre of the present-day dollar reserve currency debate is that the US is obligated to produce dollars at the rate of growth of the world, not its own rate of growth, or bearing in mind any other domestic consideration (like inflation). In the end, the leadership role of the reserve currency issuer includes an element of sacrifice for the greater good. Under the fiat money regime we have today, the reserve currency issuer courts inflation. Under the gold standard, the reserve currency country had to expend much effort to increase gold reserves – at the expense of producing all other public goods, like road and bridges. Being the reserve currency issuer may confer prestige, but it comes at a terrible cost.

The debate over gold vs. paper money

At the time of Bretton Woods, the gold coverage of the dollar was about 60%, meaning there was 60¢ of gold in reserve for every $1 of paper money. By the time the US went off the gold standard in August 1971, gold coverage had fallen to 22%. Under the gold standard, the only way the Federal Reserve could expand money supply would be to buy more gold. Abandoning the gold standard was a shock, but on the whole was a healthy development for the global economy, which expanded during the next decade at a far faster pace than before.

The change to the fiat currency basis was frightening to many. Switzerland had so big a capital inflow seeking a safe haven that it had to impose a capital surcharge on non-resident funds in June 1972. It was called a "negative interest rate," which is not strictly accurate. It was really a form of capital controls, along with a 100% reserve requirement on foreign deposits.[68] The first surcharge was 2% per quarter, raised to 3% and to 10% by February 1978.

What's so frightening about paper or *fiat* currencies? Fiat means "let it be done" in Latin, referring to government appointing itself the sole standard-setter. As economic historians and gold buffs alike are wont to remind us, governments tend to create over-supplies of fiat currencies – the Chinese did it in the 11th century – and thus create inflation. As President Hoover told incoming President Roosevelt in 1933: "We have gold because we cannot trust Governments."[69]

It is literally not practical for the reserve currency issuer to build its own reserves, whether of gold or other currencies, to support use of its currency outside it own borders. The US would have to take an amount equal to about one year of GDP to buy gold and other currencies in order to backstop the number of dollars in use outside the US around the world today. Where would it get such a sum? If the US government diverted funds from domestic spending on defence and social programs in order to build gold and currency reserves, its economy would contract and the voters would protest. More importantly, what would be the point? The real reason to build reserves to backstop global money supply would be to inspire confidence among foreigners using the dollar, which is not a platform one can easily imagine any US politician adopting.

The amount of dollars outside the US is bigger than the amount inside the US. As early as 1985, according to the Bank for International Settlements, dollar deposits in the London Eurodollar market were a larger amount than domestic money supply in the US. Note that the Eurodollar market is outside the regulatory reach of the US government and its agencies, including the central bank.

By 1997, 90% of cross-border international loans were dollar-denominated. By December 2008, the Eurodollar market was $9.7 trillion, more than US M2 money supply at the time – $8.054 trillion – even if you subtract the banknote component in M1 that is incorporated in M2.[70] (More US banknotes are held overseas than domestically.) To illustrate the reach of the dollar into foreign hands, consider during the 2008-09 financial crisis, the Federal Reserve lent to 14 central banks under dollar swap lines. According to the General Accounting Office's audit of the Fed released in July 2011, of the $16 trillion lent on a short-term basis, the Fed lent over $3 trillion to private foreign banks such as Royal Bank of Scotland, Barclays, Deutsche Bank, BNP Paribas, and UBS and Credit Suisse.[71]

Two consequences flow from the vast size of those balances outside the US economy. First, they overwhelm any illusion that the Federal Reserve has true control over money supply and thus over inflation. This is because a dollar held overseas can, with the tapping of a few computer keys, become an onshore dollar. Eurodollars held offshore are not really permanently offshore. Money is fungible, meaning a dollar in the pocket of a Cairo street urchin is exactly the same as a dollar held by a Russian bank in London or a gambler in a Macao casino. Experiments (in Belgium and elsewhere) in separating a currency into those for commercial transactions (exports and imports) and those for financial transactions have always foundered on fungibility. The only way the reserve currency issuer can discriminate between domestic money and foreign-owned money is to impose capital controls.

This is the second consequence. In order to manage the money supply and prevent all those Eurodollars from returning to the US and causing inflation, the Federal Reserve would have to brand each dollar with a domestic or international brand, like cattle. To do so is not only very difficult as a practical matter, but runs contrary to the ruling philosophy of the day, which is "let markets be free." As Russia, for example, starts using the euro as its secondary currency after the ruble, the supply of unwanted dollars goes up and value goes down. This outcome has absolutely nothing to do with the quality of Fed stewardship of the US economy and would occur even if every dollar on the planet were backstopped with gold and other currencies.

The subject of capital controls is a touchy one, to say the least. Developed countries started eliminating capital controls around 1958, ending with the last vestige in 1980 – the UK tax on ownership of dollars that resulted in the "premium dollar," which cost UK residents 10% to 20% more in sterling terms than the market value of the dollar if they wanted to invest in the US.

Relaxation of US capital controls was proposed by President Nixon in 1970 and initiated after the 15 August 1971 Sunday night announcement of the US abandoning the gold standard. We tend to imagine that free capital markets were a feature of the post-war world, but Bretton Woods co-designer Keynes believed that capital controls were an essential feature of the fixed exchange rate regime and, historically, it was Washington that adopted the free-market model that quickly became ideological orthodoxy. Today no one would support the US imposing capital controls on the dollar, whether incoming or outgoing, because the world needs dollars. Dollars are the machine oil of the global economy.

Note that during the Asian crisis of 1997-98, the IMF and World Bank frowned on capital controls as a palliative, let alone a remedy, for capital flight. Malaysia alone imposed capital controls, forbidding foreigners to remove their funds for one year. The prime minister at the time made some unpleasant remarks about speculators but capital controls were effective. The IMF changed its tune and in 2010 offered that some capital controls in emerging markets (like Brazil) are appropriate.

The real lender of last resort

The issuer of the reserve currency has another responsibility, too – not only providing a larger money supply than it wants for its own economy but also promising to lend to other central banks in the event of financial distress. This is the *lender of last resort* function. Many central banks have agreements to lend to one another. China has established so-called swap lines with about twenty countries, including Australia and India. Japan has swap lines with South Korea, India and much of the rest of Asia. The word *swap* is somewhat misleading. In practice, Central Bank A lends dollars to Central Bank B and what it gets for the other side of the swap from Central Bank B is an IOU. Most central bank swap lines are for dollars. Obviously the biggest and most reliable of sources of dollars for emergency purposes is the issuer itself, the Federal Reserve.

If the US is basically unhappy about having lost control of its money supply due to the development of the offshore dollar market, why would it make matters worse by lending more to that very market? The answer is that it's a moral obligation arising from its role as the issuer of the reserve currency. The US does not always fulfil this leadership role gracefully. As President Nixon's treasury secretary John Connally famously said, "The dollar may be our currency but it's your problem."

Foreign dollar holders are acutely conscious of the US' forced leadership role and sometimes prod the giant with a stick. In recent years, for example, China has complained that the lengthy period of ultra-low interest rates in the US is encouraging inflation down the road, not to mention depriving China of interest revenue. But were the US to have raised interest rates during the worst recession since the 1930s solely to favour China, US growth would suffer and US citizens would have a legitimate grievance. In fact, Chinese citizens may have had a legitimate grievance, too, since US unemployment would have been higher under rising US rates and thus consumer spending on Chinese imports reduced.

The bigger grievance would have been felt in Europe. The US provides liquidity to non-US parties in copious amounts in times of financial crisis – as noted above, over $3 trillion in the 2008-09 financial crisis to private banks alone. Many non-domestic parties using the dollar have a mismatch between dollar-denominated assets and liabilities, and in a liquidity crunch their own central bank cannot act as a lender of last resort without the help of the Fed. The Fed acts as a reserve currency issuer should act – as a lender of last resort to other central banks.

The Fed has to perform this role only occasionally, when markets become stressed and overseas banks decline to lend dollars to one another on even a short-term basis such as overnight. As an example, say a bank in Germany was funding its dollar loans by borrowing from other banks in the London market, but a crisis such as the 9/11 attacks on the World Trader Center in New York caused the other London banks to decline to do business. The German bank would seek funds from its central bank, the ECB. The ECB, in turn, may need to get dollars from the Fed.

After 9/11, the Fed's swap lines with the European Central Bank (ECB) and Bank of England were reactivated, having fallen into disuse, but used for only three days. In late 2007, the swap lines were re-authorised to help cope with the subprime crisis, with $20 billion named as available to the ECB and $5 billion to the Swiss National Bank. The Fed opened the lines up again on 18 September 2008, when Lehman failed, for $180 billion available to the central banks of the EMU, England, Canada, Switzerland and Japan. At the time, the Fed said there was "no upper limit on collateral," meaning it stood ready to lend essentially any amount.

Amounts actually used by these central banks can be hard to come by; the Fed shows them as "other assets." A New York Federal Reserve paper from April 2010 [72] says in the second phase of the swap expansion, from 18 September 2008 to 12 October 2008, "the Fed boosted the available amount by nearly a factor of 10, to $620 billion from $67 billion." In the third phase of the FX swap line program, from 18 October 2008 to 1 February 2010, the Fed removed the caps from the swap lines with the ECB, BOE, SNB and BOJ. On 21 December 2010, the FOMC extended the lines again to 1 August 2011, and then on 29 June 2011 they were extended to 1 August 2012. Finally, on 30 November 2011, the FOMC and the five other major central banks announced coordinated action to "provide liquidity support to the global financial system." As part of these measures, the FOMC extended the swap lines with these central banks until February 2013.[73]

What does the Fed get in return? A claim on local currency deposits at the foreign central banks. It's not hard to argue that these are of no benefit to the US at all, but don't lose sight of the alternative that failing foreign banks are of no use, either.

The gold standard is a non-starter

Critics say that if we still pegged currencies to gold, we would not need the Fed to act as lender of last resort to the rest of the world. But only about 166,000 tons of gold have been mined throughout all history, according to the World Gold Council, and of that, governments hold roughly 29,000 tons. All the gold in the world is therefore worth about $7.5 trillion (at $1500 per Troy ounce). US money supply alone is $8.4 trillion (July 2011) and there is an equal or larger amount outside the US. *We could not return to the gold standard without a severe contraction in every single economy in the world.*

This is the central problem of using gold as a backstop for a reserve currency – there is simply not enough of the stuff. The second problem is worse – we still need a *numeraire* in the form of a reserve currency in which to price transactions and settle debts. Gold is an asset, to be sure, but it is not a financial asset and it is not money. Gold fails to pass all three tests in the definition of money. Money must be more than a store of value and unit of account – it must also have transactional capability.

Moreover, a reserve currency pegged to gold would have its purchasing power determined by international market forces responding to factors outside the issuer's control, including plain old supply and demand. The issuing country's central bank would lack control over internal price stability, employment and market stability. This is the context in which Keynes issued one of his most quoted phrases: "When stability of the internal price level and stability of the external exchanges are incompatible, the former is generally preferable." Keynes went on, "There is no escape from a 'managed' currency, whether we wish it or not. In truth, the gold standard is already a barbaric relic."[74]

Note that Keynes did not say gold itself is a barbaric relic, but rather that the *gold standard* is a barbaric relic. Keynes was warning that a system dependent on something as undersupplied and subject to market fickleness as gold was inherently unstable.

Emotions run so high on the subject of the gold standard that we tend to forget what actually happened to cause the US to go off the gold standard in the first place and to float (including devaluation) two years later.

Exorbitant privilege

First, following complaints of a dollar shortage in the 1950s and early 1960s, in 1965 French president de Gaulle launched an attack on the US' "exorbitant privilege" of being the reserve currency issuer (which provided a built-in buyer of its debt and thus lower financing costs for its government). France announced it would convert $300 million of dollars into gold. Spain followed with $60 million. The 1964 trade deficit was about $3 billion and by mid-1965, US gold reserves had fallen to a 26-year low of $15.1 billion (at $35/oz).

It is thought that de Gaulle was playing the gold card to get US agreement to the French proposal for a new international reserve unit of account named the CRU (collective reserve unit). The unit would be gold-backed and of the member countries issuing the CRU, those with the most gold would have the biggest voting rights. By 1967, de Gaulle withdrew France from the US-led Gold Pool – now named the Group of Ten – set up in 1961 to provide emergency intervention funds (and managed by the Bank of England, whose pound shared reserve currency status with the dollar). The purpose of the Gold Pool was to share the costs among central banks of maintaining the price of gold at $35 an ounce rather than depleting US gold reserves. The willingness of a member, France, to act for its own individual good rather than the collective good led directly to the collapse of Bretton Woods when the dollar had to be taken off the gold standard in August 1971.

de Gaulle's timing was acute, forcing a crisis at a time of cyclical downswing. The year 1967 was a bad one for the two reserve currency countries. The US was building a fiscal deficit for an unfunded war in Vietnam, and the UK economy was weakening. Capital outflows from sterling to dollars to gold accelerated, with a record 80 tons of gold sold in London in one five-day period (and the pound was devalued later that year, by 14%, in November, the first devaluation since 1949). By the end of 1967, US gold reserves had fallen to $12 billion.

By March 1968, the Gold Pool had sent almost 1000 tons of gold to the weighing room floor at the Bank of England, with the US Air Force delivering emergency supplies of gold from Ft. Knox. On 15 March 1968, the US asked for a two-week closing of the London gold market. In April, the Group of 10 met in Stockholm, and thus was born the Special Drawing Right (SDR). SDRs were called 'paper gold' but note that they were never called money. Before going on to consider SDRs, fix it in your mind that a return to the gold standard, even if it were realistic, would open the door to a single country wreaking havoc with other countries' economies and financial systems, as France did. This cannot be an improvement in the present international financial system.

The SDR is a non-starter, too

Russia, China, various Gulf States and even the United Nations have clamoured for years for a non-dollar reserve currency choice and have put forward expanding the use of IMF special drawing rights (SDR) as a dollar alternative.

SDRs were created by the IMF "to supplement member countries' official reserves." Shares of SDRs, seen as an international reserve asset, were assigned to each IMF member country, with each member allocated both an asset (SDR holdings) as well as a liability (SDR allocation). When a country has a net asset position in SDRs, it earns interest, and when it holds fewer SDRs, it pays interest. Initially, one SDR unit was defined as an equivalent to 0.888671 grams of fine gold. Later it was changed to a base of a basket of four currencies, the euro, the dollar, sterling and yen. The IMF website says "SDRs can be exchanged for freely usable currencies."

The basket is reviewed every five years by the IMF Executive Board. In November 2010, the IMF conducted its latest review and decided that effective 1 January 2011, the SDR valuation basket would be composed of the following weights: 41.9% US dollar (versus 44% at the 2005 review), 37.4% euro (compared to 34% in 2005), 11.3% pound sterling (compared to 11% in 2005) and 9.4% Japanese yen (versus 11.0% in 2005).

> "The criterion used to select the currencies in the SDR basket remains unchanged from the 2000 and 2005 reviews: the currencies included in the SDR are the four currencies issued by Fund members or by monetary unions that include Fund members, whose exports of goods and services during the five-year period ending 12 months before the effective date of the revision had the largest value, and which have been determined by the Fund to be freely usable currencies in accordance with Article XXX (f) of the Fund's Articles of Agreement. The weights assigned to these currencies continue to be based on the value of the exports of goods and services by the member (or by members included in a monetary union) issuing the currency and the amount of reserves denominated in the respective currencies that are held by other members of the IMF."

In its current form, however, the heightened use of SDRs are a hard sell to world central banks and the IMF knows this. In February 2011 the IMF Executive Board said "an enhanced role for the SDR could potentially contribute to the long-term stability of the IMS (International Monetary System), provided appropriate safeguards are put in place and political commitment and private sector interest are mobilised."

At the same time however, the Board said, "Directors observed that, despite its theoretical benefits, an enhanced role for the SDR faces significant technical and political challenges, which call for realism in assessing its role in practice."

In other words, even the IMF acknowledges that the benefits of the SDR are theoretical. China and others propose SDRs as the new reserve currency, but SDRs are not money. They may be a useful unit of account but they do not perform the other functions of real money – to execute transactions and serve as a store of value. Individuals and corporations cannot use SDRs – only governments. In terms of replacing the UK and the US as sovereign issuers of the reserve currency, the IMF may be an improvement in the sense that it has no voters to tax or to woo and no wars to fight and to fund. But it is politically unrealistic to think that sovereigns will be able to sell the idea of yet another fiat currency to be controlled by foreigners to voters already uneasy about their own fiat currency. It is also unrealistic to think that the IMF will act without the same self-interest as individual countries; some members will always be more equal than others.

In February 2011, ECB Vice President Vítor Constâncio offered his opinion on dollar alternatives: "I do not see a major reform of the international monetary system on the horizon, as there is no real substitute for the US Dollar in medium term. The special drawing right (SDR) is not a promising option, and the insufficiently deep and liquid financial markets of emerging market economies will limit the role that their currencies can play in the foreseeable future."

Other reserve currencies

We find it interesting that the latest World Bank report on multipolarity does not propose the SDR as a reserve currency to replace the dollar. It predicts the euro and renminbi will join the dollar as reserve currencies, and we already have reports that some sovereigns are adding euro to reserves, notably China and Russia.

However, before we get carried away we have to remember that the Chinese currency is not fully convertible and the market for money market instruments is not free of government rate-setting and heavy regulation, and thus the renminbi does not yet qualify for reserve currency status. Even more important is how the Triffin Dilemma would affect the euro zone and China, which would by definition lose control over their money supply, not to mention having their public finances gone over with a fine-tooth comb, just like the US today. As the European peripheral sovereign debt crisis unwinds, we are learning more than we wanted to know about public finances in certain European countries – but we have yet to see China's books.

Ever since the euro's inception in January 1999, it was seen as the first viable alternative to the greenback. Its money market, while not as large and deep as the US bond market, is tried and true. The euro was also seen in some circles as a quasi-Deutsche Mark, making for an easy transition as well. The economic boon of having one common euro zone currency also made investors, including the world's central banks, eager to hold euro in their portfolio. It's not going too far to say the financial world became besotted with the idea of the euro zone and its currency, the euro. The bloom, of course, came off the rose for the euro in December 2009, when Greece announced that it had lied about its budget deficit for the year. In the months that followed, peripheral country spreads began to widen markedly and the euro was shunned.

The euro zone peripheral debt crisis taught investors a valuable lesson – the euro is still a nascent currency. While they might buy euro going forward as the crisis ebbed and flowed, these investors would keep an eye out for other non-dollar and non-euro alternatives.

Let us also gently suggest that while Germany, with its fiscal rectitude and rock-hard abhorrence of inflation, could no doubt easily become the replacement for the US as the reserve currency issuer, it does not have its own currency. It shares the euro with at least three countries that were in need of bailouts (Greece, Ireland and Portugal) and one that is likely to default in the end despite a second bailout (Greece). At the time of the second bailout, Greece was paying over 30% to attract investors for two-year notes. Does this look like a reserve currency replacement?

If Germany were to leave the euro zone and reissue the Deutsche Mark, it would face the same complaints of DM shortages that the dollar faced in the 1960s. The Bundesbank would be leery of increasing money supply because of its inflationary effect. World growth would slow down to a crawl. Gresham's Law would come into effect – bad money would drive out good money. In other words, we would be back to the dollar as the sole reserve currency.

So, with all due respect to the World Bank and the IMF, and to critics who long for an impossible return to the gold standard, we are stuck with the dollar, and yes, it is likely to continue a long-term secular downtrend unless and until the US reverses from a severe deficit condition to surpluses, whereupon there will be a dollar shortage and the cycle begins anew.

The changing shape of how currency reserves are held

We often see headlines suggesting that the share of the dollar as a percentage of reserves is declining. Since not all world central banks report the breakdown of their reserve holdings, it is hard to know if the dollar share is actually changing. The International Monetary Fund Currency Composition of Official Foreign Exchange Reserves (COFER) data from December 2011 put total FX holdings at $10.196 trillion in the fourth quarter. Of this total, allocated reserves stood at $5.646 trillion. Thirty-four advanced countries and 108 emerging and developing counties report to COFER. Unfortunately, China is not one of these countries. Therefore, economists assume that China allocates its $3 trillion in currency reserves in roughly the same percentages as other world central banks.

The IMF COFER data showed that the dollar's share of allocated reserves rose to 62.2% in Q4 2011 from 61.8 % in Q4 2010, while, amidst ongoing euro zone peripheral woes, the euro's share slipped to 25% from 26% at the end of 2010. The other noticeable increase was in the percentage share of claims in other currencies (not the dollar, the euro, sterling, yen or Swiss franc) which rose fractionally to 5.3% in Q4 2011 from 4.4% at the end of 2010.

Compare these percentages to COFER data from Q4 1999, just after the euro came into being. Total foreign exchange reserves were a mere $1.782 trillion, with $1.38 trillion reserves allocated. The dollar's share of reserves at the time was 71% , the euro's share was 17.9%, with claims in other currencies at 1.6%.

While the 10% decline in the dollar's share of reserve holdings over a ten-year-plus period could be viewed as disturbing, the dollar's share of reserve holdings has held fairly steady in recent years. Even in Q1 2009, when the S&P 500 was bottoming at a 12-year low of 666.92, the dollar's share of reserve holdings was 65.2%. The share later edged down in subsequent quarters as safe-haven buying of US Treasuries diminished and investors again sought out riskier assets.

Recent analysts have begun to single out the rising share of claims in other currencies, which account for a mere $295 billion of the nearly $10.4 trillion total. While the total is small, the percentage change over time is impressive. Emerging and developing economies have seen their share rise from 2.1% in the first quarter of 2009 to 5.2% in Q2 2012, which has begun to meet the accountants' criterion of *material* (5%).

China holds the ace

Analysts assume that world central banks are buying other developed country currencies such as Aussie and Canadian dollars and Korean won in an attempt to diversify their assets. What is China buying? A mere 1% shift in the country's currency allocation would mean about $30 billion hitting the currency market. While that is still a drop in the bucket of the $4 trillion daily turnover, the FX effect could be cataclysmic if China acted in such a way as to create an announcement effect.

In 2010, China announced that it had increased its Japanese government bond holdings and had begun to buy Korean bonds. Throughout the European debt crisis, China has offered a steady helping hand, buying Portuguese and Greek debt along with non-peripheral euro zone debt from time to time and the triple-

A-rated bond issues of the European Financial Stability Fund. Without China's intervention in European debt markets during the crisis, the euro would probably have fallen much further than it did. If the crisis passes without further turmoil, then China will have some attractive yields on its books, such as 7% in Portuguese 10-year bonds. Such high-yielding debt will offset what is likely to be other losses on China's and other central banks' books, as longer-dated low-yielding instruments, purchased during the US subprime mortgage crisis, begin to show losses as global yields rise.

Chinese foreign currency reserves stood at $2.85 trillion at the end of 2010, compared to $2.4 trillion at the end of 2009, and rose to $3.2 trillion as of end-December 2011. Some of the increase may be due to increased profits on China's fixed income investments, but the lion's share was seen as stemming from People's Bank of China's intervention efforts to thwart speculative yuan demand from investors. Of the $782 billion reserve increase seen from December 2009 to December 2011, only a small portion appears to have gravitated to the US. *Appears* is the appropriate word, in that China, along with other Asian and Middle East central banks, employ banks in London or the Caribbean to purchase US instruments.

Looking to gauge foreign inflows, analysts gravitate to the monthly US Treasury International Capital Systems data, called the TICS report, as well as the only recently offered, more detailed yearly TICS report. The yearly TIC report, while backward looking, offers a clearer picture of US inflows and outflows. As an example, final TICS data for 2011[75] showed that from June 2010 to June 2011 China increased its US asset holdings by $116 billion to $1.727 trillion, with the country's total stock holdings rising by $32 billion to $159 billion and total debt holdings by $84 billion to $1.568 trillion over the course of the year. The bulk (83%) of China's debt holdings were in US long-term Treasury instruments. During this same June 2010 to June 2011 period, China's FX reserves rose by $743.2 billion.

While China's total holdings remained sizable, the Treasury Department noted that on the year, "Japan, the United Kingdom, the Cayman Islands, Luxembourg, and Canada all increased their holdings by larger amounts, i.e. $192 billion or 14% growth for Japan, $184 billion or 23% growth for the United Kingdom, $146 billion or 20% growth for the Cayman Islands, $195 billion or 31% growth for Luxembourg, and $135 billion or 32% growth for Canada." While Chinese holdings of US assets increased modestly over the year, analysts red-flagged other countries' purchases of US instruments as further proof of underlying safe-haven buying and/or expectation of US outperformance.

The composition of China's foreign exchange reserves is a closely-guarded secret, but using IMF's COFER report, analysts estimate that about two-thirds of the country's reserves are likely denominated in dollars, with the euro accounting for 26%, sterling 5%, and the yen 3%.

So, if China was not buying directly from the US Treasury in the June 2010 to June 2011 period, we must assume that purchases were likely done via other centres. As mentioned above, the TICS report showed a sizeable $184 billion increase in UK holdings of US assets during this period, as well as a large $146 billion increase in Cayman Island purchases. Middle East and Asian accounts often use London banks or offshore banks to buy US assets. By doing so covertly, there is less embarrassment if there is an eventual loss on the position. And Asian banks especially do not want to report losses on their reserve holdings. In late August/early September 2010, there were reports that the PBOC may have lost as much as $430 billion on the US Treasury holdings, with select board members to be held personally responsible for the losses.

While these reports were later refuted, the understanding that losses are not acceptable remained. By investing reserve assets covertly by using UK and other centres, the PBOC can maintain its anonymity.

In a May 2012 report [76], the Treasury Department outlined "three pitfalls of the TICS data that can cause misleading interpretations of cross-border flows," with a few examples:

1. The TICS data are recorded according to the country of the first cross-border counterparty, not the country of the ultimate buyer or actual seller or issuer of the security. So if a German resident buys a US Treasury through a London broker, TICS records this as a sale to the UK, rather than Germany.

2. The TICS "measured transactions" don't fully account for deals made on behalf of official foreign investors. If the Chinese government buys US agencies via an intermediary in Hong Kong, TICS will count that as a purchase of US agency bonds by a Hong Kong account.

3. TICS does not record "important cross-border flows in securities that do not pass through standard broker-dealer channels" and does not "collect data on cross border acquisitions of stocks through merger-related stock swaps or re-incorporations because these transactions are considered direct investment transactions, for which data are collected by the BEA."

Military power and reserve currency status

Whenever the US engages in a military adventure, such as repelling the Iraqi invasion of Kuwait and the invasion of Iraq itself, the dollar rises. This is not because FX traders are particularly blood-thirsty, but because the US action reminds them of the US' hard power.

It is a historical fact that the reserve issuer has always been the dominant military power of the day, possibly starting with Babylonia but certainly from the time of the Spanish King Charles V in the 16th century, followed by the United Kingdom in the 18th and 19th centuries, to 1931. In the end, Spain squandered its gold and power, and the UK chose industrial revolution and colonial conquest over preserving and building sovereign wealth in the form of gold. But at the time, Spain and then Britain literally ruled the seas.

Since WWII, it is the United States that rules the seas. British economist R. G. Hawtrey, in *Economic Aspect of Sovereignty*, published in 1929 and again in 1952, stated that "Power is economic productivity capable of being applied as force, and is represented primarily by output of movable goods and the capacity to move them."[77] In other words, the top military power is defined by the ability of an economy to maintain military goods, to increase them very, very quickly and to deliver them where potentially needed. This is why we expect the US Navy to move closer to conflicts, whether the Sea of Japan, the Mediterranean or the Strait of Hormuz. In practice, it may not be literally the Navy showing the flag – it can be aircraft or drones or boots on the ground.

Whether we like US military supremacy or not is a judgment call involving non-economic values, but we must acknowledge that the US has it and nobody else does – at least, not yet, and not since the only other challenger to US military superiority, the Soviet Union, dissolved in 1991. Many analysts suspect that China intends to become the next world superpower. Data from the Stockholm International Peace Research Institute shows US military spending in 2010 at $698 billion in 2010 or 4.8% of GDP. From 2001 to 2010, US military spending increased by 81.3%, with China number two, with estimated military spending of $119 billion in 2010 or 2.1% of GDP. In China, military spending increased 189% from 2001 to 2010.

In the third, fourth and fifth slots are the UK, France and Russia, spending respectively $59.6 billion, $59.3 billion and $58.7 billion, or 2.7%, 2.3% and 4% (estimate) of GDP. UK military spending increased by 21.9% from 2001 to 2012, while France's spending increased 3.3% and Russia's increased 82.4%.

We literally do not know whether US military power is a necessary condition for its reserve currency status. Just because historically the reserve currency issuer was also the top military power does not mean that the two roles necessarily must go hand in hand. Much of the analysis of US military primacy as it pertains to the dollar's primacy as a reserve currency is crackpot stuff that can safely be brushed off.

We have no reason to suppose that the necessary conditions for dollar primacy – a very large economy; free, deep and liquid markets; the rule of law (including property rights); political stability, and national security – would change much if China, say, were to surpass the US as a military power, short of invasion and occupation. China has none of those other necessary conditions. If the world were to decide suddenly that the Chinese renminbi would henceforth become the reserve currency, we can imagine that some of the conditions would be created, such as deep and liquid markets, but the remaining conditions depend upon political choices (such as the rule of law, property rights, and financial market prices set by markets and not bureaucratic whim).

Hard vs. soft power

Political scientists speak of the *hard power* of the reserve currency issuer, which takes the form of being able to run current account deficits and pay lower interest rates on government bond issues, as contrasted with *soft power*, which takes the form of influence. Some influence is, in fact, pretty hard, as in the application of dollar diplomacy – supporting foreign regimes for the commercial benefit of US companies in places like Latin America, for instance, or to squash ideological opponents. After the end of the Cold War, the ideological motivation was less in play. The American sphere of influence has shifted from the military threat embedded in the Monroe Doctrine (1823) – foreigners, stay out of the Americas – to more economic, cultural and political types of influence. At the far end of the spectrum, but not trivial, is application of US soft power preventing the loud and often rude complaints about US policy decisions that somehow never make it into the communiqués of G8 summits.

One of the costs of being the reserve currency issuer is the loss of prestige and credibility under adverse conditions (like the US twin deficits in trade and public finance). Then, as Cornell University Professor of Government Kirshner writes, the long leash becomes a choke collar.

Although the political and international monetary context is distinct, the experience of sterling illustrates these phenomena. In the 19th and early 20th centuries, the pound served as the international currency of choice, with London as world's financial hub. During World War II, Britain was able to quite explicitly cash in on its key currency status, employing the sterling area to its advantage, financing billions in military expenditures in ways that would not have been possible without the mechanisms that were already in place as a result of the pound's long-standing global role.

The war forced Britain to scrape the bottom of the financial barrel, and the ability to essentially borrow at will in the sterling area and route the pounds back through London was an important element of the war effort. But after the war, the sterling balances became a vexing problem, complicating the management of Britain's relative economic decline and exacerbating its chronic financial crises in the 1960s. With sterling invariably on the ropes in international financial markets the demand for a clean bill of macroeconomic health placed British budgets – and British military spending and overseas commitments – under constant pressure as a result. It can be argued that the challenges associated with the loss of 'top currency' status were at the heart of Britain's postwar economic distress.[78] Kirshner notes, for example, that "after the war, with sterling in decline, the vulnerability of the pound left Britain exposed and forced it to abandon its military adventure over Suez in 1956."

The comparison of the UK and US as reserve currency issuers has its limitations, of course. For one thing, the world is far more integrated (flat) today. Currency rates were fixed at the time of Suez. But the hard fact remains that if a country does not have a war chest and cannot raise one quickly at an acceptable cost, its military ambitions are severely constrained.

The current loss of US prestige and power is due not only to the dollar's decline, but also to acknowledgement that political choices are yet to be made about the massive US debt, at nearly $15 trillion in mid-2011 and reaching 100% of GDP by 2012. Because of various financial crises, including the US subprime crisis and the peripheral euro zone debt crisis, the US has been able to avoid paying the piper in the form of higher interest rates. Safe-haven inflows into dollar assets, including *risk-free* US government notes and bonds, keep rates not only low, but yielding a negative real return after inflation. This is precisely the exorbitant privilege that de Gaulle complained about 50 years ago – without at the same time acknowledging the cost of being the reserve currency issuer in the form of permanent current account deficits, the need to offer liquidity to all comers, and the responsibility of sane world leadership.

At some point, it is reasonable to assume that those crying wolf will be right and an actual wolf will appear, taking the form of a risk premium for US debt. In the viral way of market thinking, the premium can appear and grow huge before policy-makers can come together to take action. Politicians and voters have to make the choice between raising taxes and cutting spending, including defence spending. If defence spending is, indeed, cut, by how much does the US lose hard influence – the ability to send the Navy in the direction of any conflict where the

US perceives it has a stake – and soft influence? No one knows. A gradual loss of power is more palatable and less shameful than a sudden one, but a sudden loss of power could easily come about in the form of China taking a military action contrary to US wishes and the US declining to engage in a showdown.

Such an event would mark only a step, if a shocking one, on the road to the dollar losing reserve currency status. As noted at the beginning of this chapter, the primary function of a reserve currency issuer is to provide liquidity to the rest of the world and to act as a banker of last resort to all the other central banks. China does not get reserve currency status for the renminbi by winning a military showdown with the US if it does not also meet this condition. It is fine for China to make the renminbi a transaction medium for regional commercial transactions and other liberalisations, but it is not until China establishes swap lines with the other central banks and they are depended upon in a real, live crisis, that China will actually get reserve currency status, whatever its military capabilities.

Evaluating China's prospects as a reserve currency issuer

We should probably assume that any rival for top reserve currency status needs to match the criteria that were used in selecting the dollar as the primary reserve currency at Bretton Woods in 1944. These are chiefly economic and political criteria, including not only the ability to lead but also the willingness. Ability resides in the size of the economy and the capabilities of the country's institutions, especially the central bank. Willingness to lead is a political matter. The reserve currency issuer has to be willing to lend emergency funds to others who insult and demean it, for the greater good of greasing the world's financial machinery.

But other factors are in play, too. Should we also assume that the successor to the US as reserve currency issuer needs to have a capitalist economy? And does it have to be a capitalist economy modelled on the US? History suggests that capitalism is likely the most enduring form of economic organisation and thus offers the best chance of institutional survival. Hernando de Soto postulates that:

> "Capital is the force that raises the productivity of labor and creates the wealth of nations. It is the lifeblood of the capitalist system, the foundation of progress, and the one thing that the poor countries of the world cannot seem to produce for themselves, no matter how eagerly their people engage in all the other activities that characterise a capitalist economy."

This is because in poor countries, title to resources is defective – people live in houses to which they do not have title and thus cannot mortgage in order to raise funds. Their businesses are unincorporated and have unmeasured assets and liabilities, and investors cannot find them. Assets are not documented and therefore cannot be leveraged or traded. De Soto calls them "dead capital".

"In the West, by contrast, every parcel of land, every building, every piece of equipment, or store of inventories is represented in a property document that is the visible sign of a vast hidden process that connects all these assets to the rest of the economy. Thanks to this representational process, assets can lead an invisible, parallel life alongside their material existence. They can be used as collateral for credit. The single most important source of funds for new businesses in the United States is a mortgage on the entrepreneur's house. These assets can also provide a link to the owner's credit history, an accountable address for the collection of debts and taxes, the basis for the creation of reliable and universal public utilities, and a foundation for the creation of securities (like mortgage-backed bonds) that can then be rediscounted and sold in secondary markets. By this process the West injects life into assets and makes them generate capital.

"Third World and former communist nations do not have this representational process. As a result, most of them are undercapitalised, in the same way that a firm is undercapitalised when it issues fewer securities than its income and assets would justify. The enterprises of the poor are very much like corporations that cannot issue shares or bonds to obtain new investment and finance. Without representations, their assets are dead capital.

"The poor inhabitants of these nations – five-sixths of humanity – do have things, but they lack the process to represent their property and create capital. They have houses but not titles; crops but not deeds; businesses but not statutes of incorporation. It is the unavailability of these essential representations that explains why people who have adapted every other Western invention, from the paper clip to the nuclear reactor, have not been able to produce sufficient capital to make their domestic capitalism work."[79]

Capital is not money. Any country can print money – look at Zimbabwe. Capital is created from property and through an institutional process that includes rules, information sharing and measurement and depends fully on a legal property system – in other words, the rule of law that confers legal rights on property owners. Further, "By transforming people with property interests into accountable individuals, formal property created individuals from masses. People no longer needed to rely on neighbourhood relationships or make local arrangements to protect their rights to assets. Freed from primitive economic activities and burdensome parochial constraints, the could explore how to generate surplus value from their own assets."[80]

De Soto has put his finger on an important difference between the two reserve currency issuers of the 19th and 20th centuries and the putative issuer-in-waiting of the 21st century, China. Formal property rights protect ownership and the security of transactions in the west. Citizens and institutions respect property titles and honour contracts. Once a party asserts title to property, he loses anonymity and can be punished by failure to respect others' property titles and to honour contracts.

But in China, title to property is often unclear, especially title to land, all of which belongs to the state. Conditions are changing and changing rapidly, but farmers do not have clear title to the land they till, nor to the crops they produce – the state can and does appropriate land and crops at will. We all know the disdain of the Chinese for intellectual property rights, from Hollywood movies to Microsoft operating systems, and the conflation of any criticism with illegal state dissent. Factory owners who produce dangerous products like tainted milk or toxic toys may either escape punishment or be hanged – the rules are unclear. The laws banning pollution that got so much publicity ahead of the 2008 Beijing Olympics were motivated by national pride and not based on the protection of individuals' property rights or a concept of a social contract promoting public welfare; as of 2010, over 250 cities had no sewage disposal system whatever and discharged raw sewage into rivers.

The concept of human rights draws its heritage from the concept of property rights, and is either absent or only nascent in China, which has no right of free speech or assembly. The US is the destination of millions of immigrants from every corner of the globe every year, many of whom become citizens. Immigrants flock to China from lesser economies in the region but not to the same extent and not from the West. China began formulating an immigration policy only in 2010.

The Chinese economy is growing at rates triple and quadruple the rate of growth in the US and West, and surpassed Japan to become the second largest economy in 2010. It is likely to surpass the US by 2027, according to research by Goldman Sachs. But foreign direct investment into China in 2010 was about $105.7 billion, less than the flows to Germany ($46 billion) and the UK ($71 billion) combined. Into the US, foreign direct investment was $228 billion.[81] To be fair, foreign direct investment ($1.24 trillion in 2010) is growing faster to emerging market and "transition" economies, at the expense of development country flows. Inflows to all of Asia rose 24% in 2010 and to China, the single largest recipient, by 11%.

Capitalism is still evolving in China and does not yet exhibit De Soto's "representational process." By this standard, China is not qualified to become the issuer of the world's reserve currency.

What's next

Former IMF chief economist Michael Mussa created a formula which measures the willingness of foreigners to hold the dollar as a reserve in the form of a trade-off between economic growth and inflation. Specifically, the ratio of net foreign liabilities to GDP will be stable when the current account deficit as a share of GDP is equal to the rate of growth of nominal income.

This is not really a brain-twister. When the current account deficit rises faster than economic growth, we correctly assume a rise in imported inflation and expect a dollar devaluation that will reduce the desirability of holding dollars as reserves. Assuming the Federal Reserve acts properly to suppress inflation, higher interest rates depress consumption, but may also depress output, which may work counter to improving the current account deficit. The trick is to get more of a drop in consumption than in output.

As Barry Eichengreen states, "Higher interest rates that depress output may then also destabilise the financial system; after all, the combination of higher interest rates and a collapsing exchange rate, occurring against the backdrop of chronic fiscal and external imbalances, is the classic recipe for a financial crisis. None of these scenarios have happy endings for the reserve currency role of the dollar."

In other words, a US recession is a good thing for the dollar as a reserve currency when external and fiscal imbalances are extreme.

The IMF seems to be right that the euro and renminbi will become co-owners of reserve currency status – there is nothing to say the world needs to have only one reserve currency, as Barry Eichengreen points out.[82] The region around China can use the renminbi and Europe can use the euro. Coexistence is not all that complicated and consists chiefly of building vast accounting systems.

But in a crisis, the central bank of last resort is the central bank of the reserve currency issuer. We see no evidence that the ECB or PBOC are gearing up for this function. For one thing, they would have to disclose the lender-of-last-resort function to their voters. It can safely be argued that US citizens do not have a clue that their central bank is performing this function – and they would not approve if they did know.

For these reasons, it's logical to deduce that the dollar will remain the primary reserve currency – unless the US shoots itself in the foot and persists in fiscal mismanagement. US indebtedness has reached the point of unsustainability, according to the ratings agencies. The downtrending dollar may be inevitable on the Triffin Dilemma, but it's accelerated by self-inflicted overspending. Adoption of serious structural deficit reduction measures would slow down the pace of dollar devaluation and probably involve a rally of some not insignificant magnitude, since investors are all to aware of the drawbacks and shortcomings of the reserve currency rivals, not least the reluctance of their central banks to step up to the plate for all comers.

CHAPTER 11 –
THE EURO AND THE NEW GOLD STANDARD

" 'When I use a word,' Humpty Dumpty said, in rather a scornful tone, 'it means just what I choose it to mean – neither more nor less.' "

Lewis Carroll, *Through the Looking Glass*

The euro was advertised as a rival to the dollar for several years before it actually come into existence in January 1999. Delegations of top European officials periodically descended upon the finance ministries of high reserve currency countries, notably China and also Japan, Taiwan and South Korea, to promote the euro as an alternative reserve currency. This is not historically abnormal – the UK pound shares reserve currency status with the US dollar today. The euro has some of the characteristics of a reserve currency – it is used as a numeraire in Monaco, San Marino, the Vatican City, Guadeloupe, French Guyana, Martinique, Réunion and Madeira, and unofficially in many other places.

The euro promotes economic efficiency and trade by removing transactional friction, not least among members. Quite apart from whether the members of the euro zone form an optimal currency union on an economic basis, the euro promotes economic, financial and political stability because it takes away control of monetary policy and some aspects of fiscal policy from politicians. Most of all, the euro is a symbol of European identity and among idealists, if not the public at large, a symbol of eventual political integration.

The fiscal and monetary rules of the several treaties that underpin the euro zone are unique in history, promising the equivalent of a new gold standard – removing inflation and devaluation due to inflation permanently from the risks faced by savers and investors. But as members violate the rules, even to the extent of sovereign default, doubts are cropping up as to whether the euro deserves to supplant the dollar. In this chapter we look at some of the characteristics of the euro that may qualify or disqualify it, starting with an examination of the nature of sovereignty itself.

The euro as a reserve currency

A sovereign state owns and protects a fixed territory, exercises control (including taxation) over its citizens, maintains a national treasury, and defines and issues money. The EMU does only one of these things – it defines and issues money. No sovereign treasury, no pan-EMU taxation, no standing army. Even the territorial scope is flexible, with new territories merging into the main body all the time, including tiny Malta (but powerhouse Turkey still waiting hopefully in the wings), a bit like colonies hoping to be conquered. And, unprecedented in all of history as far as we know, each member of the EMU continues to assert all the other bits of sovereignty, like taxation and punishment of crime, while depending for defence against invaders on a different sovereign on a nearby island (UK) and another continent (US).

The EMU could not get away with designating itself a sovereign without external defence by third parties. And why do third parties agree to accept this moral and financial burden? To keep the collective member states from warring with one another, as they have been wont to do for a thousand years and more.

The EMU as a sovereign

Clearly sovereignty is a fluid and evolving concept. The financial world is willing to accept that the old criteria are outdated, but many worry that the European Monetary Union has not adequately defined the new criteria, let alone demonstrated itself capable of satisfying the new criteria. That's because an essential component of the sovereign's ability to act is its ability to manage the affairs of the state, i.e., manage the treasury and not go bankrupt. But the EMU is not a state in the usual sense of the word. It has felt no shame in accepting bailout money from the rest of the world, i.e., the IMF, just as it feels no shame in declining to engage in military activities (such as Kosovo).

But who needs a fat treasury in a world without war? The EMU chose not to have a treasury. It doesn't have access to the individual treasuries of the member states, either, except by tapping them once in a while for specific ends, such as raising the capital of the European Central Bank (ECB), which it did in December 2010.

We can view the European Monetary Union is an experiment in sovereignty, with the EMU picking a single criterion from the sovereignty list and ignoring all the others. A fast review of the history of sovereignty yields the unhappy conclusion that the euro zone experiment may be failing, and it's failing for lack of a single critical component – a treasury, and the *raison d'être* of a treasury, the ability to tax and to fund spending by other government agencies. But the process of judging the EMU as a sovereign is not completed and we have some strong evidence that the world is willing to give it the benefit of the doubt.

Europe had plenty of time to train the world to think that it could invent a new version of sovereignty, a limited version. It started small and ended big, from the European Coal and Steel Community (1951) and the European Economic Community (Treaty of Rome, 1957) to the Maastricht Treaty (1992). Then the euro was launched in January 1999.

Notice that the EMU didn't build a wall around the member states and arm it with sentries, a different application of sovereignty from centuries past. It also did not name a head of state or impose a sovereign-wide tax on the citizens of the new sovereign state. The only real outward evidence of sovereignty is the common currency and the main institution within this new sovereign is the central bank. Tellingly, the only other institution with any clout is the Competition Commission. We say tellingly because promoting and controlling commerce for its own benefit is a characteristic of successful sovereigns (think British East India Company).

Nobody ever heard of a sovereign like this before. Normally a sovereign state is one in which you actually have a sovereign head who has exclusive jurisdiction within a specific geographic area, whether by divine right or social contract. The sovereign can do pretty much anything he likes to the subjects, including tax them or behead them, with varying degrees of restraint and moderation by constitutions and legal systems. A sovereign state holds a hoard of national wealth that it can spend on guns or butter. The sovereign always protects itself against invasion or control by other states, and maintains military forces to protect its sovereignty.

Country risk

The EMU does none of these things, and as a result, faces a different kind of risk, which we might name *component* or *country* risk. At the core, sovereign risk is the risk of default, or a nation's government deciding not to repay principal on bank loans or bonds, or refusing to make the interest payments on bank loans or bonds. For example, will Greece continue to default on its sovereign debt and so what if it does? This is the riveting question since the Greek drama started to unfold in December 2009.

Choosing default may be a political choice or a financial necessity; analysts often draw the distinction between the ability to pay vs. the willingness to pay. This bleeds into the broader concept of country risk, since a country that has the ability to pay but chooses not to pay is making a political decision, not a financial one. Russia and Argentina are the 20th century poster boys for this kind of country risk, both having defaulted several times despite having the ability to pay.

In the new post-EMU world, default is not really the issue anymore, and now we have a broader and more nuanced discussion of country risk instead of sovereign risk. How a country deals with deficit recovery, for example, is a judgmental process that affects the foreign exchange market in some very strange ways. The UK, for example, announced a budget in late March 2011 that falls far short of fixing deficit problems – but sterling remained on the upswing in congruence with the rising euro. Nobody much cared that the budget failed to meet IMF and ratings agency standards.

Dubai presented the world with a peculiar and novel kind of sovereign risk when it declined to accept sovereign responsibility for the debts of its wholly state-owned company, Dubai World, saying the company never had an explicit government guarantee. This came as a shock to bank lenders. The resolution so far consists of an equity injection into the company using proceeds from an Abu Dhabi aid package and other Dubai funds, but no state guarantee. Lest you imagine this some new special Middle East misunderstanding of the concept of the sovereign, the US has long had a similar ambiguity in the form of GSEs, or Government Sponsored Enterprises, chiefly the Fannie Mae and Freddie Mac mortgage units. (There is also a student loan facility named Sallie Mae and a farmers' mortgage loan unit named Farmer Mac.) They were explicitly not guaranteed by the full faith and credit of the US government but have been treated during the crisis as though they had been guaranteed.

If sovereign risk is a measure of a country's ability to pay and country risk widens the coverage to willingness to pay, we can also get the situation where a country has the willingness to pay but not the ability. A country's government may be honourable with respect to repaying sovereign debt but still permit corruption and/or mismanagement. Its institutions, especially financial ones, could be on shaky ground due to lax accounting standards and lack of supervision.

No one doubts that Europe in general and even Greece is particular has the wealth to pay off the Greek debt and start over. So we have the odd combination of a sovereign (the EMU) with the ability to pay but not the willingness, and its component country, Greece, taking the same stance – the ability to pay but not the mechanism, chiefly tax collection, to enable it to pay. But the reason a debtor will not pay is of no interest to the creditor. According to the old rules, both the EMU and Greece should be considered to be nearing or in default. That the private creditors in the Greek voluntary debt swap choose to consider a 70% loss not, technically, a default is both a historical aberration and an Alice-in-Wonderland re-definition of the word *default*.

In the end, the EMU is a badly formulated sovereign, but no one doubts that it is a sovereign.

Judging sovereigns

We have impressionistic ways of judging sovereigns, but we also have somewhat more systematic ways. For example, Iceland ranks high in Transparency International's evaluation of countries for perception of corruption, 13th of 180 countries covered. And yet Iceland's banking sector went down in flames in 2008-2009, leaving the sovereign with massive international debts it cannot, so far, repay, and struggling under harsh IMF-imposed budget constraints.

Transparency International judges a country on rule of law, sustainable development and quality of life. These are not financial criteria but the rule of law criterion suggests that borrowers will honour a debt contract. A high ranking implies that a country that has the ability to pay will always make the political decision to pay. The rankings – with a sample shown in Table 11.1 – are quite interesting, with New Zealand at the top of the list and Somalia, a failed state, in last place at 180th.

Table 11.1 – Transparency International Corruption Perceptions Index 2011

Ranking	Country
1	New Zealand
2	Denmark, Finland
4	Sweden
5	Singapore
6	Norway
7	Netherlands
13	Iceland
14	Germany, Japan
16	UK
24	United States
75	China
112	Vietnam
134	Pakistan
143	Nigeria
182	Somalia

Source: **cpi.transparency.org/cpi2011/results**

We generally assume that the major developed nations (G7 or perhaps G20, ex-Russia) would never make the political decision to default because it would later impose too high a funding cost on the taxpaying (and voting) citizens. And yet in November 1994, the Republicans under Newt Gingrich shut down the US government and threatened default, which was averted by the nimble Treasury Secretary Rubin, who funded interest payments from other government coffers until a political compromise could be reached. Rubin said a US default was "unthinkable" and evidently the FX market believed him. It is fascinating and inexplicable that the dollar did not fall during this episode, as illustrated in Figure 11.1. The dollar had been on a downward trend, to be sure, but one of its pullbacks to the upside came during the height of the crisis, a counter-intuitive outcome, to say the least.

Figure 11.1 – Dollar Index rises at height of default threat

The next big country to face a sovereign risk concern is Japan. Japan has total sovereign debt – government bond issuance – totalling nearly 200% of the annual GDP of the country, or about $9 trillion. The IMF estimates that by 2014, Japan's government debt will reach 246% of GDP. Ratings agencies warn that Japan faces a rating downgrade unless it brings government spending under control. S&P reduced Japan's sovereign rating from Triple A to Double A, and Moody's cut the rating to Aa2, in May 2009.

No one doubts the willingness of Japan to repay this debt as a matter of national pride, so the question is the ability to repay it, and repay it on schedule. Since Japan has $1.303 trillion in reserves as of March 2012, it could (in theory) liquidate reserves to fend off any tax shortfall and avoid default. The Japanese government could also instruct its banks to stop rolling over foreign loans and its corporations to repatriate any surplus held in foreign countries. In short, the probability of Japanese default on its sovereign debt is effectively zero. Besides, only about 8% of Japanese debt is held by foreigners, so an outright default would impoverish Japanese savers and have little effect on global bondholders. And, most telling of all, the yen does not fall when ratings downgrades and budget deficits are the headline news.

While we may be willing to give G20 the benefit of the doubt when it comes to willingness to repay, the ability to repay is being put through the shredder of the latest Great Recession. Ratings agencies already downgraded the US because of high and rising deficit funding. In fact, says former IMF chief economist Simon Johnson, "It's not just about Greece anymore." Johnson was referring to the other European countries falling into the abyss of unpayable debts, but with the exception of Canada, just about every developed country faces a ratings agency downgrade.

This is an unprecedented *simultaneous* deterioration of every country's public finances. Table 11.2 shows the IMF's projection for 2014. You can get a readable translation of the IMF's impenetrable statistics at **economywatch.com**.

Table 11.2 – government debt as percentage of GDP, 2014

Japan	246%
Italy	129%
United States	108%
UK	98%
France	96%
Germany	89%
Canada	60%

Source: *The Economist*, 27 March 2010

The US has gone deeper into sovereign debt by a stunning 20% of GDP over the past two years. The buyers are about 40% foreign, including Japan and China, with Brazil the only notable name divesting US Treasuries. In Greece, the debt-to-GDP ratio rose from 120% to 160% as the crisis worsened, so that promises to reduce it were pared to 120%, the same level that accompanied and partly defined the crisis in the first place. As for coverage, Greece was already paying 5% of GDP in interest payments in 2009 and that will rise to 8.4% in 2014. This debt load is probably unsustainable, according to Johnson. He says that if Greece had to pay 10% interest on new bonds issues (from 6% now), it would end up transferring 12% of GDP to foreign holders of its debt every year.

When every major issuer faces ratings agency downgrades and every major country has to pay some large chunk of annual GDP in debt service, what effect does this have on currencies? Hard as it is to believe, we don't know. This is an unprecedented situation. At a guess, we have to start making new judgments about country risk – not only the ability to pay, which comes from taxation or asset sales, but also the willingness to pay.

Commentators note that Ireland squeezed its deficit and the citizens are suffering real hardship, but returned to private markets ahead of schedule in 2012, while Greece's contraction plans have yet to yield any real return. The early 2012 bailout will involve EC monitors inhabiting Greek bureaucracies, including the tax office. The amount of overdue and unpaid taxes in Greece was estimated by the IMF at €60 billion in February 2012, or about half of the second bailout amount of €130 billion.

This is not a trivial point. The euro should go down on evidence that the Greek situation is impossible of solution, as economist Krugman puts it. And yet the euro has been remarkably resilient throughout the Greek crisis and subsequent developments involving Portugal, Ireland and Spain.

Hegemony and reserve currency investors

It is known that China has been adding euro to its currency reserves; why would it want to do this and invest in states that cannot defend themselves? If we consider that a sovereign state is one that seeks above else to maximise its power in order to survive, financial power may be a fine substitute for military power as long as the state has another to protect it. Japan eyes China warily and every year or so there is an incident, but nobody expects outright war. And once the Cold War ended with the downfall of the Soviet Union in 1991, Europe was no longer threatened by the Russian Bear. NATO, funded over 50% by the US, was seen as sufficient. In the old days, of course, military power and financial power went hand-in-hand, as amply demonstrated by Great Britain ruling the seas and the global financial system from the mid-18th century to World War I or World War II, depending on how you want to measure. Great Britain was more than the superpower of its day – it had *hegemony*.

Hegemony is a word now coming into more widespread usage and quite useful for understanding a new world in which the definition of *sovereign* is shifting. Hegemony comes from the Greek word for leadership and refers to a dominant group that exercises power through means other than brute military force. The leadership can be in the form of economic ideas, cultural norms, language or many other aspects of life. Thus English is the most-spoken second language on the planet, reflecting the historical hegemony of the UK and US.

To date the US is the sole military superpower and single largest issuer of sovereign debt, and thus the top sovereign state as well as the top global hegemon, distributing its cultural norms worldwide (Coca-Cola, McDonalds, Playboy, Michael Jackson) as well as its legal contracts and currency. The hegemon is often resented, even if it's not engaging in awful behaviour like imperial colonialism and Opium Wars.

Sentiment against the hegemon, or anti-Americanism, doesn't need to be based on outright bad acts of the state – it can be based on minor things like the prevalence of obesity or too much sex and violence in movies and games. Unhappily, sentiment against the hegemon contributes, albeit to a varying and unmeasurable extent, to a periodic but persistent anti-dollar bias we have observed since the devaluation of the dollar in 1971 and the floating of the dollar in 1974.

So, if the US is the top sovereign state as well as the global hegemon, what is Europe's place? Here the thinking gets a little murky. Europe presents a somewhat disorganised third way that rejects both full-bore raw capitalism and communism but is sensitive to the welfare – standard of living – of its citizens. Jobs are a right. Healthcare is a right. Higher education is a right. Environmental cleanliness is a right. So far only the UK has embarked on an examination of Bhutan's concept of 'gross national happiness', but the European mentality is open to the idea. Ideologically, Europe wants to have its cake and eat it, too – socialistic ideals being implemented in the context of a mostly free-market environment. Every American tourist to France or Italy returns with an appreciation of a superior way of life (better manners and certainly better cuisine), but without accepting European leadership in these matters as something that must be acted upon right away.

The new gold standard

Europe's claim to hegemony lies not in standards of humaneness, courtesy and good food, but rather its principle that national debt should not exceed 60% of GDP and that the topmost goal of the state is to prevent inflation. EMU fiscal principles are like a new religion, as former British Prime Minister Brown said. The absence of this fiscal rule can be said to have toppled many an empire and threaten many existing regimes today. Avoiding inflation is the Number One priority of all savers and fixed income investors throughout history, whether inflation arises from bad monetary policy or overindebtedness.

In a word, the EMU has devised the new gold standard of sovereign financial governance – monetary and fiscal excellence. No other sovereign in the history of the world has explicitly promised to its debt-holders that they will be safe from depreciation via inflation.

Turn the picture to the other side. Imagine the US adopting an unbreakable law – a Constitutional amendment, maybe – requiring national debt not to exceed 60% of GDP and the central bank to manage inflation to within a specific range. (In practice, we have the inflation mandate, but it's a policy choice of the current Fed board, not a law.) Given the US' superpower status and top hegemon ranking, the dollar would be as though gold-based. Gold is what some misinformed people imagine would save us from overspending and from inflation. In fact, adopting a gold standard would be a disaster on a par with California falling into the sea – we have so little gold ($300 billion) compared to money supply ($8 trillion) that the economy would have to contract drastically. Instead, why not adopt the EMU's gold standard?

If Europe can emerge from austerity with its fiscal principles in working order, why would China not be lured into investing its trillions in euro-denominated reserves? This is an even more enticing prospect the longer the US fails to adopt the *gold standard* of fiscal excellence. In sum, Europe's *gold standard* has the hegemonic power to rule international finance for the next century or more. It may not matter if a state or two has to fall by the wayside and out of the Union, presumably Greece being the first of these.

Economists and armchair observers alike accept that the EMU has rejected the transfer mechanism that makes the US federal system work. Therefore, it's almost irrelevant that Europe has the wealth to pull itself out of the sovereign debt crisis. The amount the component countries will devote to the rescue operation, at €750 billion as of the first quarter of 2012, is a tiny portion of the total wealth available in these countries, although curiously close to combined official reserves. It's the standard country risk problem – ability to pay but unwillingness to pay. Instead, the EMU wants and expects investment from established nations like Japan, emerging markets like China and the rest of the world in the form of the IMF.

The IMF is an integral part of the European bailout equation and it is funded over 50% by the US. That means the euro zone depends on the US for external defence and on the US for bailout funding. What kind of sovereign is this? More to the point, what kind of sovereign would agree to do this for a fellow semi-sovereign, and one who would not return the favour if the tables were turned? This is a deal that is too good to be true – the euro zone gets its longed for reserve currency status from China and does it on the back of the US, the country it is endeavouring to supplant as the reserve currency issuer.

Is the world going to let Europe get away with it? Is the US? The answer is probably yes. The founders of the EMU wanted the union as an economic growth mechanism and also as a preventer of wars. That has always been explicit. These are the countries that started two world wars. Now they are holding the US hostage to that history, demanding not only external defence at low or no cost but also emergency financing. The world is enchanted with the EMU's new gold standard of fiscal excellence.

Evaluating the euro zone debt crisis

The historically normal path to sovereign default includes, first, over-indebtedness by the state and sometimes the private sector as well, and second, some kind of crisis of confidence that triggers a bond and currency sell-off. Usually the state responds by intervening to support the currency, and when that fails, as it usually does, devaluing the currency. This was the pattern in the Asian crisis that started in 1997 as well as others. When the IMF is brought in, its standard policy prescription consists of just a few initiatives – float and devalue the currency, raise interest rates, and slash government spending, all in the context of free markets and with the explicit goal of restoring investor confidence and foreign capital inflows.

The 1997 Asian crisis that spread to Latin America and Russia brought forth tens of billions in IMF lending – although it proves virtually impossible to get the exact amounts by country at the IMF website or anywhere else. It's astonishing that barely 15 years after this first global exercise in moral hazard, you can't readily find the cost. The $57 billion for South Korea was the biggest to date at the time and possibly more than half of a total estimate of $100 billion.

If we look at the on-going euro zone crisis in the context of the Asian crisis, right away we see differences. The IMF did not advise the devaluation and higher interest rates that are the staple in emerging market crises. Moreover, the euro zone did not intervene to prop up the euro on those occasions when the FX market showed signs of a crisis of confidence. Rather than intervene, each time the euro was being sold off, the euro zone leadership came up with an institutional fix or at least the promise of a fix. The European tactic of "kicking the can down the road" with public figure sound bites instead of actually spending money on intervention has been derided – and yet it has worked for several years.

As the euro was undergoing one of its periodic sell-offs in July 2012, for example, ECB president Draghi said "To the extent that the size of these sovereign premia [for Spanish bonds] hamper the functioning of the monetary policy transmission channel, they come within our mandate. Within our mandate, the ECB is ready to do whatever it takes to preserve the euro… Believe me, it will be enough."

The comment was interpreted as an announcement that the ECB would intervene in the sovereign debt market. The immediate effect was a drop in Spanish 10-year bond yields by over 50 bp and a rise in the euro by almost 300 points in a single day, even though previously Draghi had substituted two tranches of Long-Term Repo Operations for the bond-buying Securities Market Program, which had totalled only about €200 billion up to then. In other words, professional FX analysts and traders had good cause not to believe Draghi, and even to think he may not have appreciated the implications of what he was saying, but they traded the euro as though Draghi's words were a realistic promise. This is in sharp and stunning contrast to the effect of officials making similar promises in other countries under the same circumstances, who have never yet succeeded in halting a crisis of confidence with mere words.

This is an instance in which declining to intervene in favour of the euro in the midst of a sell-off is a signal to the FX market that intervention is not warranted. It's a clever and presumably well-thought-out tactic, since intervention is a sign of desperation and acknowledgement that fundamental imbalances are so bad that policy fixes will be too little and too late. The fixed income and FX markets are so enamoured of the euro zone's new gold standard status that they are willing to give the benefit of the doubt to officials offering little more than promises. Each time the euro undergoes a major sell-off, it recovers after some new institutional fix is promised or devised, even when the fix falls far short of need and is demonstrably inadequate. Table 11.3 shows some instances of this, but these are just the tip of this iceberg.

Table 11.3 – major euro/dollar declines halted by institutional events

Date	Euro high	Euro low	High-low range	Action
25 November 2009 to 4 June 2010	1.5145	1.1956	3189 points	European Financial Stability Facility
4 November 2010 to 11 January 2011	1.3973	1.2904	1069 points	Japan buys EFSF bonds as Portugal nears bailout
5 June 2011 to 19 July 2012	1.4588	1.2229	2359 points	Draghi promise to re-activate SMP

A second feature of the euro zone-as-sovereign is that its official reserves are untouched by multiple crises. Instead of each sovereign having to intervene in its own bond market and in defence of its own currency, running down reserves, the euro zone countries have evaded both actions and succeeded in getting others to do the heavy lifting, including its own supra-national bailout fund, the EFSF and its successor, the European Stability Facility (ESM). We may say that the member countries are contributing to the bailout funds and thus accepting liability, but in practice what they are contributing is credit, not cash. Euro zone member reserves are high and have stayed high throughout the crisis. This is a distinct departure from the usual consequences for a sovereign in crisis. Most sovereigns lose their treasure in the course of fighting a crisis. Not so in the euro zone. So far, the cost of the euro zone crisis is not affecting sovereign wealth.

The euro zone member states have plenty of actual foreign exchange and gold reserves, about $786 billion, according to the IMF. While only five members qualify on the 60% of debt-to-GDP criterion (Estonia, Luxembourg, Slovenia, Slovakia and Finland), the euro zone is collectively seen as very, very rich. Table 11.4 shows the foreign exchange and gold reserves of euro zone countries.

Table 11.4 – FX and gold reserves of selected euro zone countries

Country	US $m
Germany	239,522
Italy	173,245
France	171,479
Spain	52,160
Netherlands	51,723
Portugal	21,516
Austria	27,624
Finland	10,732
Greece	6878
Austria	1034
Ireland	1595
Luxembourg	25,628
Slovakia	2396
Slovenia	937
Estonia	269
Cyprus	1229
Malta	638
Total	**788,605**

Source: IMF (**www.imf.org/external/np/sta/ir/IRProcessWeb/colist.aspx**)

It has never been made explicit that these reserves are a backstop of the bailout facilities, although historically, one might think they should be. Having said that, consider that US sovereign debt is on the order of $15.9 trillion while IMF-reported official reserves are $148.5 billion, or a leverage factor of 1000. No wonder the euro zone seeks to have the euro become a reserve currency! As noted in Chapter 10, reserve currency status confers extraordinary privilege – other counties must buy sovereign paper for reserve purposes far beyond the proven ability to repay out of the reserve currency issuer's reserves. This is one way to understand the euro zone leaders' resolve to soldier on – it will have a tremendous payoff in the end, quite apart from the prestige factor.

Contagion

So far the cost to the still-performing component members of the EMU and the rest of the world, i.e. the IMF, is quite low. That could change if questions about adequacy get put to the ultimate test – contagion to other countries like Spain and Italy. Consider that contagion is more than a psychological phenomenon and far from irrational. With banks in each European country exposed to sovereign debt in other European countries, a cascade of failures would swiftly paralyse the financial sector in all of Europe. As of end-2010, according to the BIS, euro zone banks accounted for over 50% of all bank exposure to imperilled countries (Greece, Ireland, Portugal and Spain).

France and Germany alone had the most exposure, despite their own economies being in fine fettle. Total euro zone bank exposure to the four peripherals adds up to well over €1 trillion.

The cure for contagion is not known in the context of financial markets, but is assumed to be somewhat similar to the treatment for infectious disease in medicine – first, isolate the inflicted. In the case of potential default, bring in the private creditors under the mantle of their guild and let the specialists determine solutions, as the International Swaps Dealers did in the case of Greece. Then, consistent with disaster-relief methods, apply every tool in the new central bank toolkit, especially vast quantities of cash. The ECB's two doses of three-year ultra-cheap liquidity at end-December 2011 and again in February 2012 is analogous to massive doses of penicillin and chicken soup.

Most of all, the fight against contagion entails affirming the monetary policy that fights inflation, lest investors imagine that not only the threat of default lies ahead but also perhaps inflation. In early 2012, most of the members of the European Union approved a new fiscal compact that does little more than repeat the aspirations and goals of the original Maastricht Treaty, except that fiscal rectitude is to be better enforced. It can't be put more clearly than by German Finance Minister Schaeuble, who said:

> "We have to assume responsibility. If we can't defend our currency effectively as a stable currency, the economic and social consequences for our country and the people in our country would be incalculable. It is extremely important to show in Germany that what is being discussed so much internationally is indeed possible: to fight in a measured way the main causes of the crisis – excessive deficits in public budgets and liquidity bubbles in financial markets."

Conclusion

The EMU is not qualified to be the issuer of a reserve currency by the standards of centuries past. It seems implausible that a new reserve currency can be born out of a single principle – control of inflation and public debt to specific levels – without all the other features and benefits of a reserve currency, especially a rock-hard unwillingness to default on sovereign debt. And yet the EMU is permitting default while getting the rest of the world to name it something else and the rest of the world is willing to buy into the fiction because it is so enchanted with the new gold standard. The holder of all the best cards are the merchants, who may choose to accept the euro as the new numeraire, and their governments, such as China, who may choose to continue diversifying reserves into euro. The US – arguably paying for some of this development – doesn't get a vote.

The long journey of the euro to reserve currency status that started in 1999 was thrown off course by the peripheral debt crisis and it remains to be seen whether the detour will deliver the euro to its final destination. Judging from the remarkable resilience of the euro in the face of crises that would have felled a lesser currency, and from the euro zone members' ability to hang on to their reserves and get others to pay for repairs, the euro may well arrive at reserve currency status one day, just later than the founders wanted and foresaw.

CHAPTER 12 –
THE CENTRAL BANK TOOL KIT AND HOW IT AFFECTS FOREIGN EXCHANGE

"Banking establishments are more dangerous than standing armies."

Thomas Jefferson

In earlier chapters, we say that to the FX trader, the central bank is the single most important institution. The trader studies economic and other data specifically to get an understanding on how it may affect the central bank's policy stance. Until recently, world central banks adhered to tried and true methods of implementing monetary policy. This involved raising and lowering benchmark interest rates, using open market operations to adjust liquidity, and in some cases providing domestic banks with a discount window to borrow from. Occasionally, a central bank would adjust reserve requirements or intervene in foreign exchange markets.

Then the subprime mortgage crisis and the euro zone peripheral debt crisis forced central banks around the world to seek out new tools to keep financial markets running smoothly. This chapter looks at the old and new tools in the central bankers' tool kit and the effect on foreign exchange. We will discuss quantitative easing, intervention, capital controls, FX pegs and engineered interest rates – all non-standard monetary policy measures.

Non-standard measures

An IMF working paper from June 2011[83] lists unconventional central bank balance sheet policies as:

- liquidity provision to funding and credit markets
- foreign exchange liquidity provision to local markets
- bond purchases
- large-scale foreign exchange intervention
- credit provision to the private sector

"In summary, most of the unconventional balance sheet policies used by the major central banks appear to have been effective, albeit to varying degrees. Against these apparent benefits must be weighed the risks posed by the overlaps of these policies with other policy spheres, the need for an exit strategy, and risks to the balance sheet," the working paper said.

"More specifically, the policies used to support *financial stability* broadly warrant inclusion for use to counter systemic financial stress. Liquidity provision to funding and credit markets and the provision of foreign exchange liquidity to local markets reduced the impact of financial stress on the real economy, and have for the most part been wound down without disruption. Further, the systemic importance of financial markets can be, if anything, expected to increase, and thus they warrant a broad set of liquidity provision tools. Some of the elements of the broadening of liquidity provision put in place during the crisis could be kept on permanently, depending on what the new financial landscape looks like. Inclusion of liquidity provision policies to the tool kit should be complemented by fully effective regulation and supervision to mitigate against the moral hazard problem," the paper said.

While unconventional tools may be necessary and beneficial in some circumstances, there is a danger that this cure brings its own form of disease. In this vein, the IMF working paper offered "a cautionary final thought" for world central banks to consider:

"Central banks and governments are faced with the challenges of exiting smoothly from balance sheet and other crisis intervention policies, clarifying the new wider set of central bank policy responsibilities, and reducing in some cases very large fiscal burdens. This setting raises the potential of a downside scenario involving the misuse of balance sheet policies and a loss of central bank independence. The preservation of the historically large measure of credibility gained by central banks during the pre-crisis golden age will hinge on meeting successfully these challenges."

Quantitative easing

While the term *quantitative easing (QE)* became mainstream during the latest financial crises in the US and Europe, its roots lie with the Bank of Japan.

It came from Japan

Japanese growth bottomed near -4% in mid-2009 and has not been over 2% since. In fact, growth is jumpy, up one quarter and down the next. Meanwhile, inflation hit the lowest low in October 2009 at -2.5% and has not been over 0.5% since. Japan's deflationary recession that started after the stock market crash in 1990 and ensuing multiple banking sector crises is characterised by the failure of conventional monetary policy. Many efforts to boost morale and economic activity have been tried and all have failed. Keynes called trying to use conventional stimulus measures in a deflationary environment "pushing on string." Before he was Fed chairman, in the 1990s and in 1999 at a conference, Bernanke called on Japan to take less timid unconventional monetary policy measures.

What does a central bank do when it has run out of monetary policy *bullets*? When interest rates are already zero or near zero and there is nothing else to do on the interest rate front to jumpstart the economy? Such was the dilemma facing the BOJ in late 2000/2001.

In January 2001, with its discount rate at 0.50% and the uncollateralised overnight rate at effectively zero (0.25%), then central bank governor Masaru Hayami set the stage by issuing a statement saying that the staff would examine ways to improve liquidity provision to the market.

The BOJ lowered the discount rate to 0.35% on 9 February 2001 to enhance the effectiveness of a newly created (Lombard type) lending facility. The BOJ also increased outright operations of short-term government securities and prepared for the introduction of Bill Purchasing Operations at all business offices. The BOJ lowered the official discount rate again on 28 February to 0.25% and encouraged the uncollateralised overnight rate towards 0.15%. In March 2001, the central bank left rates unchanged and acknowledged the effectiveness of the Lombard-type lending facility. The BOJ said the facility would remain in place until CPI excluding perishables stabilised at zero or saw a year-on-year increase. Balances outstanding on the bank's current accounts were increased to Y5 trillion from Y4 trillion and the uncollateralised overnight rate was encouraged towards zero.

In August 2001, with the discount rate now at 0.15%, the BOJ's balances outstanding were increased to Y6 trillion. The BOJ also announced an increase in government bond purchases to Y600 billion per month from about Y400 billion per month. By December 2001, with the discount rate at 0.10%, the BOJ raised the main operating target for balances outstanding on the bank's current account to Y10 trillion to Y15 trillion. When the BOJ ended quantitative easing in March 2006, the main operating target for current account balances outstanding stood at Y30 to Y35 trillion. The BOJ still encouraged the uncollateralised overnight rate to remain at zero.

With Japanese interest rates low and BOJ QE starting, the yen began to weaken more markedly. Dollar-yen rose from about Y113.60 the first week of January 2001 to just shy of Y135 in 2002. Then the pair reversed course and edged lower as the US fed funds rate was lowered to new life-time low levels. The Fed began an easing cycle in January 2001, by moving the fed funds rate from 6.50% to 6.0%. The easing cycle ended with fed funds being lowered to 1.0% in June 2003. Dollar-yen bottomed around Y115.00 in mid-May 2003.

By late 2008/early 2009, the BOJ officials were again digging QE measures out of the toolkit. But this time, they had the company of other central banks.

Other banks use QE too

The Federal Reserve, the Bank of Japan, the European Central Bank (ECB) and the Bank of England joined the BOJ in adopting a form of quantitative easing, which was used to stimulate the economy, or in the ECB's case, was purportedly crafted to maintain their single mandate to maintain price stability. The ECB could get around the mandate by pointing to Article 2 of the Treaty on European Union which states that the European Union aims to promote "economic and social progress and a high level of employment and to achieve balanced and sustainable development." The ECB notes on its website that, "The Eurosystem contributes to these objectives by maintaining price stability."

At the start of the world financial crisis, it was clear that global money markets were becoming dysfunctional and that banks had a hard time borrowing, even in liquid currencies such as the dollar.

A New York Federal Reserve Staff report[84] (No 429) from January 2010 (revised February 2010), entitled 'Central Bank Dollar Swap Lines and Overseas Dollar Funding Costs' discusses how dollar funding costs shifted in the wake of the US financial crisis. Despite the advent of the euro in January 1999, the foreign currency exposure of European banks increased markedly from 2000 to 2007, the report noted.

"European Union, United Kingdom, and Swiss banks' on-balance sheet dollar exposures were to exceed $8 trillion in 2008. Prior to the crisis, this exposure was funded from money market funds ($1 trillion), central banks ($500 billion), and the foreign exchange swap market ($800 billion), while the remainder was funded by interbank borrowing, flows from US-based affiliates, and other sources," the Fed report said.

European and other non-US banks lacked a dollar-denominated retail deposit base and had increasingly relied on wholesale funding to meet US dollar funding needs.

Spreads drive policy

In the fall of 2008, after Lehman Brothers declared bankruptcy in September, LIBOR-OIS spreads began to widen, as did the spread between the implied dollar funding cost of a foreign exchange swap and Libor. There were even discrepancies in US fed funds, with morning fed funds more expensive than afternoon fed funds. To address this spread widening, the Federal Reserve and select other world central banks first entered into *reciprocal currency arrangements* (initially established in December 2007 between the ECB and Swiss National Bank) and then *central bank dollar swaps*. Eventually, 14 central banks entered into swap agreements with the Fed.

"Net dollars outstanding through the CB dollar swaps peaked at nearly $600 billion near the end of 2008, as banks hoarded liquidity over the year end, with some of this demand for dollars unwinding in the post year-end period. Amounts outstanding at the dollar swap facilities declined to under $100 billion by June 2009, to less than $35 billion outstanding by October 2009, and to less than $1 billion at the program's expiry on 1 February 2010," the Fed report said.

A chart of the euro over this period (Figure 12.1) shows how spread widening and narrowing played a key role in FX direction. About two weeks after the ECB raised interest rates by 25 basis points to 4.25%, in July 2008, the euro peaked at $1.6040. The pair slipped in subsequent months as dollar funding costs tightened and players preferred a dollar long position. After falling below $1.2330 in October 2008, the euro spiked toward $1.47 into year-end after the Fed decided to lower the fed funds rate from 1% to a historic low range of zero to 0.25% in mid-December. In addition to announcing plans to buy agency and mortgage-backed debt, the Fed also said it would implement the Term Asset-Backed Securities Loan Facility or TALF in early 2009. Expectations about these unconventional measures seemed to have a disproportionate effect on the EUR/USD beyond spreads alone.

Figure 12.1 – EUR/USD and Central Bank rate moves (2008)

The euro again came under downward pressure in the first quarter of 2009, as massive deleveraging of all instruments sent US stock and commodity markets plummeting. The S&P 500 bottomed at 666.92 in March 2009, down over 57% from its lifetime peak of 1565.15 seen 9 October 2007. The Thomson Reuters-Jefferies CRB index fell 46% from peak to trough also. The euro crept higher in Q2 2009, as US stocks recovered and the Fed announced plans to heavily expand its balance sheet. The recovery continued into the end of 2009, when peripheral debt jitters began to weigh and the euro again came under downward pressure.

To address the widening of the peripheral (Greek, Italy, Ireland, Portugal, Spain) country spreads, the ECB was also forced to consider unconventional tools. This included stepped-up buying of member nation debt. In December 2010, the central bank announced plans[85] to nearly double its capitalisation from €5.76 billion at the time to €10.76 billion.

> "The capital increase was deemed appropriate in view of increased volatility in foreign exchange rates, interest rates and gold prices as well as credit risk. As the maximum size of the ECB's provisions and reserves is equal to the level of its paid-up capital, this decision will allow the Governing Council to augment the provision by an amount equivalent to the capital increase, starting with the allocation of part of this year's profits. From a longer-term perspective, the increase in capital – the first general one in 12 years – is also motivated by the need to provide an adequate capital base in a financial system that has grown considerably."

The national central banks were instructed to pay their share of €1,163,191,667 in three instalments, the first on 29 December 2010 and the remainder at the end of 2011 and 2012, respectively.

On the currency front, the euro edged up over $1.4500 at the start of 2010, but soon succumbed to massive selling as market players began to price in the prospects of an EMU breakup. The announcement in early May of a €750 billion joint stabilisation plan between the European Union and the International Monetary Fund provided only short-lived support to the euro and the pair soon edged lower to close the month around $1.2300. The euro closed 2010 around $1.3377, with the gains driven by improved risk appetite and the belief that euro zone peripheral issues could be contained and dealt with.

QE2

The Federal Reserve implemented a second quantitative easing program in November 2010. QE2 by the Fed served to underpin risk appetite, which in turn served to underpin the euro and other currencies as the prospects of lower US yields weighing on the dollar into year-end.

In 2011, the euro began to rebound, despite increased spread widening in the peripherals, because of expectations of ECB tightening. The ECB did indeed raise the minimum refi rate by 25 basis points rates in April 2011, and while not "pre-announcing" further hikes, kept the door open for additional tightening, which was later seen in July. In response to the ECB hike and the assumption that the Federal Reserve would not raise rates until 2012, or at least Q4 2011 under the best of circumstances, the euro rose to then 16-month highs over 1.4940 and then stalled as new peripheral spread widening and concerns about peripheral debt began to weigh on investor sentiment. The euro traded in a $1.40-$1.45 range throughout the early part of the second half of 2011, with the euro and the dollar both vying to be the winner of the "ugly" currency contest. Eventually, the dollar won on its safe-haven status and the euro lost due to escalating peripheral debt jitters and broke below $1.3 before the year was over.

Capital controls

Capital controls have been used in some form ever since foreign exchange began to be actively traded, albeit controls are more widely used in emerging markets, where economies tend to live or die by exports. So it came as no surprise to see countries, such as Brazil and South Korea, turn to capital controls in recent years to bolster their economies as their currencies began to rise markedly versus the dollar. Brazil, Korea and many other emerging markets saw huge investor inflows because these countries had more attractive yields and better growth prospects than the United States offered.

Brazil began the process of limiting these flows by raising the IOF tax on select foreign purchases of Brazilian assets to 2% from zero in October 2009. In subsequent months and years, Brazilian officials would again raise the IOF tax and resort to other measures such as requiring all over-the-counter derivative operations be registered with a clearing house and imposing an IOF tax on the net long position of institutions' and individuals' new currency derivative operations. South Korea in November 2010 moved to reimpose taxes on foreign purchases of local government bonds. Other Asian countries, such as Thailand, Taiwan and China, either implemented new capital controls or strengthened old ones around the same time.

Emerging market country officials, in their attempt to move their country toward becoming a developed rather than developing or emerging nation, normally would prefer not to use capital controls unless absolutely necessary, wary of the taint of the use of these measures. However, in light of the trying times seen in the wake of the US financial crisis and later the euro zone peripheral crisis, capital controls have been given a pass, by the highest authorities, as sometimes being necessary, and effective.

"Capital controls are a little bit in the eye of the beholder, but they are certainly a part of the toolkit," observed Caroline Atkinson, the International Monetary Fund's director of External Relations in January 2011[86]. She noted that "some capital controls are more focused on macro-prudential measures, others are more focused on, for example, shifting the length of the maturity of inflows as they're taxing short-term and encouraging longer term flows." Atkinson said the IMF viewed the steps taken by Brazil as "macroprudential measures aimed to strengthen the banking system in Brazil in the face of big capital inflows and those can be part of the toolkit."

And in a May 2011 interview[87] with Market News International, Jonathan Ostry, deputy director of the IMF Research Department, said while the conventional wisdom is capital controls do more to impact the composition of capital flows than their aggregate levels, "there is a range of cross country studies that do suggest some effectiveness on the aggregate level, i.e. in moderating the extent of surges." Ostry said IMF research indicates that measures such as those Brazil is taking, provided a country also has sound fiscal policies and a currency that is not undervalued, are likely to increase its resilience to a possible reversal or reduction in capital flows.

In the above cases, the capital controls served only to stem, rather than halt, the tide of foreign investor demand for EM currencies. Until there was a viable alternative in either the US or the euro zone, global emerging markets would remain hot.

During the height of uncertainty in the summer of 2011, portfolio managers remained overweight in global emerging market equities. The September 2011 Bank of America/Merrill Lynch fund managers survey noted that a net 30% of global portfolio managers were overweight global emerging markets, down from a net 33% in July and at the long-term average. Back in November 2010, a net 56% of fund managers were overweight GEMs.

The year 2011 was to be the year when developed economies were to recover. Accordingly fund managers exited their EM holdings in late 2010 and early 2011, only to edge back into long positions later in the spring. As an example, dollar-real closed 2010 around BRL 11.6600 and, despite the various capital controls being put in place, still managed to fall to a 12-year low around BRL 11.5275 in late July 2011. Of course a 12.5% Selic rate did not detract from the Brazilian real's allure. It was only in late September 2011 that there was a larger exodus out of risk assets in general and emerging market assets saw widespread selling. This did not last long, however, with other investors happy to *bottom-fish* at bargain basement prices at the start of 2012.

Emerging markets have come a long way since the Asian crisis of 1997/1999. They are now considered a must-have in an investor's portfolio, if only a small allocation to enhance the returns of more developed markets. This makes the job for the emerging market central banker even tougher.

Peg-o-my-heart

The SNB's battle to control the franc's strength

Emerging market central banks are not the only ones having a hard time dealing with currency strength.

The Swiss National Bank has had an especially tough time in recent years in preventing the Swiss franc from gaining versus the dollar, as well as the euro, its key trading partners' currency. In the summer of 2008, the euro-Swiss cross held in a tight range above CHF 1.6000 before safe-haven demand for the Swiss franc began to push the cross lower. The pair closed around CHF 1.4930 that year.

In early 2009, euro-Swiss bottomed near CHF1.4600 and then stabilised just over CHF 1.5000 for most of the year – that is until December 2009, when Greece announced the truth about its deficits. Even before Greece's admission, it was clear that the Swiss franc, deemed the non-euro euro, would be a favourite for investors seeking safe-havens. The yen was another favoured current account surplus – albeit low yielding – currency attracting investor demand.

The SNB aggressively intervened to prevent the Swiss franc strength from March 2009 to June 2010. In January, the central bank announced[88] a loss of "some CHF 21 million" for the year 2010, with a CHF 26 million foreign exchange loss offset to a degree by "just under CHF 6 billion gold valuation gain."

Then SNB Governor Philipp Hildebrand[89] said of the loss admission:

> "In view of these losses, it is very tempting to argue that the SNB should not have purchased any foreign exchange. However, the purpose of the SNB is not to make a profit. The decision on whether monetary policy measures in the form of foreign currency purchases are necessary is based on an evaluation of the threat of deflation and the monetary policy expansion needed in order to counter this. Monetary policy inaction during the dramatic phases of 2009 and 2010 was not an option."

In 2011, dollar-Swiss and euro-Swiss continued to press lower and posted new life-time lows of CHF 0.7068 and CHF 1.0075 respectively in early August, before rebounding in response to a series of aggressive actions taken by the central bank.

On 3 August, after the euro-Swiss cross had broken below the psychological CHF 1.1000 level, the SNB lowered the three-month Libor rate to "as close to zero as possible, narrowing the target range for the three-month Libor from 0.00-0.75% to 0.00-0.25%" and increased the supply of liquidity to the Swiss franc money market. The SNB also expanded the bank's sight deposits at the SNB from currently around CHF 30 billion to CHF 80 billion.

On 10 August, a day after new life-time Swiss highs were seen versus the dollar and the euro, the SNB further expanded the sight deposits to CHF 120 billion and announced it would conduct foreign exchange swap transactions. In the forward FX market, the SNB would sell Swiss francs spot and then buy Swiss francs at some forward date, effectively creating a lower Swiss franc interest rate, at times a negative yield, through its transactions. On 17 August, the SNB raised the sight deposit level to CHF 200 billion and stressed it would continue to buy outstanding SNB bills and use FX swaps. The central bank kept the door open for other measures. "Furthermore, the SNB reiterates that it will, if necessary, take further measures against the strength of the Swiss franc," the 17 August statement warned.

Analysts at the time debated the SNB's next move, with talk of a euro-Swiss peg or trading band, at levels such as CHF 1.30 or even CHF 1.40. On 6 September 2011, the SNB did indeed announce[90] that the central bank would no longer tolerate a EUR/CHF exchange rate below the minimum rate of CHF 1.20 and stressed that "the SNB would enforce this minimum rate with the utmost determination and is prepared to buy foreign currency in unlimited quantities."

Before the announcement of the cross peg in September, capital controls, last used by the SNB nearly 40 years ago, were also viewed as on the table. The use of capital controls by a major developed country in the new millennium was shocking to the market. This was especially so because the SNB's use of these measures during the 1970s was deemed ineffective in the long term.

Ineffective use of capital controls by the SNB in the 1970s

A US Congressional Budget Office report from August 1985[91] noted that measures taken in early 1973 and 1975:

> "included negative interest rates on Swiss franc deposits of nonresidents at an annual rate of 40%; discriminatory minimum reserves, higher than those prevailing in Germany, on the growth and level of nonresident bank liabilities; requirements for banks to balance their position in foreign currency daily, not only overall but also vis-à-vis each of nine major foreign currencies; a limitation on the forward sale of Swiss francs by foreign

residents; and a prohibition on nonresidents' investing foreign funds in fixed-interest securities denominated in Swiss francs between June 1972 and February 1974."

These measures were not as effective as Swiss authorities would have liked, and in 1976, additional measures "were placed on interest payments on nonresidents' savings deposits denominated in Swiss francs; forward exchange regulations were tightened to reduce transactions in Swiss francs unrelated to trade; and substantially enlarged reporting requirements were introduced on banks' foreign assets and liabilities positions, both spot and forward," but still the Swiss franc kept strengthening.

In October 1978, the SNB adopted yet other measures "including the encouragement of capital exports and provisions concerning interest rates and liquidity." Finally that month, the SNB "decided to abandon setting norms for money supply growth and to concentrate on stabilising the exchange rate instead. This policy remained in effect until 1981," the CBO said.

Time will tell if the SNB's latest attempt to stem Swiss franc strength, the euro-Swiss peg at CHF 1.2000, will be successful or the central bank will have to resort to more draconian measures.

Pegs have a place

Currency pegs do have their place, as evidenced by the long-held yuan-dollar peg revived by the People's Bank of China during the US financial crisis. After years of nagging by G20 nations to allow the yuan to be more "flexible," which was code word to allow the yuan to strengthen versus the dollar, on 21 July 2005 China freed the yuan from its long standing peg to the dollar in favour of a managed float with a reference to a basket of currencies. In January 2007, the PBOC began setting a daily central parity rate and later that year widened the daily fluctuation band for the yuan-dollar exchange rate to 0.5% from 0.3% on either side of the central parity level.

As the US financial crisis escalated in the summer of 2008, the PBOC unofficially returned to the peg and kept the yuan holding largely in lockstep with the dollar. Two years later, on 19 June 2010, the central bank pledged to increase the flexibility of the yuan after pegging it to the dollar for the two prior years. Of course the thinking at the time was that the world economy was improving and that was why the PBOC allowed the yuan to then strengthen again. The yuan continued to strengthen in 2011, but this time, the central bank was perceived to be allowing yuan strength in order to combat inflation.

Intervention

Traders tend to think of government intervention in the FX market as a rare and exotic event, but in practice intervention has a very long history and occurs more often than thought. Intervention by big countries may be fairly rare, but you can find intervention every year by some country.

In the days of fixed rates before the dollar was floated in 1974, intervention took the form of one-off revaluations, often to the downside. The UK pound was devalued in 1967. The French and Belgian francs were devalued numerous times during the 1960s and 1970s. In 1978-79, the US intervened to support the dollar. In 1985, G7 intervened to weaken the dollar and in 1987, G7 intervened to strengthen it.

Until a policy change in Japan in 2002, intervention amounts were a big secret. The Plaza Accord (1985) and later the Louvre Accord (1987) involved undisclosed sums in G7 intervention, with most of the shift in rates achieved through the *announcement effect*. Later, in his 1992 book *Changing Fortunes*, former Fed chairman Volcker revealed that the 1985 intervention was about $10 billion, of which $4.8 billion was done by the Bundesbank (at first unilaterally) and $600 million by the US Federal Reserve.

In 1992, the UK was forced to leave the Exchange Rate Mechanism, in part because of the assault by speculators (including George Soros) who judged the level of the GBP against the DM was economically unsustainable. Bank of England intervention ahead of leaving ERM cost £3.3 billion but this information was not revealed until 1997. And after the European Monetary Union was formed and issued the first euro in January 1999, G7 intervened in 2000 to halt its slide from $1.1746 at the launch to $0.8444 around 20 September. The amount of the intervention was reported at the time at about €3 billion by the ECB and $1.5 billion by the US.

Cold hard cash vs. jawboning and the announcement effect

Aside from the Bank of Japan's massive intervention in 2003-2004, which cost about $300 billion and the BOJ's still sizable intervention in March 2011 and October 2011, estimated at about $58 billion and $128 billion respectively, most intervention amounts are small when compared to the trillions per day traded in FX – they are usually in the $3 billion to $10 billion range. Most central banks refrain from reporting intervention, including the BoJ and Fed, until later when emotions are steadier. Many researchers enjoy rooting through the official statistics of bank reserves and short-term capital flows to deduce intervention amounts and, in practice, often find flows that might derive from intervention even when not labelled as such or attributed to intervention. The Eurosystem is accused of having a lot of such entries, especially around the time of the September 2000 intervention.

Because of the absence of hard data, we can't add up the cash cost of the combined G7 interventions over the years. It is probably about several trillion dollars since the dollar was floated in 1974 if we include emerging markets. We have yet to see a definitive list of interventions with the amounts listed alongside and with the currency price effect quantified, too. It can be argued that the exact amounts don't matter, anyway, because what matters is the announcement effect on the market.

The Japanese have honed their warnings about possible intention to intervene, also known as jawboning, to a fine art. They say the Ministry of Finance is "watching the FX market carefully," which can get ratcheted up to "the Ministry of Finance will act if FX market conditions become disorderly." Another code word is "excessive volatility." Japan is not alone. It was our experience in the late 1970s that the Fed made many "moral suasion" phone calls to bank treasurers, and we have no reason to suppose central banks today do not continue to twist arms behind the scenes.

Intervention – Does it work? Yes and No

The efficacy debate

We discuss intervention in Chapter 5, where it is positioned as a policy response to free markets failing to equilibrate exchange rates as theory says they should. Traders don't spend much time contemplating the value of intervention. It is a fact of life, like lightning storms and public transportation strikes. Central bankers and academics, however, debate intervention pros and cons carefully. They are fully aware that the need for intervention means the pretty fiction of free markets always producing the best price is just that; a fiction. The ideal is that advanced economies with well-functioning financial markets should be able to let the market establish exchange rates.

Intervention is a dirty business. It not only stinks of failure, it also imposes losses on the market players who are positioned wrong when intervention takes place, and these players include regular commercial interests such as exporters and importers as well as FX traders. Besides, intervention per se cannot and does not alter the underlying conditions that caused the imbalances that now necessitate intervention.

Conventional wisdom has it that intervention in financial markets is a waste of the taxpayer's money because it hardly ever has a lasting effect in the absence of a change in interest rates, and sometimes not even then. This was the conclusion of a G7 report on intervention demanded by French President Mitterrand at the June 1982 summit in Versailles and published in April 1983. The committee was chaired by French ministry of finance official Philippe Jurgensen and named for him (the Jurgensen Report), with the key chapter written by the Fed's international economist Edwin M. Truman.

In addressing the subject of intervention 20 years later, Truman wrote[92] "Exchange market intervention has definite limits as a policy instrument. Its effectiveness is uncertain and imprecise, and therefore it is at best a blunt or blunted instrument." He said, "Intervention is not a separate instrument of policy that can be used regardless of the stance of other economic and financial policies; it is not effective in achieving discrete adjustments in exchange rates, moving them from one level to another and holding them there." FX intervention is like a drug that works sometimes for reasons we don't understand and that can be accompanied by unforeseen side effects, "It is dangerous to prescribe the use of intervention except in extreme situations, and it is certainly not recommended for everyday use."

The Jurgensen Report has been added to but its conclusions have not changed since 1983, including a report by the Bank for International Settlements in December 2004 that was published as a set of essays by economists from the BIS and several central banks[93]. Since then, academics have built on the intervention literature with studies of interventions by Mexico, Argentina, South Korea, Thailand, Indonesia – and, of course, China.

Is it correct to lump together intervention in fixed or managed-float currencies with intervention in floating currencies? Yes, because the motivation is the same – to obtain or restore a competitive advantage without changing the monetary and fiscal policies that contributed to the currency crisis in the first place.

In addition, intervention is triggered by perception of disorderly or disruptive FX market conditions that contaminate other markets, especially stock markets. The intervention by the Hong Kong Monetary Authority in the stock market, during the 1997-98 Asian crisis, was designed specifically to fight back against speculative pressure against the Hong Kong dollar, which is fixed against the US dollar. We might even say that a key motivation in many instances of FX intervention is to prevent stock market slides, since currency devaluation tends to drive away foreign equity market investors. In the case of Japan, everything is upside down – it's a rise in the yen that harms the stock index, since stocks are dominated by exporters.

Japan

Most of what we know about FX market intervention comes from our experience with the Japanese, who have intervened more often and by bigger amounts than any other country. In fact, before the G7 intervention in March 2011, Japan had already intervened in September 2010 – and was heavily criticised by the rest of G20, which was meeting in Seoul at the time. That time, Japan meekly stopped. On other occasions, the Japanese Ministry of Finance has intervened heavily, repeatedly, at vast expense and without regard for others' disapproval.

For instance, Japan intervened from September 2001 to March 2004, spending ¥40.76 trillion. This steady Japanese intervention from the fall of 2001 to the early spring 2004 sent a clear message to traders, even if at times they chose to defy official wishes and buy yen anyway. The message was to slow down the pace of yen appreciation, which had earlier seen a shocking rise from ¥260 in February 1985 to ¥80.50 by April 1995. Did intervention work in the 2001-04 period? Yes and no.

The yen continued to rise, but first benefited from the Asian crisis that was already starting in 2005. The yen did not reach the export-killing 1995 level again until 2011. Given the long timeframe of Japanese policy-making, this should probably be seen as a success. We also saw that the Plaza Accord intervention and relentless official harangues worked, too. The dollar/mark fell from a high of DM 3.3602 in March 1985 to DM 2.3815 by January 1986. The pragmatic Swiss National Bank, intervening in recent years in the EUR/CHF pair, would not continue to intervene if it didn't get results.

It's hard to avoid the conclusion that central bankers say intervention doesn't work in the face of the evidence because intervention uses up a country's wealth for no obvious direct benefit to the citizens. Intervention runs counter to other policy objectives, like the US wishing to promote exports in 2010 and 2011 and wind down QE2 by June 2011 (the thought at the time of intervention).

The concerted intervention undertaken in March 2011 came after a perverse run up in the value of the yen in the wake of the 9.0 on the Richter scale Tohoku earthquake and the subsequent tsunami that devastated northeastern Japan. Dollar-yen had been holding in roughly in a Y81.50 to Y84.50 range before the quake hit on 11 March. The trader's instinct at the time was to sell the yen, i.e. the currency of the country experiencing such an unexpected blow to the economy. In this case however, the market became less worried about a investor exodus out of Japan and more worried about Japanese insurance companies selling overseas holdings to repatriate home.

By the time the BOJ and other central banks stepped in on 18 March 2011, dollar-yen had posted what was then a new life-time low of Y76.25. While the pair peaked at well over Y85 in coming weeks, it was not long before it crashed again.

Dollar-yen dipped below Y80 in June 2011, and bounced, but then a few weeks later broke below that psychological level. While there was no official intervention in subsequent months, there was ongoing talk of standing bids by Japanese accounts any time the pair traded on a ¥76 handle. This was not enough to stop dollar-yen from falling below ¥76 on 19 August and the BoJ was forced to intervene again in the fall of 2011 – and on a larger scale than had been seen in years.

China

No discussion of intervention would be complete without including China's sizable intervention to prevent the yuan from rising. As we have mentioned in this chapter, after much prodding by other countries in the early years of the new millennium, China begrudgingly allowed the yuan to strengthen. At the end of December 2011, the yuan gains versus the dollar since July 2005 stood at a bit over 31%. The yuan was up 8.36% versus the dollar since the de-peg in June 2010. China's currency reserves have increased from $711 billion in June 2005 to $3.2 trillion in Q4 2011. The sharp rise in reserves was driven largely by seemingly unstoppable investor inflows. If the PBOC had not intervened, it is likely that dollar-yuan would not be CNY 6.3500, but rather something closer to CNY 5.5000, analysts have said.

As discussed in Chapter 4 on interest rates and interest rate expectations, this steady increase in Chinese and other emerging market central bank reserve holdings created the interest rate conundrum described by then Federal Reserve Chairman Alan Greenspan in 2005. What China and other countries do with their sizable reserve holdings, now still mostly in US Treasuries, will largely dictate FX direction going forward.

Conclusion

Unlike monetary policy of yesteryear, the central bank toolkit of 2008-2012 included non-standard measures that a few years before would have been unthinkable. In early 2000, the thought of the Federal Reserve and the Bank of England doing quantitative easing, like the Bank of Japan, would have inspired guffaws. For Europeans, the notion of the ECB buying peripheral bonds or the creation of a euro zone bond market raises eyebrows. In short, no one foresaw that conventional monetary policy would run out of tools or that boosting domestic demand via unconventional means would spill over to FX in quite the way it did, more powerful than plain old central bank rate "guidance."

The subprime mortgage and euro zone crises forced the world's central bankers to become more proactive and adaptable as they try to deliver the appropriate dose of monetary policy for the economy. Unfortunately, however, like the 'roach motel', once a central bank walks through the door of non-conventional measures, there is no guarantee that they can easily walk out the other side.

This raises the profoundly uncomfortable issue of what comes next after central bank balance sheet manipulation has been exhausted. The FX market does not like intervention and capital controls, since like all interference in free markets, they tend to distort prices, often in unforeseen ways – the famous unintended consequences of government meddling. And yet history teaches us that one sure-fire way to boost economic activity is to devalue the currency and thus to promote export-oriented industrial activity.

When every major country is doing the same thing on the interest rate front and those unconventional stimulus measures do not suffice to boost activity, it's hard not to imagine that policies targeting devaluation have to come next. This is the thesis of many a commentator, and they are not entirely crackpot. It may be going too far to imagine that major countries intend to conduct *currency wars*, or competitive devaluation, but *beggar-thy-neighbour* devaluations were a standard part of the central bank toolkit before rates were floated in 1974. One wonders how many central bankers today ever cast an eye in that direction.

The only central bank that openly talks about the level of its currency in the context of overall economic health is the Bank of England, although central bankers in Canada and Australia occasionally mention currency levels as inherent to policy discussions. If and when the non-standard tool kit becomes exhausted, we may expect more explicit talk from other countries about the role of currencies in the economy.

Consider that back in 1999, among the suggestions Bernanke had for the Japanese was to devalue the yen, using intervention if necessary, as well as more aggressive unconventional monetary policy. We cannot say that Japanese intervention worked to devalue the yen over the past two decades, but the comment indicates that central bankers are fully aware that devaluation is an unconventional tool, too, just one that is a lot harder to implement in the floating rate world.

References

Chapter 1 – The Matrix Concept

[1] Matthew C. Harding, 'Application of Random Matrix Theory to Economics, Finance and Political Science', Department of Economics, MIT Institute for Quantitative Social Science, Harvard University, SEA'06 MIT: 12 July 2006 (**web.mit.edu/sea06/agenda/talks/Harding.pdf**).

[2] Robert Slater, *Soros, The Unauthorized Biography, The Life, Times and Trading Secrets of the World's Greatest Investor* (McGraw-Hill, 1995).

[3] James Burke, *The Pinball Effect* (Little Brown, 1996).

Chapter 2 – Risk Indicators

[4] Birgit Uhlenbrock, 'Financial markets' appetite for risk – and the challenge of assessing its evolution by risk appetite indicators', Bank for International Settlements, IFC Bulletin No. 31.

[5] Laura E. Kodres and Matthew Pritsker, 'A Rational Expectations Model of Financial Contagion', **www.federalreserve.gov/pubs/feds/1998/199848/199848pap.pdf**

[6] Craig S. Hakkio and William R Keeton, 'Financial Stress: What Is It, How Can It be Measured and Why Does It Matter?' Kansas City Fed Q2 2009 Economic Review.

[7] **research.stlouisfed.org/publications/net/NETJan2010Appendix.pdf**

[8] **www.federalreserve.gov/pubs/feds/2011/201102/201102pap.pdf**

[9] **thomsonreuters.com/content/financial/pdf/i_and_a/indices/trj_crb_overview.pdf**

Chapter 3 – Global Risk

[10] Alexandra Schaller, 'Continuous Linked Settlement: History and Implications', Ph.D. Thesis, University of Zurich, Zürich, Switzerland, December 2007.

[11] **www.cls-group.com/Media/Pages/NewsArticle.aspx?id=85**

[12] Peter Norman, *The Risk Controllers* (Wiley, 2011).

[13] Carmen M. Reinhart and Kenneth S. Rogoff, *This Time is Different, Eight Centuries of Financial Folly* (Princeton University Press, 2009).

[14] Ibid.

[15] Ibid, p.176.

[16] Erik Snowberg, Justin Wolfers, and Eric Zitzewitz, 'Partisan Impacts on the Economy: Evidence from Prediction markets and Close Elections', NBER Working Paper 12073, 2006 (**www.nber.org/papers/w12073.pdf**).

[17] **www.ny.frb.org/fxc**

Chapter 4 – Interest Rates and Differentials

[18] **data.worldbank.org/indicator/FR.INR.RINR**

[19] Federal Reserve Semi-annual Monetary Policy Report to Congress, 16 February 2005.

[20] N. Gregory Mankiw, Ricardo Reis and Justin Wolfers, 'Disagreement about Inflation Expectations', National Bureau of Economic Research Working Paper 9796, 2003 (**www.nber.org/papers/w9796**).

[21] **www.clevelandfed.org/research/workpaper/2011/wp1107.pdf**

[22] 'Treasury Inflation Protected Securities (TIPS)', Treasury Direct website (**www.treasurydirect.gov/indiv/research/indepth/tips/res_tips_faq.htm**).

[23] Federal Reserve of San Francisco Economic Letter, 3 October 2005.

[24] 'Liquidity Risk Premia and Breakeven Inflation Rates', Federal Reserve of Kansas City Q2 2006 (**www.kansascityfed.org/Publicat/econrev/PDF/2Q06Shen%28rvd%29.pdf**).

[25] 'Estimates of Inflation Expectations', Federal Reserve Bank of Cleveland, June 2010.

[26] Fact Sheet: A Historic New 5Y TIPS Auction (**www.centerforfinancialstability.org/research/TIPS042011.pdf**).

[27] The text of the Federal Register notice can be found at **www.treasurydirect.gov/instit/statreg/auctreg/FRUOCMinIntRate03012011.pdf**

[28] The Federal Reserve Board, Remarks By Ben S Bernanke before the Investment Analysts Society of Chicago, Chicago Illinois', 15 April 2004.

Chapter 5 – Forecasting FX

[29] Kenneth Rogoff, 'Dornbusch's Overshooting Model After Twenty-Five Years', Second Annual IMF Research Conference Mundell-Fleming Lecture, 30 November 2001 (revised 22 January 2002) (**www.imf.org/external/np/speeches/2001/112901.htm**).

[30] Michael R. Rosenberg, *Currency Forecasting – A Guide to Fundamental and Technical Models of Exchange Rate Determination* (Irwin, 1996).

[31] Andreas Schabert, 'Money Supply and the Implementation of Interest rate Targets', ECB Working Parier Series No. 483, May 2005 (**www.ecb.int/pub/pdf/scpwps/ecbwp483.pdf**).

[32] Nick Silver, 'IMF Applications of Purchasing Power Parity Estimates',

IMF Working Paper, November 2010 (**www.imf.org/external/pubs/ft/wp/2010/wp10253.pdf**).

[33] **epp.eurostat.ec.europa.eu/cache/ITY_PUBLIC/2-28062011-AP/EN/2-28062011-AP-EN.PDF**

[34]**epp.eurostat.ec.europa.eu/tgm/table.do?tab=table&init=1&plugin=1&language=en&pcode=tsier020**

[35] J. B. Taylor, 'Discretion versus Policy Rules in Practice', *Carnegie-Rochester Conference Series on Public Policy* 39, December 1993, pp. 195-214 and J.B. Taylor (ed.), *Monetary Policy Rules* (Chicago: University of Chicago, 1999).

[36] www.frbsf.org/economics/economists/grudebusch/el2009_17data.xls

[37] Athanasios Orphanides, 'Taylor Rules', Staff Working Paper in the Finance and Economics Discussion Series (FEDS), 2007-18 (www.federalreserve.gov/Pubs/FEDS/2007/200718/200718pap.pdf).

[38] James Rickards, *Currency Wars, The Making of the Next Global Crisis* (Penguin, 2011).

[39] www.whitehouse.gov/the-press-office/remarks-president-g20-closing-press-conference

[40] www.newyorkfed.org/aboutthefed/fedpoint/fed44.html

[41] www.michelbeine.be/pdf/paris10.pdf

[42] Michael M. Hutchison, 'The Role of Sterilized Intervention in Exchange Rate Stabilization Policy', June 2002, for the conference 'Stabilizing the Economy: Why and How?' sponsored by the GeoEconomics Center of the Council on Foreign Relations, New York City (www.blackwellpublishing.com/specialarticles/Hutchison.pdf).

[43] www.imf.org/external/pubs/ft/issues7/index.htm

[44] Edwin M. Truman, 'The Limits of Foreign Exchange Intervention' (Chapter 12), *Dollar Overvaluation and the World Economy* (Institute for International Economics, 2003).

Chapter 6 – Positions and Flows

[45] International Monetary Fund COFER data released March 2012 (www.imf.org/external/np/sta/cofer/eng/cofer.pdf)

[46] Sovereign Wealth Fund Institute, May 2012 (www.swfinstitute.org/fund-rankings)

[47] TheCityUK Fund Management, October 2011 (www.thecityuk.com/research/our-work/articles-2/uk-funds-under-management-reach-a-record-4-8-trillion-but-down-in-2011).

[48] Celent Study by Sreekrishna Sankar, August 2011 (www.celent.com/reports/retail-fx-entering-phase-mature-growth).

[49] fxtrade.oanda.com/analysis/open-position-ratios

Chapter 7 – Intermarket Analysis

[50] John Murphy, *Intermarket Technical Analysis: Trading Strategies for the Global Stock, Bond, Commodity, and Currency Markets* (Wiley, 1991).

[51] John Murphy, *Intermarket Analysis, Profiting from Global Market Relationships* (Wiley, 2004).

[52] Board of Governors of the Federal Reserve System International Discussion Paper 976, June 2009 (www.federalreserve.gov/pubs/ifdp/2009/976/ifdp976.pdf).

[53] Ashraf Laidi, *Currency Trading and Intermarket Analysis* (Wiley, 2009).

[54] www.whitehouse.gov/blog/2012/03/01/our-dependence-foreign-oil-declining

[55] Gorton, Gary B. and Rouwenhorst, K. Geert, 'Facts and Fantasies about Commodity Futures' (28 February 2005). Yale ICF Working Paper No. 04-20. Available at SSRN (**papers.ssrn.com/sol3/papers.cfm?abstract_id=560042**).

[56] Jim Rogers, *Hot Commodities: How Anyone Can Invest Profitably in the World's Best Market* (Random House, 2007).

Chapter 8 – Technical Analysis

[57] Edwards and McGee, *Technical Analysis of Stock Trends* (St. Lucie Press, 1948) and Welles Wilder, Jr., *New Concepts in Technical Analysis* (Trend Research, 1978).

[58] George Soros, *The Alchemy of Finance* (Simon & Schuster, 1988).

Chapter 9 – FX Gets Wired

[59] Podcast: 'Birth of FX Futures', CME Group 2008.

[60] Dagfinn Rime, 'New Electronic Trading Systems in Foreign Exchange Markets', (**www.norges-bank.no/upload/import/english/research/published/rime_electronic.pdf**).

[61] Sreekrishna Sankar, 'Technology Systems in the Global FX Market', (**www.celent.com/node/28625**).

Chapter 10 – Reserve Diversification

[62] Jason Goodwin, *Greenback – The Almighty Dollar and the Invention of America* (Henry Holt, 2003).

[63] World Trade Organization, 'World Trade 2010, Prospects for 2011', Press Release, April 2011 (**www.wto.org/english/news_e/pres11_e/pr628_e.htm#chart1**).

[64] **blogs.worldbank.org/prospects/a-new-multipolar-world-economy**

[65] Barry Eichengreen, 'Sterling's Past, Dollar's Future: Historical Perspectives on Reserve Currency Competition', Tawney Lecture, April 2005.

[66] Robert Triffin, *Gold and the Dollar Crisis* (Yale University Press, 1960).

[67] Charles Kindleberger, *Historical Economics – Art or Science?* (University of California Press, 1990) p. 231.

[68] Paul Meggyesi, 'Reflections on Negative Interest Rates in Switzerland', JP Morgan Global FX Strategy, May 14, 2010 (**mm.jpmorgan.com/stp/t/c.do?i=E0003-F&u=a_p*d_414632.pdf*h_-1vgm7fk**).

[69] Peter L. Bernstein, *The Power of Gold, A History of an Obsession* (Wiley, 2000), p. 346.

[70] **www.federalreserve.gov/releases/h6/hist/h6hist1.txt**

[71] General Accounting Office, Report to Congressional Addresses, Federal Reserve System, July 2011 (**www.gao.gov/products/GAO-11-696**), p. 144.

[72] **www.newyorkfed.org/research/current_issues/ci16-4.pdf**

[73] www.federalreserve.gov/newsevents/press/monetary/20111130a.htm

[74] John Maynard Keynes, *A Tract on Monetary Reform* (Harcourt Barce & Co, 1924).

[75] www.treasury.gov/resource-center/data-chart-center/tic/Documents/shla2011r.pdf

[76] www.treasury.gov/resource-center/data-chart-center/tic/Documents/frbulmay2012.pdf

[77] Hawtry quoted in Charles P. Kindleberger, **Power and Money** (Basic Books, 1970), p. 57.

[78] Jonathan Kirshner, 'Dollar primacy and American power: What's at stake?', *Review of International Political Economy* 15:3, August 2008, pp. 418–438 (**web.rollins.edu/~tlairson/seminar/dollarprime.pdf**).

[79] Hernando de Soto, *The Mystery of Capitalism, Why Capitalism Triumphs in the West and Fails Everywhere Else* (Basic Books, 2000), Chapter 1.

[80] Ibid., p. 55.

[81] UN Conference on Trade and Development, World Investment Report 2011, p. 28 (**www.unctad.org/en/docs//wir2011_embargoed_en.pdf**).

[82] Barry Eichengreen, *Exorbitant Privilege, The Rise and Fall of the Dollar and the Future of the International Monetary System* (Oxford University Press, 2011).

Chapter 12 – Central Bank Toolkit   83-93

[83] Mark Stone, Kenji Fujita, and Kotaro Ishi, 'Should Unconventional Balance Sheet Policies be Added to the Central Bank Toolkit? A Review of the Experience So Far' Working paper 11/145 (**www.imf.org/external/pubs/ft/wp/2011/wp11145.pdf**).

[84] Linda S. Goldberg, Craig Kennedy and Jason Miu, Federal Reserve Bank of New York Staff Report 429.

[85] European Central Bank Press Release, 16 December 2010.

[86] Press briefing 6 January 2011 by Caroline Atkinson Director, External Relations Department, International Monetary Fund in Washington.

[87] 'IMF Official To MNI: Brazil Capital Controls Likely Effective', Market News International, 26 May 2011.

[88] Swiss National Bank press release, 14 January 2011.

[89] 'The Swiss National Bank and the financial crisis', speech by SNB Chairman Philipp Hildebrand, 20 January 2011.

[90] Swiss National Bank press release, 6 September 2011.

[91] 'The Economic Effects of Capital Controls', Congressional Budget Office Staff Working Paper August 1985.

[92] Edwin M. Truman, 'The Limits of Exchange Market Intervention', The Peterson Institute for International Economics Special Report, Chapter 12, 16 February 2003 (**www.petersoninstitute.org/publications/chapters_preview/360/12iie3519.pdf**).

[93] www.bis.org/publ/bppdf/bispap24.htm

Index

www.ingramcontent.com/pod-product-compliance
Ingram Content Group UK Ltd.
Pitfield, Milton Keynes, MK11 3LW, UK
UKHW020010190325
456458UK00002B/32